RACING POST
ANNUAL 2019

Racing Post Floor 7, The Podium, South Bank Tower Estate, 30 Stamford Street, London, SE1 9LS. 0203 034 8900

Irish Racing Post The Capel Building, Mary's Abbey, Dublin 7. 01 828 7450

....

Editor Nick Pulford
Art editor David Dew
Cover design Jay Vincent
Chief photographers Edward Whitaker, Patrick McCann
Other photography Alain Barr, Debbie Burt, Gerry Cranham, Mark Cranham, Getty, John Grossick, Martin Lynch, Caroline Norris
Picture artworking David Cramphorn, Liam Hill, Stefan Searle, Shane Tetley
Feature writers Scott Burton, David Carr, Steve Dennis, Richard Forristal, Jonathan Harding, Jack Haynes, Ben Hutton, David Jennings, Tom Kerr, Lee Mottershead, Julian Muscat, Tony O'Hehir, Lewis Porteous, Nick Pulford, Peter Scargill, Brian Sheerin, Alan Sweetman, Peter Thomas, Kitty Trice, Robbie Wilders
Contributors Paul Curtis, John Randall, Martin Smethurst, Sam Walker

....

Advertisement Sales
Racing Post: Floor 7, The Podium, South Bank Tower Estate, 30 Stamford Street, London, SE1 9LS. 0203 034 8900. Charlie Allen, charlie.allen@racingpost.com

....

Archant Dialogue
Advertising Sales
Gary Stone, 01603 772463, gary.stone@archantdialogue.co.uk
Advertising Production Manager
Kay Brown, 01603 772522, kay.brown@archantdialogue.co.uk
Prospect House, Rouen Road, Norwich NR1 1RE. 01603 772554
archantdialogue.co.uk

....

Distribution/availability
01933 304858 help@racingpost.com

....

Published by Racing Post Books
27 Kingfisher Court, Hambridge Road, Newbury, Berkshire RG14 5SJ

Copyright © Racing Post 2018

ISBN 978-1-910497-73-9 [UK]
ISBN 978-1-910497-74-6 [Ireland]

Printed in Great Britain by Buxton Press. Every effort has been made to fulfil requirements with regard to copyright material. The author and publisher will be glad to rectify any omissions at the earliest opportunity.

racingpost.com/shop

C HOOSING the lead story for this eighth editio[n] difficult. Turn to pages four and five and you w[ill] only bring to life the most memorable contest[s] of racing's very soul: two horses, two jockeys[, one] course, giving their all, never flinching, for the [very] best.

Native River v Might Bite was not just the race of the year, it was one for the ages, an instant classic. It reminded us why a race named after the 12th Earl of Derby came into being at Epsom in 1780 and why a wager in 1752 between Cornelius O'Callaghan and Edmund Blake led to the first recorded steeplechase across country in County Cork from St John's Church in Buttevant to St Mary's Church in Doneraile.

That epic duel for the Cheltenham Gold Cup set the tone for the year. Almost seven months later, on the Flat in Paris, there was another unforgettable race from which both the winner and runner-up emerged with great credit. Yes, Enable won and Sea Of Class lost – just as Native River won and Might Bite lost – but there was a sense of a greater glory.

In between, there were many other memorable races. The Grand National, Eclipse, Nunthorpe Stakes, Irish Champion Stakes, Irish Oaks, King George VI and Queen Elizabeth Stakes . . . none of these great contests was decided by more than a neck. In the Ayr Gold Cup, another age-old race, there was a dead-heat for the first time.

Of course, racing is not all about exciting finishes. It is also a search for excellence, for dominance, and that was found in 2018 with the likes of Cracksman in his Champion Stakes repeat, Alpha Centauri in her record-breaking Coronation Stakes, Roaring Lion in the Juddmonte International, Altior in the Queen Mother Champion Chase and across the pond in Justify's Triple Crown.

There were also reminders that we should keep all these things in perspective, that racing remains a great triviality in comparison with Richard Woollacott's tragic death, Pat Smullen's fight with cancer and George Baker's battle to build a new life.

I wish you all enjoyable reading over the next 208 pages but, above all, good health and happiness.

Nick Pulford, Editor

CONTENTS

44

78

BIG STORIES

68

FINAL FURLONG

Native River outstayed Might Bite in a mighty battle for the Cheltenham Gold Cup where both protagonists emerged with great credit

EPIC DUEL

By Steve Dennis

"About the best thing in racing is when two good horses single themselves out from the rest of the field and have a long-drawn-out struggle"

THE Edwardian dictum of champion Flat trainer George Lambton, lifted from his autobiography Men and Horses I Have Known, stands up well to modern scrutiny. Its sentiments were underlined by the 2018 Cheltenham Gold Cup, which was nothing less than Lambton's idea of the best thing in racing. It was, simply, everyone's idea of the best thing in racing.

There were 15 runners in the

▸ *Continues page 6*

Timico-sponsored Gold Cup, the absolute apex of the jumps season, but really there were only two. In the blue corner, Might Bite. In the red corner, Native River. The other 13 horses were spectators, just among those present, no more than the crowd that gathers in the playground around two plucky scrappers. Djakadam, Definitly Red, Our Duke, Road To Respect, Total Recall and all the others; this doesn't concern you.

It was a soft-ground Gold Cup, attritional, wearying. The wet spring would have its say in the outcome. Nico de Boinville, rider of 4-1 favourite Might Bite, the King George-winning speed factor whose fleet-footedness might be traduced by the mud, woke on Gold Cup morning with the weather on his mind.

"It had been raining off and on all week and I was a bit worried leaving the track on Thursday night that it was going to be plenty soft enough, heavy in places, and that would not play to our strengths but to Native River's strengths," he says.

"I walked the course in the morning – there was a lovely fresh strip of ground saved for Gold Cup day – and I was quite happy with that. But when I walked from the last fence to the line I found the bad, chewed-up ground

where the different courses cross, and I knew then that it was going to be hard work for my horse."

Native River thrived on hard work. His stamina was assured – he had won a Welsh National – and his jockey Richard Johnson, proceeding inexorably towards a third title, was relishing the prospect.

"I'd been looking forward to riding him since he was third in last year's race. I woke up confident that he'd run a massive race. I had it on my mind to get a good start, to get into a nice rhythm, and he is the most straightforward horse to ride anyway, he pops out and I let him get on with it.

"The ground was on the slow side, but [trainer] Colin Tizzard always felt he didn't want the ground too soft anyway – it's in his favour because of his stamina, but as he's got older I think he copes with anything."

Both riders had a plan in mind – essentially the same plan, to ride a positive race and see what lay in store – and when the tape rose they enacted it. When they reached the first fence Native River was marginally in the lead, Might Bite at his right shoulder, a wingman with every intention of shooting down his rival. There, in the breadth of a sentence, lies condensed

GOLD CUP WINNERS BY RPR

Year	Horse	RPR
2018	**Native River**	178
2017	**Sizing John**	171
2016	**Don Cossack**	182
2015	**Coneygree**	178
2014	**Lord Windermere**	168
2013	**Bobs Worth**	179
2012	**Synchronised**	171
2011	**Long Run**	181
2010	**Imperial Commander**	182
2009	**Kauto Star**	185

▲ The Racing Post front page after Native River's Gold Cup triumph

the story of the 2018 Cheltenham Gold Cup. The race within a race was on.

"It felt like a match race even then, after jumping the first," says De Boinville, with more than three miles to run. "I had him in my sights, I knew we were going a good gallop, I couldn't really hear them too much behind, and we were both jumping so well that I knew we'd be taking lengths out of the others."

And so the scene was set, the pattern established. The first circuit – the equivalent of those ten paces in opposite directions before the turn and fire – passed without variety, mesmerising in its monotony. Native River led the way, Johnson in the vivid yellow, red and purple silks of Garth and Anne Broom. Might Bite never left his side, De Boinville garbed in the riotous raiment of the Knot Again Partnership, blue, yellow, orange and black. We couldn't have taken our eyes off them if we'd tried, so surely were those colours burned into the retina.

At the seventh, the storied ditch at the top of the hill, Native River put daylight between himself and Might Bite. Might Bite did the same to Djakadam. The ties that bound them stretched, recoiled. Neither put a foot

wrong, their jumping – as De Boinville advised, putting pressure on those behind – was immaculate. By the tenth they were together again, in lockstep, with five or six lengths back to Djakadam at the head of the chasing group, the vainly chasing group.

****

AS they passed the post for the second time with a circuit to run, a cheer broke loose from the packed grandstands and floated like a cloud across the green Cotswold fields towards the bulk of Cleeve Hill. The sense of something unusual taking place, something special, began to take hold. At the same time, Johnson made the first move toward the endgame.

"I felt we hadn't gone stupidly fast over the first circuit – perhaps some riders didn't want to take me on with a horse who'd definitely stay very well – but turning down the back straight I thought I needed to build the race up a little bit," he says.

"Because he jumps so well, it makes it easy to put pressure on other horses without even asking him to go quicker. Some might say it was a fantastic ride but I just let him get on with it. The worst thing I could have

done was to start telling him what to do, getting in his way."

The pace picked up. "I could feel it quicken," says De Boinville. "We were both jumping so well, at that stage I knew if we could maintain it we were in with a right shout."

On they went, down the back straight. At the last open ditch, clear water began to open between the front two and the pack. In a race, the decisive moment is almost never in the last few strides. Destinies are decided somewhere else, a good jump here, a change of pace there. Native River and Might Bite were now in their own little bubble, oblivious to the world outside, like chess players puzzling over some tricky gambit, like lovers lying in bed with the rain beating ceaselessly on the window, like duellists.

"From halfway down the back I knew Nico was following me, but I was in the perfect position, maybe he was in the perfect position for him, and the other horses weren't too much of a factor," says Johnson.

Five out, and even the most ardent fans of those horses in behind were writing it off as a bad business. Native River still in front,

▲ Battle scenes: from left, Native River leads Might Bite in their virtual match race; the contest is decided up the hill as Native River forges clear; Richard Johnson celebrates and is congratulated by Sean Flanagan

▼ Johnson salutes the crowd on Native River

Might Bite half a length behind, the rest increasingly nowhere. At the next, Johnson asked Native River for a big jump and got it. Might Bite was still at his shoulder, and now Johnson's arms started to move, to cajole, to request the next move from his willing partner.

"Coming down the hill I was happy to sit quiet and not ask for too much effort, he came down the hill like a dream," says De Boinville. "When top-class horses are jumping and travelling like that you take lengths out of the others, that's the difference between those at the top and those in the second rank.

"After the downhill ▶ Continues page 8

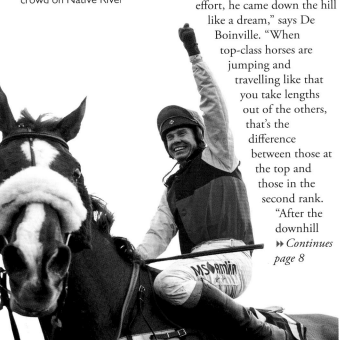

fence Richard started to get Native River going, off he went, and I was happy to sit at his girths and cruise away. I was just cruising."

****

ANY observer would have concluded that the rapier was just about to best the bludgeon, that Might Bite was cruising where Native River was being pushed along, and at some point soon Might Bite would sweep majestically past and on to glory. Over the third last.

"The key point in the race was three out," says Johnson. "I could feel him there, and that's when the race was properly on." De Boinville nods. "Turning in I still had a load of horse," he says.

On the run to the second last Johnson went to the whip. De Boinville sat as still as a birdwatcher, counting his strides, waiting for his moment. They met the second last as one horse, no quarter asked, none given. Two to jump and the race to win.

"We flew two out, and I felt I was starting to get the advantage. The more I asked, the more he gave. He's such a tough horse," says Johnson. "And when Might Bite jumped upsides that's when I asked Native River for everything. I didn't know how much Nico would find and I knew I'd stay, the hill was my friend, I had that up my sleeve, it was an unknown for Nico but not for me."

Momentarily, the old order changed. Might Bite poked his nose in front. The crucial moment, the hinge upon which the race swung, had arrived. Johnson gave his willing mount a couple more cracks, De Boinville's encouraging push became determined shove. At the last they rose together, the race between these two, as it had been since the beginning. And then it wasn't.

"We both met the last on the same stride, and then we landed, we came off that fresh strip of ground, we hit that bad ground and I knew it was over," says De Boinville. "I could feel him falter. We were done, just like that.

"Jumping the last upsides is a tremendous feeling because you're there or thereabouts but you haven't quite got there yet, but a couple of

▲ Sweet feeling: Richard Johnson savours the moment on his second Cheltenham Gold Cup winner

strides after the fence I knew it was gone."

There was suddenly a gap, and this time Might Bite could not hold his place on Native River's shoulder. The gap widened, and now the race was lost and won.

"Might Bite began to find it hard and Native River just kept going," says Johnson, his face alight with the memory of it.

"You never know what might be coming from behind, and I wasn't going to start looking round, but he was giving me everything. There's a mixture of relief and joy as you pass the line, we'd been in front for so long I'd have been mortified if something had grabbed us on the line. The race couldn't have gone any better, it was perfect."

One man's perfect is another's ruined. Behind him, De Boinville was rescuing what he could from the situation. Might Bite was running as though through dry sand, his great power blunted. For almost the first time, De Boinville became aware of the rest of the opposition.

▶ Continues page 10

TRIPLE CHAMPION

Native River added a golden glow for Richard Johnson as he completed a hat-trick of British titles since Sir Anthony McCoy's retirement in 2015.

Johnson's third triumph was achieved with 176 winners, his lowest winning total after racking up 235 and 189 in the previous two seasons. His 34-winner margin of victory over Brian Hughes, runner-up for a second consecutive season, was comfortable enough but down from 106 in 2015-16 and 55 the following season.

Part of the reason for the reduction was that Philip Hobbs, who has been Johnson's main supporter down the years, had an uncharacteristically thin season, with the usual 100-plus winners down to 63.

With Hughes the top rider in the north and Harry Skelton – third last season with a career-best 128 – backed by the increasingly powerful stable of his brother Dan, Johnson is set to face his strongest challenge yet.

Johnson has turned 41 – a year older than McCoy when he retired – but remains determined to stay at the top. "I promise you nothing's changed. When you've got one [championship] you want two; when you've got two you want three; and when you've got three you want a fourth as much as you wanted the first. I'm still just as competitive and I'll be trying as hard as ever."

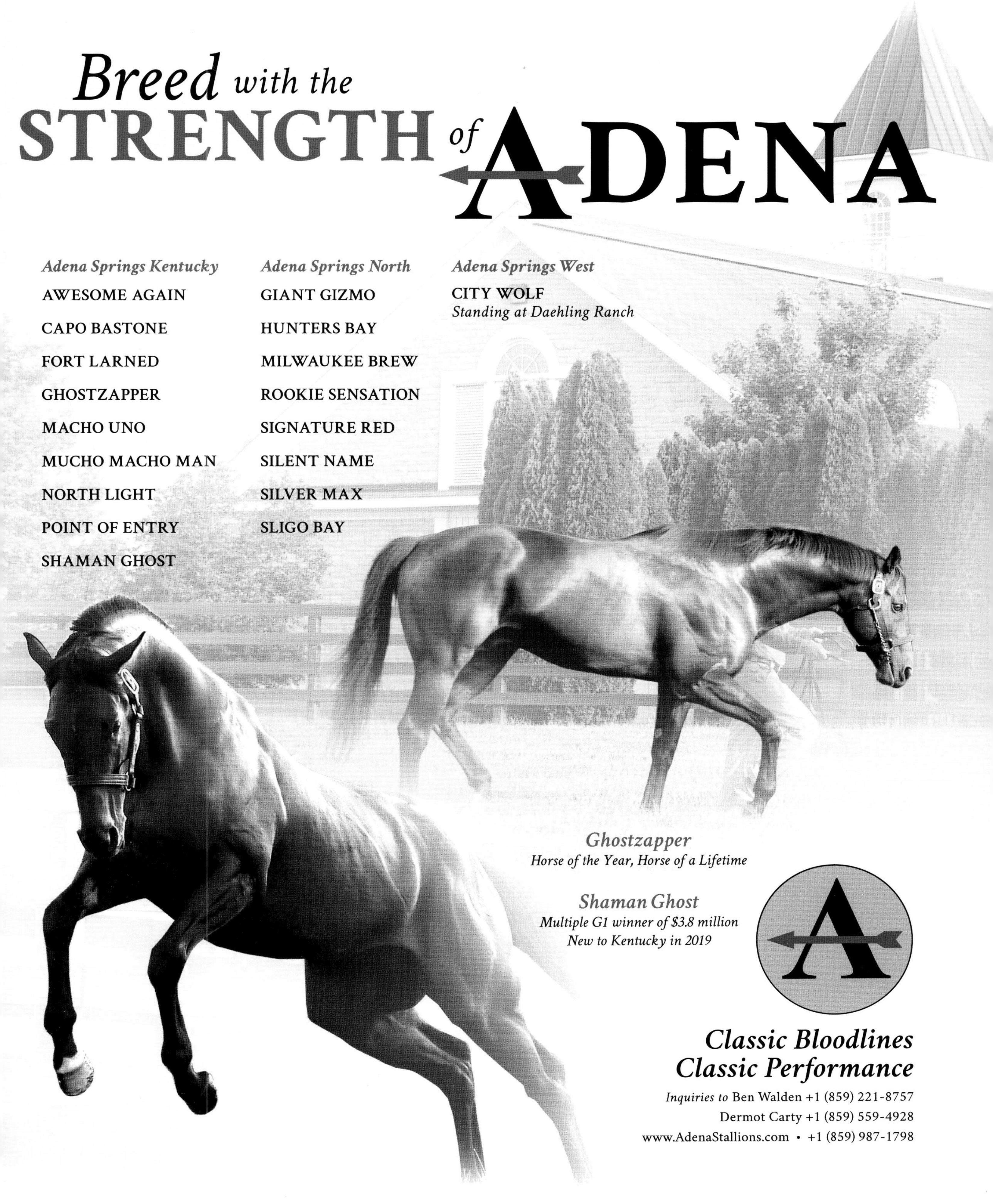

Breed with the
STRENGTH of ADENA
Adena Springs Kentucky
AWESOME AGAIN
CAPO BASTONE
FORT LARNED
GHOSTZAPPER
MACHO UNO
MUCHO MACHO MAN
NORTH LIGHT
POINT OF ENTRY
SHAMAN GHOST
Adena Springs North
GIANT GIZMO
HUNTERS BAY
MILWAUKEE BREW
ROOKIE SENSATION
SIGNATURE RED
SILENT NAME
SILVER MAX
SLIGO BAY
Adena Springs West
CITY WOLF
Standing at Daehling Ranch
Ghostzapper
Horse of the Year, Horse of a Lifetime
Shaman Ghost
Multiple G1 winner of $3.8 million
New to Kentucky in 2019
Classic Bloodlines
Classic Performance
Inquiries to Ben Walden +1 (859) 221-8757
Dermot Carty +1 (859) 559-4928
www.AdenaStallions.com • +1 (859) 987-1798

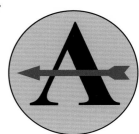

"I was just thinking that we had to try to hold on for second, but without beating him up. Native River was gone. It was the ground, he simply couldn't get his feet out of that ground. Instead of giving him a really hard race, I thought it best to let him plug away, hold on for second. There are always other days.

"Take nothing away from the winner, he just ground us out. I've watched the race a few times and it doesn't get any better."

****

THE usual post-race ceremonies took place, the hand-slapping, the back-patting, the words of congratulation and condolence. Johnson, who had won the Gold Cup with Looks Like Trouble in 2000, recalled his younger self, turned himself into human blotting paper to soak up every second.

"I was 22 and I didn't appreciate it then. In a weird way this time it sank in quickly, I knew what it was all about and I knew enough to make sure I enjoyed it. I really wanted to enjoy the moment.

"The crowd was amazing. My wife and my mum were there, times like that are unique in your life. Eighteen years earlier I hadn't appreciated that at all – I thought I'd probably win the Gold Cup the next year as well.

"It was a great race, and on the day we came out on top. It's a feeling that never wears off."

For De Boinville, the feeling was very different. He too had a Gold Cup on his sideboard – Coneygree in 2015 – but to come so close, on such a willing partner, in such a race, might make a maniac of the mildest man.

"Crossing the line I didn't think I could have done anything different, I felt we'd given as good as we could. I was very proud of Might Bite, he'd battled so hard, but it wasn't to be.

"I don't dwell on it. If a horse has run to his very best there's no more you can do. There's no point carrying it around with you. The only time I get annoyed is when I feel I haven't got the full potential out of a horse, and Might Bite ran to his full potential in those conditions.

"It felt great. I lost, but it was fantastic being in a top-class race like that."

There is the spirit that moves us. Both jockeys, winner and loser, describe the 2018 Cheltenham Gold Cup as a great race. It was indeed an epic contest, a duel that will live long in the memory and will be rekindled whenever folk meet to talk about great men and horses.

There are also things that this Gold Cup was not. It was not epochal, life-changing, as when Arkle beat Mill House. It did not forego an ecstasy of emotion, as in Desert Orchid's year, or Norton's Coin's. It did not vouchsafe the thrill of a desperate finish, like The Dikler v Pendil, or Cool Ground v

'THIS IS SO SPECIAL'

THE ultimate achievement of Colin Tizzard's training career transformed a challenging season that had brought big-race disappointment with Thistlecrack, Cue Card and Fox Norton amid concerns over his Dorset stable's overall form.

Native River proved the toughest of them all to claim the Gold Cup after finishing third the previous year. Having been injured then, he was kept out of the fray until warming up for Cheltenham with victory in the Denman Chase at Newbury in February.

"This has been the plan for Native River since last year's Gold Cup when he picked up the ligament problem. He couldn't run until at least Christmas and we decided he would run at Newbury and then the Gold Cup," Tizzard said. "Our horses went out of form at Christmas, which coincided with the flu injections, so we eased off with them a bit and that may have helped them going into the spring campaign."

Tizzard, 62, added: "To win a Gold Cup is so special. I came here as a 17-year-old farmer who stood in the hut by the last fence never thinking I would have a runner or even be a trainer. The Gold Cup is everything and the fact that we've won it is unreal.

"Garth and Ann Broom [owners, Brocade Racing] have been big supporters of our yard, so it's great to provide them with a winner in the Gold Cup."

▼ Hero's welcome: Native River with Colin Tizzard (right) and travelling head lad Richard Young as they celebrate Gold Cup victory among stable staff and wellwishers outside the Virginia Ash pub in Henstridge Ash, Somerset

The Fellow, and it did not make history in the same way as Michael Dickinson's Famous Five or Dawn Run.

But it will be remembered as these are. It lived up to a maxim stated by an old-time trainer and still carried around in our hearts to this day, along with the knowledge that these things are rare, precious, life-affirming. The 2018 Cheltenham Gold Cup was an epic encounter, it was a thrilling affair, but more than this and more than anything, it was a *race*.

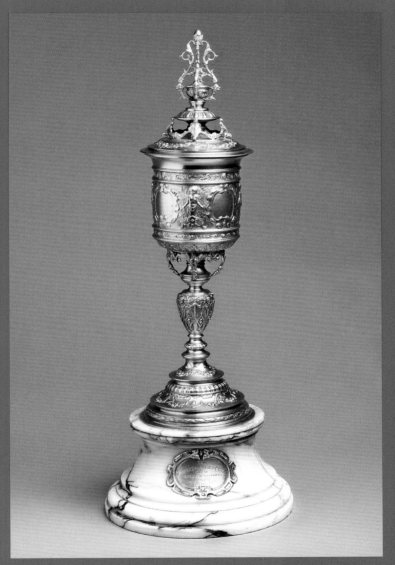

THE BIGGER PICTURE

A blue supermoon over Mandown gallops in Lambourn on the night of January 31. A blue moon is a second full moon in a calendar month and a supermoon is when the moon is unusually close to Earth, making it appear bigger and brighter
EDWARD WHITAKER (RACINGPOST.COM/PHOTOS)

Presenting Percy put on quite a show in the RSA Chase and now the aim is the biggest stage of all to take on Native River and Might Bite

PRESENTING . . .
The next big thing

By Brian Sheerin

IT seems there is a downside after all to owning one of the best jumps horses in training: it's not good for the ticker. The 2018 RSA Chase didn't take a lot out of Presenting Percy as he whooshed up the famous Cheltenham hill in style but, back in the winner's enclosure, Philip Reynolds was left examining the damage, and for a brief moment he might have wondered if he had died and gone straight to heaven.

"I'm in pieces," said the owner, before touching on Presenting Percy's far from conventional route to back-to-back Cheltenham Festival glory. "I'm speechless. I just can't believe it. I was hoping he was a Graded horse and was so thrilled for him when he won the Galmoy Hurdle [at Gowran Park] because he's got a bit of a slagging for being a handicap horse and I knew he was a Graded horse.

"But to come here and do what he did," Reynolds added, wiping a tear from his eye, "as you can see it's mind blowing and it means so much to me. It's incredible. I'm in pieces."

In that short interview, Reynolds got to the core of what racing is all about. He may be the son of former Taoiseach Albert Reynolds but to have a horse like Presenting Percy and to compete with – and beat – mega-owners Michael O'Leary and Rich Ricci is a once-in-a-lifetime experience for an owner like him. The stuff of dreams.

Not that Cheltenham success is anything new to Reynolds *(below)* or Pat Kelly, the small-time Galway-based trainer who seldom stops to chat with the media and says so little that he would make some of Pablo Escobar's most loyal men look like motormouths.

What Kelly lacks in charisma he more than makes up for as a 'target' trainer at the Cheltenham Festival, which happens to be the most difficult target to hit for most people but which Kelly has made routine for three years in a row. Twice he had taken aim at the Pertemps Handicap Hurdle, with the Reynolds-owned Mall Dini and Presenting Percy, and both times he found the centre of the bullseye. For his next shot, he moved Presenting Percy up to Grade 1 novice chase company and did it again.

The RSA Chase is one of the most arduous three-mile tests for any novice chaser but the manner in which Davy Russell's mount sauntered around on the bridle, before cruising to the front turning in and quickening up the hill, screamed 'future Gold Cup winner'.

This success was different to any of the others and connections knew it. So did the bookmakers, who installed Presenting Percy as the new favourite for the 2019 Gold Cup, a position he continued to hold after the Native River-Might Bite epic two days later and through the rest of the 2017-18 festival season.

With Kelly preferring the background after the RSA Chase, Reynolds, beginning to get his breath back, said: "Pat is incredible and he should be up here talking to you because he deserves all the credit. Pat is quiet. He's an incredible genius. I know that word is used very loosely but where Pat Kelly is concerned it's fitting.

"He has a very small number of horses in training, thankfully a good few of them for me. One field is where he trains them. I must be doing a very bad job advertising his wares because I can't understand why he doesn't have 150 in training."

****

REYNOLDS, a hugely successful businessman, is astute enough to have put his faith in Kelly and to know not to question his judgement. To everyone on the outside, the unorthodox Kelly seemed to chart a bonkers path to Cheltenham with his star chaser, but Reynolds left him to it.

The road to the festival began conventionally enough in October when Presenting Percy opened his account over fences in style in a 2m6f beginners' chase at Galway before suffering defeat behind Jury Duty and Shattered Love when upped to Grade 2 company at Punchestown the following month.

This was where Kelly deviated from a normal path. Instead of heading towards the Christmas programme for novice chasers, he ran Presenting Percy in the Porterstown Handicap Chase over 3m5f at Fairyhouse in early December. The step up in trip by nearly a mile – and well beyond the distance of the RSA – was eyecatching but Presenting Percy's performance was even more so as he dished out an 11-length beating to experienced handicappers.

In the new year Kelly took aim

▸▸ *Continues page 16*

at the three-mile Galmoy Hurdle at Gowran Park, where Presenting Percy gained his first Graded success, and then went back to the track for the Grade 2 Red Mills Chase on heavy ground, where his novice was a close second to second-season chaser Our Duke, who came into the race off the back of an underwhelming campaign.

It was an unusual preparation for the RSA but Kelly's method was proved right. "It's incredible," said Reynolds, explaining the thinking behind such a crazy campaign.

"That's three Cheltenham winners, three years in a row. We ran at three miles five at Fairyhouse to know he would stay three-plus miles, which you need to do to win an RSA, and we ran him in open company twice to toughen him up. I had no qualms with Pat. He had good reasons for doing what he did and you've seen the result."

Many would have gone full steam ahead towards the Punchestown festival in the knowledge that the odds would be firmly in their favour of landing another Grade 1 success, but a more cautious approach was decided upon.

With Cheltenham success still on his lips, Reynolds revealed: "We're going to pull the plug for this season. To have one as good as

Presenting Percy, you need to mind him and look after him and we're going to give him every chance."

Having such an exciting and talented horse clearly wasn't lost on the owner, who couldn't wait to get his pride and joy home to his farm in County Westmeath so that he could "go down and drool over him all summer". After that he handed him back to Kelly for the ultimate dream, a crack at the Cheltenham Gold Cup.

"For Pat to do what he's done, with the number of horses he has in training, is just phenomenal," Reynolds said. "People might think I've gone out and blown out the lights and bought really expensive horses to put into training with Pat, but that's not the case at all. The word genius is used far too often, but Pat is exactly that and he was a genius before I ever had horses with him."

****

THERE'S an old Irish saying, 'it's not off the ground you licked it', which roughly refers to a characteristic or interest acquired through the influence of others, and it certainly applies to Reynolds. A love of horses was instilled in him by his late father and, perhaps most significantly, it

was Albert who first introduced his son to Kelly in the early 1990s, at a time when the trainer managed the careers of Natalies Fancy and No Tag, winners of the Galway Hurdle in 1992 and 1995 respectively.

The relationship lay dormant until Kelly suggested Reynolds have another horse with him some years ago. That horse turned out to be Mall Dini and luck has been on the duo's side ever since they got back together. The road, as long as Kelly is driving, is meandering, but scarcely does the trainer fail to reach his destination.

"Percy has been back in Pat's since before Galway and everything has gone well with him and the plan is the Gold Cup," Reynolds said in the autumn. "That's the plan anyway, but we all know plans can change with Pat. I'll leave him to his own devices with the horse as he's a genius and he doesn't need me interfering. It's surreal having the Gold Cup favourite but it's also not very good for the nerves."

With Native River and Might Bite lying in wait, and 2017 Gold Cup winner Sizing John on the comeback trail, quite a race is in prospect if they all get together. Maybe it should come with some sort of health warning.

HIGH MARK

Presenting Percy's prospects of jumping to the next level are enhanced by his standing in the 2017-18 Anglo-Irish Jumps Classifications, where he was ranked the top staying novice chaser with a rating of 165.

In recent years that mark has been bettered only by Coneygree and Thistlecrack, both of whom had greater opportunity to achieve high ratings by being tested in open company as novices. Coneygree won the Cheltenham Gold Cup in his novice season, taking him to 172 in 2014-15, while Thistlecrack landed the King George VI Chase as a novice and was rated 170 at the end of the 2016-17 season.

The only other staying novice chaser to rate higher than Presenting Percy since the classifications began was Gloria Victis with a mark of 166 in 1999-2000, the inaugural season. The ill-fated Gloria Victis also ran outside novice company, winning the Racing Post Chase before falling fatally two out when in contention for the Cheltenham Gold Cup.

Staying novice chase champions rated lower than Presenting Percy in the classifications include top-class performers Denman (161), Beef Or Salmon (161) and Bobs Worth (160).

▾ Jumping ahead: Presenting Percy clears the last under Davy Russell on his way to RSA Chase victory

HORSE OF THE YEAR

by Candy Ride out of a half sister to Horse of the Year Saint Liam

6 time Grade 1 Winner by a combined 30 lengths

Breeders' Cup Classic (G1) • Pegasus World Cup (G1) • Woodward Stakes (G1)
Whitney Stakes (G1) • Stephen Foster Handicap (G1) • Clark Handicap (G1)

Arguably one of the best pedigrees in the stud book

st Dam
QUIET GIANT, by Giant's Causeway. 7 wins in 12 starts at 3 and 4, $405,389, Hill 'N' Dale Molly
   Pitcher S. **[G2]**, Lady's Secret S., Rare Treat S., Cheap Seats S., Lady on the Run S., 2nd
   Ladies H., Polly's ___ ___ m of _oals, 2 to race, 1 winner--
GUN RUNNER (c. ___ ___le (G1). 12 wins, 2 to 5, 2018, **$15,988,500. Horse of the**
   Year in U.S. ___ ___der ___ **Male Horse in U.S.** Won Breeders' Cup Classic
   [G1] ___us ___ ___vita___ S. **[G1]**, Whitney S. **[G1]**, Woodward S. **[G1]**,
   S___ er ___ ___winspires.com Louisiana Derby **[G2]**, Veterans
   ___r S ___ ___ **[G_]** Razorback H. **[G3]**, 2nd Emirates Airline
   ___eders' Cup Dirt Mile **[G1]**, Pennsylvania Derby
   ___ S. **[G1]**

2n___
QUIET ___NCE ___ 4, $224,240, Gala Lil S., 2nd Demoiselle S.
   [G2]. Dan___
SAINT LIAM ___ to 5, $4,456,995, **Horse of the Year in U.S.**,
   Champion ___ ___s' Cup Classic **[G1]** Stephen Foster H. **[G1]**,
   Donn H. **[G** ___d S. **[G1]**, Clark H. **[G2]**, 2nd Whitney
   H. **[G1]**, Woo___ ___. Sire.
QUIET GIANT (f. ___ ___see above.
DANCE QUIETL__ ___0, Busanda S., 2nd Wanda S.
   3rd Pike Cree___
CONGRESSION ___2,413, Bay Meadows Derby
   [G3]. Sire. ___
Miss Besilu (f. b ___29, 2nd Ginger Brew S.,3rd
   Alabama S. ___
American Danc___ ___d TRI, $174,395 (USA), 3rd
   Remsen S. **[G2** ___
Quiet Now (f. by Tizn___ ___
   LULL (f. by War ___ 3, 20___ ___6,057, Kentucky Downs Ladies
      Sprint S., Exa___ ___ Fillies S___ ___an Clemente H. **[G2]**, JPMorgan
      Chase Jessam___ ___ng Softly S.
   Irsaal (g. by Mo___ Re___ wins, 2 to ___ ___laced at 7, 2017, $340,398, 2nd
      Birdstone S., ___sy Goe___ ___azil S., Be___ ___en S.
Beaten Buster (f. by ___ ___ng C___ ___raced, ___ of--
   BUSTER'S RE__ ___ Mo___ Rea___ wins at 2, ___3, $364,834, Mother
      Goose S. **[G___** ___ ___2nd ___ ___Out Pl___ ___roducer.

THREE CHIMNEYS
859.873.7053 • www.threechimneys.com

f ⊙ 𝕏 @three_chimneys

BREED TRUE

GUN RUNNER

Gun Runner shown winning the
$16 Million Pegasus World Cup (G1)

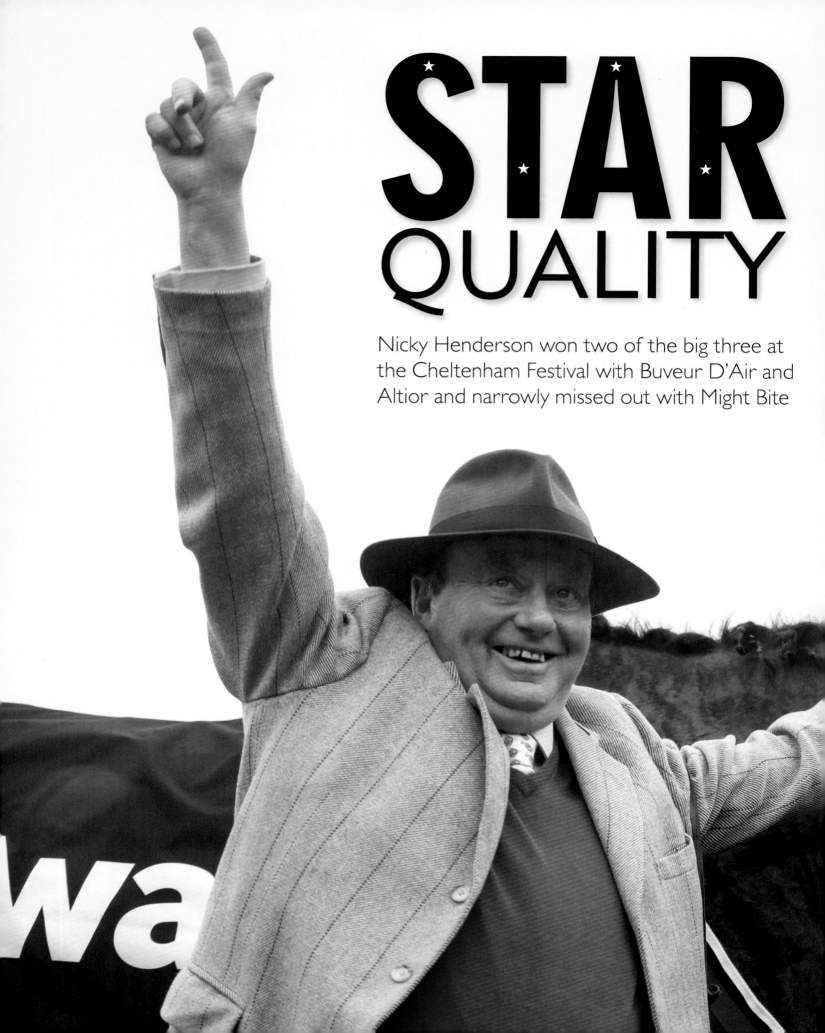

STAR QUALITY

Nicky Henderson won two of the big three at the Cheltenham Festival with Buveur D'Air and Altior and narrowly missed out with Might Bite

By Peter Thomas

WHEN the dust settled on the 2018 Cheltenham Festival, the picture that emerged with the sharpest focus and the brightest colour was the dominance of the Irish; the tale told with the greatest vigour recounted the exploits of Willie Mullins and Gordon Elliott, of how they came, saw and conquered, 15 times between them, as they led a raiding party that made off with no fewer than 17 of the 28 prizes up for grabs.

It was humiliation bordering on whitewash for the home team, but if the celebrations of the Hibernian hordes were loud and raucous, there was no suggestion that they kept Nicky Henderson awake at night. He and his fellow Brits may have been bested on quantity, but the quality went the way of the home team and it was the master of Seven Barrows, with a Champion Hurdle and a Champion Chase, who did most to steady the ship.

It was nothing more than might have been expected from the man who, since his first success with three-time Champion Hurdle hero See You Then in 1985, has racked up an astonishing 60 winners at the festival. Whenever he has seemed becalmed by the shifting of the wind or washed up on the tide of fashion, he has come back with a big year, and if 67 seems an advanced age at which to be asked to see off the rampant Celtic Tiger in the shape of Mullins, Elliott, Gigginstown and Rich Ricci, then Henderson has shown no sign of fading, passing the £3 million mark in prize-money for the first time last season and landing a fifth trainers' title.

"I imagine everyone thinks I should be retiring but I can assure you I'm not," he smiles, as he looks back but, more importantly, forward. "I bought ten three-year-olds last week in Ireland and you won't be seeing them for three years, by which time I'll be 110, so if I don't carry on I'll have been wasting my time.

"Yes, you have to keep your eye on the ball all the time, but we had an amazing year and the title is very good for morale. I'm at the helm of the ship but it's a big ship with a lot of people on board and success means a lot to all of us.

"What's more, my owners are all friends and we're in this to have fun, believe it or not. That's what we're trying to provide for them because if it isn't fun there's no point in it."

More than all the statistics, Henderson was back where he belonged, in the public eye as the trainer of the best two-milers in the land at the biggest meeting in the game. Anybody who thought he would never match the ancient deeds of Remittance Man and Travado, or emulate the recent triumphs of Binocular, Punjabi, Finian's Rainbow and the peerless Sprinter Sacre, were proved wide of the mark as Altior and Buveur D'Air backed up their 2017 festival triumphs with wins in the Champion Chase and Champion Hurdle respectively.

Had the enigmatic Might Bite been able to match the relentlessness of fellow Brit Native River in the Gold Cup, we would

▸ *Continues page 20*

have been lauding a unique clean sweep of the major prizes, but the trainer certainly wasn't complaining, even if the victories came after an eve-of-meeting scare that caused palpitations in the camp.

"I hadn't even thought of the treble until it was mentioned a fortnight before that it hadn't been done and we had three chances," he recalls, "but I remembered being at Fred Winter's when we had the three favourites one year, Lanzarote in the Champion Hurdle, Crisp in the Champion Chase and Pendil in the Gold Cup, and we walked away with zero, so I know how difficult it can be – and if you'd have seen this place on the Monday of Cheltenham week you wouldn't have believed it was possible.

"We Have A Dream had a temperature of God knows what and Altior came out of his box on three legs and you thought the world had come to an end, but I have brilliant farriers, they found the corn in Altior's foot straight away, put a poultice on it, we were on top of it within an hour and by Tuesday morning it was 100 per cent. There was nothing to say because we knew what we were doing, but that's when you have to earn your corn as a trainer."

****

MENDED to the trainer's satisfaction, Altior headed to Cheltenham to further his already sky-high reputation. He had emerged at Seven Barrows at a crucial juncture, just as Sprinter Sacre was fading into sepia-tinted memory, and for Henderson, whose capacity to recruit, satisfy and hang on to well-heeled owners borders on the remarkable, finding a replacement in the same league seemed to happen as a seamless transition.

By the end of the season Altior's sequence stood at 14 unbeaten runs on the trot, with his Champion Chase sandwiched between a gutsy win in the mud at Newbury, which put him spot-on for the festival, and a second consecutive Celebration Chase at Sandown's finale. Min and Douvan formed a strong team from the Mullins yard in the Champion Chase but Douvan's jumping let him down four from home and Min was, quite simply, seven lengths inferior to the even-money favourite. As has become his custom, Altior threatened to make hard work of the victory, being niggled along by Nico de Boinville three out, but soon found his stride and forged clear impressively up the hill.

He showed signs of either laziness or cuteness – depending on your level of leniency – when overcoming the 20lb inferior San Benedeto by little more than three lengths in the Celebration Chase and he began the new season as the most eagerly anticipated horse in the jumping ranks, with Henderson trying hard to overcome the temptation to explore his outer limits.

"Luckily he had the Sandown race waiting for him, but I'd have loved to try him over a bit further," says Henderson, "two and a half miles at Aintree maybe, and if he'd have won that I suppose I'd have been tempted to try and do something stupid the next year,
▸ *Continues page 22*

Nicky Henderson had this to say about his big guns in September

Altior "It'd be almost certain he'll start in the Tingle Creek and we've been talking about a King George entry. If it closed today I'd probably put him in it and one day we might need to branch out, but it's very difficult to do that when they put such a good two-mile programme in front of you. I'm pretty sure he'll get further. How much further I don't know, but unless he gets three miles there's not really any advantage coming out of two miles. [Two and a half miles] brings you into the Ryanair, which is a great race, but it's not the Champion Chase or King George."

Buveur D'Air "I'm not sure he was at his very best at Cheltenham; he's better than that. I'm full of admiration for that new meeting in Ireland [Dublin Racing Festival in early February] but I'm not sure an overseas trip and almost certainly a hard race – because the best opposition is over there – is the right thing when we're trying to get ready for Cheltenham. It's a commendable meeting, but I'm just not sure about the timing as far as we're concerned and his only objective is a third Champion Hurdle."

Might Bite "His priority is another King George. He's got to have a race before that, so we'll try to go for the Betfair Chase. He was very good last year and his best performance and when I was the proudest of him was in the Bowl at Aintree. He was the only one out of Altior and Buveur who categorically bounced out of Cheltenham and said, 'I'm ready to go again', and yet he'd had the hardest race of the lot."

◀ First class: Altior and Nico de Boinville after their victory in the Champion Chase; previous page, Altior in the winner's enclosure with Nicky Henderson

Grade 1 meets
Delicious treats
Dublin beats

Celebrate the best of our proud and famous city, in one famous city venue.

Two days of exhilarating racing, including the BHP Insurance Irish Champion Hurdle and the

Unibet Irish Gold Cup, with over €1.5 million in prize money, performances from the best Dublin

Entertainment and Dublin's finest food, all for only €30 each day.

February 2nd & 3rd. **Book now at leopardstown.com**

Dublin Racing Festival at **LEOPARDSTOWN**

like trying him over even further, so you're probably better off not doing it. If it ain't broke, why fix it, I suppose, and he's the best at what he does.

"It was a bit unlucky last season in that we had to miss the first half and I had to rush at him a little bit. After the wind operation we were definitely up against the clock and everything had to go right, but luckily the recuperation went well and the build-up to Newbury went well.

"Politologue had had a ball mopping up in his absence and I was petrified because if Altior was going to get beaten, that was the day it was going to happen – then we get out of our hospital bed to remind him who's the top dog.

"You can't believe your luck. One minute you're saying goodbye to a true champion and in the next breath you're holding on to the next one, who's done nothing but grow in stature and follow in Sprinter's footsteps. I think he'd need to win another Champion Chase and then we can start calling him a true champion as well."

TOP OF THE FORM

Nicky Henderson took his fifth trainers' championship in 2017-18 – and the second in a row – while Altior was the top-ranked two-mile chaser and Buveur D'Air the best two-mile hurdler in the Anglo-Irish Jumps Classifications.

British jumps trainers' championship
Nicky Henderson £3,477,473
Paul Nicholls £2,513,233
Colin Tizzard £1,975,899
Nigel Twiston-Davies £1,896,192
Dan Skelton £1,738,235

Two-mile chasers
Altior 175
Un De Sceaux 168
Fox Norton 167
Min 167
Footpad 166

Two-mile hurdlers
Buveur D'Air 166
Melon 165
Supasundae 164
Mick Jazz 162
The New One 161

▲ Heat of battle: Buveur D'Air (nearside) jumps the last in unison with Melon before winning his second Champion Hurdle

▼ Altior basks in the autumn sunshine at Seven Barrows with Robin Land

****

BUVEUR D'AIR approached his festival test as reigning champion and at 4-6 the hottest favourite for the race since the great Istabraq in 2000. While his critics ascribed those odds to the paucity of credible opposition rather than the unassailable brilliance of the winner, there was no denying his superiority on the day, or his admirable battling qualities in the face of brutally heavy ground.

A neck defeat of Melon – with 25-1 shot Mick Jazz and Identity Thief at 50-1 filling the places – may not have been the kind of form to send handicappers into raptures, but the seven-year-old was racking up his tenth straight win since being beaten by Altior in the 2016 Supreme Novices' Hurdle, with six of them coming in Grade 1 company.

With a brief experiment over fences having long since been abandoned, he had been freed to fulfil his ▶▶ *Continues page 24*

Stallions

BOLT D'ORO *NEW*
BRODY'S CAUSE
CAN THE MAN
CINCO CHARLIE
CROSS TRAFFIC
DANZA
DOMINUS
FLAT OUT
FREE DROP BILLY *NEW*
GOLDENCENTS
GORMLEY
HIT IT A BOMB
INTO MISCHIEF
ITSMYLUCKYDAY
JIMMY CREED
LORD NELSON
MALIBU MOON
MEDAL COUNT
MOR SPIRIT *NEW*
NORMANDY INVASION
PALACE
RACE DAY
SHAKIN IT UP
TEMPLE CITY
WICKED STRONG

SPENDTHRIFT
THE BREEDERS' FARM
spendthriftfarm.com
884 Iron Works Pike | Lexington, KY 40511
859 294 0030

SHARE THE UPSIDE and SAFE BET PROGRAM
EST 2018

destiny as the best two-mile hurdler in the business, and with his technique honed to a slick, twig-tickling, heart-stopping nicety, he delivered, setting up a 2019 bid for the treble that would match See You Then's exploits and send him – although whisper it softly within earshot of Irish disciples – into Istabraq territory.

"The Champion Hurdle again will be the intention," says Henderson, unperturbed by any criticism of his champion, "and you know what, I don't think we saw the best of him at Cheltenham last time. He hadn't had a race all season, and when We Have A Dream in the box next door to him got sick, it went through my mind what effect that might have had. Listen, he won the Champion Hurdle, so there wasn't a lot wrong with him, but I wonder if he was at his very best.

"People are always going to say the opposition is weak in these races, but he's beating them because he's better than them and he's a very good horse. It might not be a vintage era but the novices keep coming through and come the Champion Hurdle, it

'With a Gold Cup as well it would have been an extraordinary year but I was just as proud of Might Bite finishing second in the Gold Cup'

doesn't matter who you are or what you are, they're still bloody hard to win."

****

WHILE Might Bite was the one who failed to deliver the final leg of what would have been a unique treble, his trainer has nothing but admiration for a horse who dug deep at Aintree next time to land the Grade 1 Betway Bowl. The son of Scorpion may have earned himself a reputation for quirky antics in a finish, but there was no disguising the performance of a hardened warrior on this occasion.

"With a Gold Cup as well it would have been an extraordinary year," reflects Henderson, "but I was just as proud of him finishing second and, while Altior didn't have to go to Aintree and Buveur D'Air didn't want

to go to Aintree because he'd had a hard race, Might Bite, who people might have said was the most delicate of the three, was the one to bounce back and do the job really professionally."

All of which gives the veteran trainer the strongest hand in the big races. If Might Bite can squeeze another ounce of achievement out of himself, and both Altior and Buveur D'Air can do what they've done before, the treble is on the cards and Henderson's retirement will be pushed back another year.

"I still wake up every day wanting to go and get on with it," he says, "and if you didn't you'd need to be giving it up completely. Of course you have to take the rough with the smooth because you know there's going to be plenty of rough and it absolutely kills you sometimes. And there are a lot of hungry lions out there and they'll soon have you if you're not at the top of your game. But I won't be packing it in all the time I've got these very good horses – that's what makes the difference."

▼ True grit: Might Bite claims a determined victory in the Betway Bowl at Aintree

THE CHAMP

Willie Mullins outpunched Gordon Elliott
in a dramatic showdown at Punchestown
that settled the Irish jumps trainers' title battle

THE champ came out swinging from the first bell. With his title at stake, he had no choice. The first punch landed a hefty blow and, even if that did not betray weakness in his younger opponent, the champ continued to attack relentlessly. Punch after punch rained on the challenger, sometimes in singles, often in combinations, until he could take no more. Long before the final round, the challenger was out for the count, a brave but beaten man. The champion, arms aloft, took the title again. Undefeated now in 11 years.

The latest title showdown between Willie Mullins and Gordon Elliott was one hell of a battle fought over many months, but in the end it boiled down to a dramatic final slugfest at the Punchestown festival and once again it was Mullins who came out on top as he turned a substantial deficit into an even more commanding advantage to claim his 11th consecutive Irish jumps trainers' championship and his 12th in all.

The Mullins figures that week were remarkable: he outscored Elliott by 18 winners to four, won nine of the 12 Grade 1 races and, most crucially of all, took €1.75m in prize-money, around 60 per cent of the bounty on offer. No wonder, in the midst of it all, Mullins said in his usual understated way: "You couldn't make up what's going on this week."

****

FOR much of the 2017-18 jumps season, Elliott seemed to hold sway over Mullins with a series of notable successes at home and abroad. Having started the calendar year with a lead of more than €500,000 in prize-money, Elliott stretched further clear when he landed the biggest prize in Irish jump racing – the €500,000 BoyleSports Irish Grand National – in early April when General Principle got up to deny the Mullins-trained Isleofhopendreams by a head.

Meanwhile, across the water, Elliott took the top trainer award at the Cheltenham Festival for the second year in a row, beating Mullins 8-7, and narrowly denied his big rival again in the Randox Health Grand National at Aintree when Tiger Roll held on by a head from Pleasant Company.

With the tide seemingly turning in Elliott's favour, he started Punchestown week as the 8-11 favourite to claim his first Irish championship. His lead stood at €521,413 but nobody could forget how he had been denied victory in the final stretch the previous year when Mullins outscored him by nearly €600,000 at Punchestown. This was not going to be easy.

Mullins signalled his intent right from the start. In the first race he contested, the Herald Champion Novice Hurdle, the champion saddled four of the ten runners and the mob-handed approach paid off as 25-1 shot Draconien, the

outsider of his quartet, came home in front. Just over an hour later he took the biggest prize of the opening day when Un De Sceaux and Douvan scored a one-two for the stable, with Min fourth for good measure and Elliott only third with A Toi Phil.

The biggest drama – not just of the week but possibly of the entire season – came in the third and final Grade 1 on the Tuesday, the Growise Champion Novice Chase.

Approaching the final fence, Al Boum Photo seemed on course to take the honours and earn more valuable prize-money for Mullins, but events then took a bizarre twist. Paul Townend at first seemed to start easing down Al Boum Photo and then looked over his right shoulder before urging his mount in that direction, as if he was trying to bypass the final fence. Al Boum Photo crashed through the plastic wing, taking himself as well as the unfortunate Finian's Oscar out of the race, and to rub salt in the wound it was Elliott's runners who took full advantage.

The Storyteller galloped past the post in front under Davy Russell, followed by Monbeg Notorious and Jury Duty, giving Elliott a scarcely believable one-two-three worth €87,000. "We've had a good bit of luck there, but we needed it," Elliott admitted, although Russell, with tongue firmly in cheek, said: "I was never in doubt. I was always going to win."

Mullins beat Elliott 3-2 on the

day but the Al Boum Photo reverse meant he had only managed to chip away at Elliott's overall advantage, which still stood at €405,838, and the leader remained 8-11 favourite. The turning point was at hand, however, and the second-day headlines would be all positive about Mullins and Townend, who was quick to seize his chance of redemption.

Once the opening handicap hurdle had passed with no significant involvement by either title challenger, the day belonged entirely to Mullins. He won six races on the bounce, including the three Grade 1s with Next Destination in the Irish Daily Mirror Novice Hurdle, Bellshill in the Coral Punchestown Gold Cup – with Djakadam runner-up – and Tornado Flyer, who led home a one-two-three in the Racing Post Champion INH Flat Race.

Next Destination's victory, by a neck from the Elliott-trained Delta Work, was especially sweet for Townend after his brain fade the previous day. "Paul has been cool under pressure and the crowd are delighted for him. It shows how highly he's thought of," Mullins said. At the end of the Wednesday card, having taking the lead by €48,162 in spectacular style, the trainer reflected on his own comeback. "It's been fantastic and has hugely exceeded expectations. I didn't expect to be in front in the championship by Saturday, never mind by the end of today."

▶▶ *Continues page 28*

****

THE odds reflected the dramatic turnaround, with Mullins now 1-8 for the title and Elliott out to 11-2, and the reigning champion pressed home his advantage on day three. Once again he outscored Elliott, 3-1, and crucially took the day's Grade 1 prizes when Faugheen led another one-two-three in the Ladbrokes Champion Stayers Hurdle and Footpad cruised to victory in the Ryanair Novice Chase.

That stretched Mullins' lead to €424,148 and the game was up for Elliott midway through Friday's card when Samcro crashed out of the Betdaq Punchestown Champion Hurdle. Mullins did not win the race – that honour went to Supasundae for Jessica Harrington – but he had the second, third and fourth and that was enough to take his advantage to an unassailable €550,648.

Incredibly, considering the size of the task he faced at the start of the week, Mullins had needed only three and a half days to turn the title race on its head and claim another championship. Even he found it hard to believe how events had played out, from the Al Boum Photo disaster on the Tuesday to the wonderful Wednesday that turned the tide.

"Going home in the car on Tuesday evening wasn't a nice feeling and I'm sure Gordon went home on Wednesday with a similar feeling," he said. "We had a Grade 1 go up in smoke and Gordon had the first, second and third. I thought that was it. I said to people that we couldn't come back from that, but then Wednesday and the way that day worked out was unprecedented.

"Gordon was the first man to congratulate me," he added. "Obviously I'm pleased to win, but I don't take any pleasure from beating Gordon because he's such a great competitor and I know how he'll be feeling. It's a tough position to be in when you know your chance is gone. It's not nice at all and I know that because we've experienced it in the past when we were up against Noel Meade."

It was indeed tough on Elliott, who enjoyed a tremendous season apart from that difficult final week and struck in the very next race after

▸▸ *Continues page 30*

▸▸ Punchestown Grade 1 aces: (clockwise from top) Un De Sceaux, Tornado Flyer, Next Destination and Draconien

GO RACING IN IRELAND 2019

Wherever you are in Ireland, you're never far from a race meeting and if you want to understand one of our country's great passions, choose from over 300 race meetings at any of the 26 racecourses around the country. Play the odds, raise a glass and enjoy good times with friends – you'll have a day out you'll always remember. So what are you waiting for?

It's time to go racing... because nothing else feels like this.

2019 RACING FESTIVALS

LEOPARDSTOWN
Dublin Racing Festival
2nd – 3rd February

CORK
Easter Festival
20th – 22nd April

FAIRYHOUSE
Easter Festival
21st – 23rd April

PUNCHESTOWN
National Hunt Festival
30th April – 4th May

KILLARNEY
Spring Festival
12th – 14th May

CURRAGH
Guineas Festival
24th – 26th May
(now 3 days)

DOWN ROYAL
Ulster Derby
21st – 22nd June

CURRAGH
Irish Derby Festival
27th – 29th June

BELLEWSTOWN
Summer Festival
3rd – 6th July
(now 4 days)

KILLARNEY
July Festival
15th – 19th July
(now 5 days)

CURRAGH
Irish Oaks Weekend
20th – 21st July

GALWAY
Summer Festival
29th July – 4th August

TRAMORE
August Festival
15th – 18th August

KILLARNEY
August Festival
21st – 24th August

LAYTOWN
Beach Racing Festival
11th September

LISTOWEL
Harvest Festival
8th – 14th September

**LEOPARDSTOWN
& CURRAGH**
Longines Irish
Champions Weekend
14th – 15th September

GALWAY
October Festival
26th – 28th October
(now 3 days)

DOWN ROYAL
Festival of Racing
1st – 2nd November

PUNCHESTOWN
November Winter
Racing
16th – 17th November

FAIRYHOUSE
Winter Festival
30th Nov – 1st Dec

LEOPARDSTOWN
Christmas Festival
26th – 29th December

LIMERICK
Christmas Festival
26th – 29th December

HORSE RACING
IRELAND

▲ Unstoppable: Willie Mullins scores further Grade 1 victories at Punchestown with (clockwise from top left) Faugheen, Benie Des Dieux, Bellshill, Saldier and Footpad

Samcro's fall when Dortmund Park took the Grade 1 Profile Systems Champion Novice Hurdle. He was magnanimous in title defeat, saying: "It's a credit to Willie Mullins. We'll be there to fight another day. We'll just have to put our head down and keep trying."

He could do nothing to stop Mullins on the final day, however, as the champion put the icing on the cake with four more winners, including both Grade 1 prizes with Benie Des Dieux in the Irish Stallion Farms Mares Champion Hurdle (in a one-two with Augusta Kate) and Saldier in the AES Champion Four Year Old Hurdle (this time saddling the first four).

****

THAT gave Mullins a record 18 winners for the week and took him level with Tom Dreaper, Arkle's legendary trainer, with a dozen titles. "I'm humbled to be alongside him in the statistics. He was sort of God when we were growing up," Mullins said.

Dreaper, of course, worked in an era where the top trainers relied on quality over quantity. Mullins is blessed with both and it showed at Punchestown, where he wheeled out big guns like Un De Sceaux, Douvan, Faugheen, Footpad and Min at the head of a mighty battalion that included 13 runners in a handicap hurdle, equalling the world record for one stable in a race set by Elliott in the Irish Grand National.

For those who maintain title battles are a sideshow to the racing, this may have been instructive. Two years

earlier Mullins sent many of his stars to Aintree's Grand National meeting in vain pursuit of a British title, fielding 19 runners in the Grade 1 contests, but Elliott's increasingly strong challenge for the domestic crown has ensured that Mullins prioritises having his best horses fit and firing at Punchestown. Mullins sent all nine of his top-rated performers in the 2017-18 season to the Kildare track, while running only two of them at Aintree as well.

With Elliott doing the same in his bid to secure a first title, Punchestown racegoers were treated to a galaxy of stars at the five-day festival and a feast of exciting races. "I hope this trainers' championship has been good for racing," Mullins said.

He could be sure it was, especially after that breathtaking finale.

THE
BIGGER
PICTURE

Children play in the puddles as Waqaas (Lisa O'Neill, farside) denies Royal Admiral in a tight finish over seven furlongs at Laytown in September. Ireland's famous beach venue celebrated its 150th anniversary in 2018
PATRICK McCANN (RACINGPOST.COM/PHOTOS)

Enable had to miss the summer but the mighty filly came back with a bang to land her second Arc in dramatic fashion

By Lee Mottershead

AUTUMN HARVEST

THE amount of time afforded us to enjoy Enable during 2018 was short. So, too, was the margin by which she famously became a back-to-back winner of the Prix de l'Arc de Triomphe. It was not much, but it was enough, and it turned a magnificent filly into one of the greats.

What we did not know in the days before the Arc's Longchamp homecoming was the extent to which Enable needed everything to go right. In a year when fate had not smiled kindly on her, she deserved a change of luck. She got it.

Perhaps crucially, she benefited

from a favourable stalls draw. In that regard, the filly who always looked likeliest to provide the principal danger was not so fortunate. Yet while it was easy to ruminate on the obstacle Sea Of Class so nearly overcame, Enable had faced a mountain of her own. The annals of the world's most prestigious Flat race now show she reached the summit.

Measured in pounds and ounces, what Enable achieved at Longchamp on October's first Sunday was some way removed from the stunning performance that lit up Chantilly 12 months earlier. Dig deeper, however, consider the circumstances, the context and the final countdown, and it is quite possible to argue Enable's second French foray was even more meritorious than the first.

Had things worked out differently, Khalid Abdullah's champion would have been winning Group 1s as a four-year-old long before defending her Arc crown. Connections had spoken of taking in the Prince of Wales's Stakes at Ascot, where she was so sublime when thumping Ulysses in the 2017 King George, a contest that could again have been on her agenda. There had been even more mentions of aiming the John Gosden-trained filly at the Juddmonte International, the race that with each passing year further cements its status as Britain's premier all-aged prize.

In May a short statement revealed Enable had sustained a setback. Some filling had been found in a knee. The horse who had been supposed to be the summer's star would not run until at least August. In a slight amendment to the headline used above the piece on the superstar filly in last year's Racing Post Annual, she was suddenly ready, willing and unable to run.

As we moved closer to the Ebor festival it became increasingly obvious she would not appear there. A new point of return was identified. Enable would prepare for the Arc on sand.

▸▸ *Continues page 36*

She had raced on an all-weather track once before, when making a striking racecourse debut at Newcastle in November 2016. This time she would go to Kempton for the September Stakes, an event her trainer had won with another leading light, Jack Hobbs, in 2015. That colt had frightened off all meaningful opposition. The expectation was that Enable would do the same. We expected wrong.

When the September Stakes entries came out they featured, to widespread surprise, the name of Crystal Ocean, who had rattled off a series of notable successes before being edged out of the King George by his Sir Michael Stoute-trained stablemate Poet's Word. The highlight of Kempton's Flat programme seemed, at first glance, an unusual diversion for Crystal Ocean, so much so a common assumption was that he would not be declared to run. But he did run, and Enable ran all over him.

This was the finest race ever staged on a British all-weather racecourse. As the stalls crashed open Crystal Ocean held a superior official rating to Enable, his 129 trumping her 128, but he was also being asked to shoulder a 5lb penalty that, on top of the 3lb sex allowance, meant he needed to concede 8lb to the then five-time Group 1 winner. Bookmakers did not believe he could do it, sending off Enable the 8-15 favourite. They were right and she was wonderful.

It was all remarkably simple. Frankie Dettori sent his girl straight into the lead, they dictated proceedings, kicked on off the home bend and then drew clear for an easy three-and-a-half-length romp. After some troubled times this was the perfect reintroduction to racing.

"I was confident she would do that, yeah," said Gosden just after Dettori had dismounted from his equine sweetheart and given her an affectionate kiss that prompted some of those assembled around the

▲ September success: Enable powers clear of Crystal Ocean on her Kempton return

DUAL ARC WINNERS

Enable became the eighth to complete a double since the Arc's inception in 1920 and the third filly after Corrida and Treve. Of the 13 three-year-old fillies to have won the Arc, only Treve and Enable have returned to strike again at four.

Ksar 1921, 1922
Motrico 1930, 1932
Corrida 1936, 1937
Tantieme 1950, 1951
Ribot 1955, 1956
Alleged 1977, 1978
Treve 2013, 2014
Enable 2017, 2018

paddock to go "aaahhh" in unison. Gosden then suggested it was a blessing for Dettori's wife Catherine that Enable has four legs. If the filly could have understood, she would have taken it as a compliment. Before dashing off to Heathrow and a flight to the States, Gosden heaped upon her further praise.

"She was determined to come back, so it's all down to her and nothing to do with us," he said. "All our staff have worked very hard but she's a great person to deal with and really wanted to come back."

****

THE day could hardly have gone better. The four weeks that bridged Kempton and Longchamp did not go nearly so well. That may explain why in a pre-Arc interview on ITV Gosden had appeared strangely downbeat, not sounding like a man about to field a scorching hot favourite for the most coveted test in European Flat racing.

It transpired Enable had suffered

▸ *Continues page 38*

SIX MACHINE

Frankie Dettori became the seventh jockey to ride four Arc winners when he scored on Golden Horn in 2015 and now he stands two clear after his double strike on Enable. His six victories have been gained for two trainers and with a 13-year gap between his third for Saeed Bin Suroor and his winning spree for John Gosden

DETTORI'S RECORD ARC HAUL

Year	Horse	Trainer
1995	**Lammtarra**	Saeed Bin Suroor
2001	**Sakhee**	Saeed Bin Suroor
2002	**Marienbard**	Saeed Bin Suroor
2015	**Golden Horn**	John Gosden
2017	**Enable**	John Gosden
2018	**Enable**	John Gosden

VIEWS FROM THE SADDLE

How the Arc was won and lost – in the jockeys' own words

Frankie Dettori, Enable

This was my 30th time riding in the Arc and it was without doubt the most nervous I've ever been. It was one hell of a long morning, let me tell you. I was very excited.

Things went according to plan early. I knew the O'Brien runners would go an end-to-end gallop to suit their stayers and that's what they did. I found myself in a fantastic spot.

The first part of the race she was only okay. She wasn't carting me along like she sometimes can. Then, along the false straight, the life in the old girl came back.

The leaders came back to us and I knew then we were in business. I waited as long as I could and, at the 300-metre marker [a furlong and a half out], she showed her trademark turn of foot.

The rail at Longchamp on good ground is a big help and we got it after we hit the front.

I had a glance at the 300-metre mark and I'm three lengths clear. I said to myself, "I've won this". I put my whip down and tried to get one last drop of energy to get her head down at the line. In the last 50 yards we were on our hands and knees. I was trying to squeeze everything I could out of her and we got there.

James Doyle, Sea Of Class

We had a bad draw but she's got a unique run style and, if you change that, you risk losing the ability she's got. So we had to ride her to her run style.

Unfortunately I got caught behind Kew Gardens, who just struggled for tactical speed at a key point of the race, which meant the race got away from me a bit.

She's a tremendous filly and I'm sure with a better draw we wouldn't have had to sit as far back as we did and the result might have been different. But for Enable to do that on her second start of the year is pretty spectacular, so full credit to her.

another setback in the days after her glorious comeback. Gosden had not been happy with the filly's temperature or blood but chose to keep the information within a tight circle. "I did not bother people with it," he told members of the media in the post-Arc press conference. "It's my job to manage it. You don't need it in the paper. I just had to back off a bit and I had to miss a bit of work. That's tough, but if you then push at the wrong time you pay the price."

Some will feel Gosden, so often praised for his communication skills, should have informed the punting public that a horse they were betting on was not in peak condition. Moreover, it was laid bare during the race, and in Gosden's words afterwards, that he had known she could not deliver a peak performance. "She wasn't at her best today," he said. It is a mark of Enable's reserves of talent, and indeed of Gosden's genius at getting her to Paris as well as he possibly could, that Enable not at her best was still good enough to win the Arc.

The Arc she had to win was not vintage by any means. Nor was the Arc-day experience a vintage one for the many racegoers who found an afternoon spent in Longchamp's new Lego-like grandstand to be deeply unsatisfactory. There were also far fewer of those racegoers at Longchamp than had been present when Golden Horn scored for Dettori and Gosden in 2015, just one day before the bulldozers began to do their job. On that occasion 52,000 people were in attendance. This time there were only 35,000, the figure no doubt influenced by a massive increase in the general entrance fee to €85. Despite the problems those 35,000 folk witnessed a pulsating spectacle up the wonderfully wide Longchamp home straight.

Aside from Enable, the evens favourite on industry starting prices, only three other horses began the mile-and-a-half journey at single-figure odds. There was St Leger winner Kew Gardens, one of five candidates for Aidan O'Brien, cosy Prix Foy victor Waldgeist, part of an Andre Fabre trio, and Sea Of Class, a first Arc runner for William Haggas in 22 years.

The Tsui family had been represented in the Arc only twice before. They won it in 1993 with their latest challenger's granny, Urban Sea, and they won it again with her father, Sea The Stars, in 2009. Their prospects of winning it for a third time were hit hard when

▲ Happy day: Enable and Frankie Dettori are the centre of attention after their Arc repeat

▼ John Gosden and wife Rachel Hood are all smiles at Longchamp

Sea Of Class landed stall 15. The statistics showed overcoming a wide draw in a big-field Arc staged on decent ground was, if not mission impossible, then mission improbable. Sea Of Class had been sublime in taking the Irish and Yorkshire Oaks, unleashing a searing turn of foot having been ridden off the pace by James Doyle. Here, with Enable beginning from much closer to the rail in stall six, she was at a significant disadvantage.

When Haggas spoke on the eve of the deciding day there was already dejection in his voice. He dropped a clear hint Sea Of Class would be ridden patiently, as usual, no doubt aware of what his wife Maureen had been advised by her father Lester

▸▸ Continues page 40

ARC WINNERS BY RACING POST RATINGS OVER THE LAST TEN YEARS

	Enable (2018)	Found (2016)	Solemia (2012)		Treve (2014)	Golden Horn (2015)	Danedream (2011)	Enable (2017)	Workforce (2010)	Treve (2013)	Sea The Stars (2009)
RPR	122	123	124	125	126	127	128	129	130	131	132

KARAKONTIE

FIRST-CROP YEARLINGS
SOLD FOR:

$220,000, $150,000,
$130,000, $125,000,
$120,000, $120,000,
$100,000, etc.

Colt out of Judy In Disguise (GB)

GAINESWAY / GAINESWAY.COM / 859.293.2676

Piggott. "When we got the draw," she revealed, "I rang my father and said, 'what do we do?' He said: 'Don't change the tactics. Drop her out the back and pray'." Their prayers were so nearly answered.

****

AS soon as the 19 runners commenced their tour de Longchamp, Doyle took a pull on Sea Of Class, steered right and began to wait. He managed to get his mount to a ground-saving position on the fence, but heading down the false straight she had only a single horse behind her. Enable, kept close to the leaders by Dettori, was fired to the front a furlong and a half from home. Behind her, but beginning to close, was Sea Of Class.

Having weaved her way into daylight following a blessedly smooth passage, one Newmarket-trained filly was bearing down on another. Sea Of Class was closing. Enable was stopping, her lack of fitness finally telling in the last 50 metres. Granted one more stride, or two at most, Sea

Of Class would have got up and won the Arc. Instead, Enable made history by a short neck.

She had become the eighth horse to win two Arcs, emulating Treve's achievement from four years earlier. She was the first horse ever to win the Arc off the back of only one run that year and the first to win it at two different tracks. Dettori had extended his own record haul to six triumphs. Abdullah was present to witness it all happen. Gosden was pleased it was all over.

"It has been a nightmare year," he said. "I'm feeling a deep sense of relief – the elation will come later."

Dettori had just won the Arc and was in no mood to defer elation. He seldom is. "I can't believe it, I'm actually lost for words," he said. "She wasn't the Enable of last year but she has got the job done and that's all that matters.

"There was almighty pressure on all of us. The world was behind me. Everybody wanted her to win. I wasn't riding a 10-1 shot, I was riding the

▲ Driving finish: Enable goes for home while Sea Of Class (right) starts her run before coming agonisingly close to a famous Arc victory

▼ The Racing Post's front page the day after Enable's Arc repeat

favourite in the most famous race in the world. I'm looking forward to watching the replay."

For the Sea Of Class camp, full of pride and pain, the replay would have made less pleasurable viewing. Maureen Haggas was close to tears, her first thoughts with Doyle, who had executed such a sublime race after wasting down to a weight painfully below his normal minimum. Doyle's thoughts were for those thinking of him. "It was absolute agony," he said. "I was heartbroken, more so for everyone that has been connected with her – her owners and William and Maureen."

They had come so close. They had also been beaten by an exceptional athlete. In that nightmarish year of which Gosden spoke, so much went wrong for his stable star, but on the day that mattered most, the day that had been of paramount importance since the first Arc was won, Enable overcame adversity.

Britain has only one dual Arc winner. A very special one indeed.

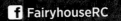 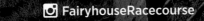

CLASS ACT

Sea Of Class sparkled with two Group 1 victories and her gallant charge in the Arc

By Lee Mottershead

HER season was topped and tailed by near misses, one in a Craven meeting maiden, the other in the Prix de l'Arc de Triomphe. In the intervening time Sea Of Class won four races, two of them at the top level, and confirmed herself a thoroughbred of the highest order even with that agonising defeat at the very end.

What there was not during the journey from Newmarket to Longchamp was a crack at the Investec Oaks. Had she gone there she would have been one of the favourites and, judging from her later form, might easily have won. She would have been going there on only her third outing, however, and by making the brave call to swerve Epsom, William Haggas played the patience card and displayed an understanding of his filly that paid off splendidly as the year progressed.

Haggas, entrusted with training Sea Of Class by Ling Tsui and her son, Christopher, knew the Oaks would be too much, too soon for a filly whose owners paid 170,000gns for her as a yearling. That now looks a bargain. They also raced her father Sea The Stars and his mother, the 1993 Arc heroine Urban Sea, whose own story rarely strayed from the extraordinary, with another remarkable chapter written in the 2018 Arc when she was granddam or great-granddam of the first eight finishers.

Sea Of Class was quick to demonstrate her own talent, breaking her black-type duck on just her second outing. From that tail-swishing second place in a mile maiden at Newmarket, Haggas took her to Newbury for the ten-furlong Oaks trial and the filly dazzled in that Listed contest, unleashing a turn of foot that could not fail to catch eyes.

She became prominent in the Oaks betting and was kept in the race at the six-day forfeit stage, but you sensed Haggas was desperate not to run her. When rain fell on Epsom, turning the ground soft, he took her out.

His valuable asset instead went back to Newbury and claimed her second consecutive mile-and-a-quarter Listed heat at the venue. With more precious education gained, the time had come for a proper test and it came in the Irish Oaks. It shone a light not just on the prowess of Sea Of Class but also her jockey James Doyle.

Haggas and Doyle became a powerful combination in 2018, and at the Curragh the Godolphin rider executed waiting tactics with a confidence and bravura that had to be seen to be believed. Although he began to push his mount along with more than two furlongs to run, he never did more than push. Yet despite at no point resorting to the whip, it was only in the final blades of grass that Sea Of Class put her neck in front of Epsom's Oaks winner Forever Together.

"I fancied her today," Haggas admitted. "I asked James to be brave because she has a good turn of foot but I didn't think he would be that brave!"

That turn of foot was again evident when Sea Of Class went to her trainer's favourite racecourse for the Yorkshire Oaks. What was so breathtaking was the speed with which she went from being a few lengths down to a few lengths in front. In a matter of strides she stamped her authority all over Group 1 opposition. It was exhilarating to watch.

It also made it nigh on inevitable she would be supplemented for the Arc, despite the €120,000 cost of buying a late ticket. She almost won in Paris, thundering down the track and getting to within a short neck of Enable having had to make up acres of ground. Had she not been drawn horribly wide in stall 15, and therefore forced to race from so far back, Sea Of Class surely would have won the Arc.

In the immediate aftermath those connected with the valiant runner-up could not have been more sporting or gracious. A few days later Haggas spoke of the reverse as "gut-wrenching" but added: "I'm so proud of the way she performed and proud of the way the jockey performed."

There was good reason to be proud. Looking forward to 2019 there is also good reason to be excited.

ALPHA FEMALE

Alpha Centauri was the mile star who shone bright through a glorious summer

By Richard Forristal

HINDSIGHT tends to make visionaries of even the dullest minds, but there was a prophetic ring to Jessica Harrington's musings on Alpha Centauri's stellar impact shortly before Irish Champions Weekend.

"It's all amazing," she said. "When it's actually happening you get the buzz and all that, but you don't really take it in. It wasn't until after Moscow [Flyer] retired that I really looked back at what he did – and I was in awe of what he had done – and I'd say it will be the same with Alpha. What she has done is amazing, but we're sort of on the rollercoaster at the moment and I don't want to get off it."

At the risk of evoking the spirit of Donald Rumsfeld, Harrington has been in this game long enough to know that you never know what's around the corner. The known unknowns sort of thing.

She hasn't endured at the top of her profession for 30 years without acquiring some sage-like wisdom. Harrington and the team surrounding Alpha Centauri revelled in the once-in-a-lifetime nature of the filly's brilliance but that fear of tempting fate is ever-present when you are dealing

with fragile animals in a sport as fickle and unpredictable as horseracing.

For all that she inferred otherwise, the simple fact that Harrington conveyed those sentiments illustrated that she was acutely conscious of the incalculable value of the grey thoroughbred daughter of Mastercraftsman, not in a monetary sense but in an opportunistic one. Far better financially resourced stables with access to the most select pedigrees have never happened upon a filly remotely as good as Alpha Centauri.

Lamentably, within a day of those utterings, the Kildare trainer's caution was realised at Leopardstown. Alpha Centauri seemingly came there to win her race in the Matron Stakes, only to take a misstep that visibly stalled her momentum.

The Niarchos family's filly then

took another and the wind was knocked from her sails. It emerged that she had chipped a joint in her fetlock, and it did not take long for connections to call time on her terrific career. It's hard to interpret what happened without inadvertently implying that Laurens didn't prevail on merit. That is a pity, but it's also not necessarily unfair.

Without getting bogged down in form, the proximity of Clemmie to Alpha Centauri at Leopardstown bears out the point. The Ballydoyle filly got to within a length and three-quarters of the

runner-up that day. In their three encounters in the previous four months, Alpha Centauri's margin of superiority varied from five and a half to 12 lengths.

Laurens duly went on to confirm herself a filly of tremendous class, but circumstances conspired to hinder Harrington's exceptional filly from showing her true colours when they clashed in Dublin, for all that it made a stirring spectacle.

Although the Moone handler was magnanimous in defeat, the nature of Alpha Centauri's swansong served only to enhance her estimation of the filly. "For her to sustain the injury she did – and everyone could see when she did it – and still run on to finish second to another very good filly says it all," said Harrington (left). "Let's not take anything away from Laurens, but I saw her do it and knew straight away we were in trouble."

Reinforcing just how much she appreciated the epochal clout of the equine heavyweight she had at her disposal, Harrington added: "It was incredible to have her, and no-one can take away what she's done. I had an amazing summer with her. She gave me my first Classic winner, my first Royal Ascot

▸▸ Continues page 46

winner, my first French winner – she did an awful lot of firsts for me."

Had Alpha Centauri prevailed at Leopardstown, she would have emulated the mighty Sea The Stars by claiming a fifth Group 1 in as many months. Fellow fillies of the calibre of Enable, Black Caviar, Zenyatta and Winx all won five times in succession at the highest level, so that's the realm for which she was headed.

****

GIVEN her name, an Icarus parallel might be apt, for she did fly that close to the sun. Alpha Centauri is the star grouping closest to the solar system and the equine version absolutely lit up the summer from the moment she emerged in the Irish 1,000 Guineas.

Her victory at the Curragh was a shock and it wasn't. Odds of 12-1 reflected the bumpy flight Alpha Centauri had taken, but there had long been a sense that she was destined for something special. She just took a bit longer than expected to get there. While we had seen how much talent she had as a juvenile, the testing ground she encountered on her final start of 2017 in the Moyglare Stud Stakes and her first start of 2018 in a Guineas trial at Leopardstown tempered the initial fervour.

Back on good ground at the Curragh on Guineas day, she ran out a decisive winner under Colm O'Donoghue to reignite the spark of hope that here indeed was a rare talent.

"I've finally got the Classic!" Harrington gushed after the race. "To win a Classic is a dream come true. It's almost as good as winning a Gold Cup at Cheltenham – it's probably better. They're on a par. To win a race like this is absolutely fantastic."

Things were about to get even better. Come Royal Ascot, expectations were off the scale. For all that Harrington was well versed in coping with such high-pressure scenarios over jumps, and she had handled a horse of Group 1 calibre before when landing the National Stakes with Pathfork in 2010, this was new territory for her. She subsequently admitted to being aware of what was at stake, but if it affected

HIGH CLASS

Alpha Centauri achieved an RPR of 124 in three consecutive races – the Coronation Stakes, Falmouth Stakes and Prix Jacques le Marois – and that mark has been bettered only by Goldikova among three-year-old miling fillies in Europe this century.

European 3yo fillies over a mile since 2000

Horse	Year	RPR
Goldikova	2008	125
Alpha Centauri	2018	124
Darjina	2007	124
Attraction	2004	123
Divine Proportions	2005	123
Immortal Verse	2011	123
Minding	2016	123
Russian Rhythm	2003	123

her judgement in any way it can only have done so in a positive sense.

Alpha Centauri absolutely pulverised the opposition in the Coronation Stakes, setting a track record of 1min 35.89sec for the new round mile course, and no other filly in recent times had won the race by further than her six-length knockout. The winners of the British and French 1,000 Guineas, Billesdon Brook and Teppal, were obliterated, and Racing Post Ratings expert Paul Curtis ranked it the best edition of the race for 15 years.

The universe had a new star. "I'm relieved," a breathless Harrington admitted. "I got very wound up. I was very nervous – I know she's very good. It was nice going into the Irish Guineas very much under the radar but I had confidence in her. Today was different. She was favourite and we were there to be shot at. I've had Ascot winners, but I've never had a Royal Ascot winner and it's absolutely fantastic."

Again, things were about to get better – and better. Harrington

▼ Record breaker: Alpha Centauri comes home in glorious isolation in the Coronation Stakes at Royal Ascot

pointed her newly crowned Coronation queen in the direction of Newmarket and, under an O'Donoghue steer of tremendous conviction, the filly bossed the Falmouth Stakes from the front.

It was a performance of sheer majesty, somehow both graceful and merciless. That dichotomy was something that seemed to define Alpha Centauri, a towering individual who tipped the scales at 530kg when she arrived in Moone. It was a scarcely credible mass for a yearling that famously prompted Harrington to have her weighed twice more, and nearly to get the scales recalibrated. Yet this athletic filly floated over a sound surface with the elegant lightness of a nimble ballerina. She was a freak of nature.

"She's absolutely unbelievable," Harrington enthused after the Falmouth. "She was just hacking along and quickened up. Maybe she didn't win as far as she did at Ascot, but she had to do the donkey work

and make all the running – she's amazing. For the size of her, she loves that ground. She has a high cruising speed and that's what really helps her. I'm very lucky to train her."

They went from Newmarket in July to Deauville in August, when another superlative display confirmed this was an alpha female to rank among the best. In the Prix Jacques le Marois, a race sponsored by the Niarchos family, she pulverised both colts and fillies, with Recoletos, the Prix d'Ispahan and subsequent Prix du Moulin winner, unable to lay a glove on her in second. It was her piece de resistance.

Harrington would later reflect: "She was at her most spectacular in the Coronation Stakes, I suppose, and she consolidated in the Falmouth. But really I think she was at her best in France. She beat top-class colts very easily. In form book terms I would think it was a genuinely superior performance."

⏭ *Continues page 48*

▲ Colm O'Donoghue celebrates winning the Irish 1,000 Guineas
▼ Joy in the winner's enclosure after victory in the Falmouth Stakes

****

IF THAT was Harrington's gut reaction, the official assessors thought similarly. After the Marois, Alpha Centauri was handed a rating of 124, which was the highest figure for a three-year-old filly trained in Ireland since Ridgewood Pearl's seminal campaign 23 years earlier. John Oxx's filly ended up on a mark of 126 after her heroics in the Breeders' Cup Mile, and Alpha Centauri might have threatened that pinnacle had fate not intervened.

The dramatic final act at Leopardstown also denied her the chance to emulate her great granddam, Miesque. The Niarchos family's original mile sensation won back-to-back Breeders' Cup Miles in 1987 and 1988, and the plan was to keep Alpha Centauri in training as a four-year-old as well. But it wasn't to be. She went out on her shield at Leopardstown, beaten but not bowed, leaving a legacy that will endure for a time to come.

"She has given the Niarchos family enormous pleasure and has added another chapter to the story of a wonderful equine family," their racing manager Alan Cooper reflected.

"The connection to Miesque brought back great memories 30 years on. It was a thrill to be associated with Jessie's first Classic winner. Her Coronation win in record time was spectacular and her win against the colts in the Marois confirmed her as a special talent. It was a sad way to end, but she was immensely brave in defeat at Leopardstown. Now we look forward to her making her mark as a broodmare."

O'Donoghue, who rode Alpha Centauri in each of her ten races en route to accruing £1,254,827 in prize-money, also paid tribute to the filly who had burned so bright. "She was the leading three-year-old all year – an incredible filly," he said. "She didn't just beat them, she annihilated them. She broke horses' hearts and she was immense for my career. It was a privilege to be associated with her."

Quite the rollercoaster. Now that they're off it, they can look back with pride and awe at the luminescent supernova that was Alpha Centauri.

O'DONOGHUE'S STARRING ROLE

FOR Colm O'Donoghue, Alpha Centauri was the horse he had been waiting for and needed.

After 20 years as an intrinsic cog in the wheel at Ballydoyle, O'Donoghue began his association with Jessica Harrington in 2016. It would be another year before he cut the cord completely with the most successful racing and bloodstock operation in the world, but he knew he had to take a leap of faith.

A trusty deputy for Aidan O'Brien, he took every chance he had been given at Ballydoyle, plundering ten Group or Grade 1s, including three British and Irish Classics. Still, having served under every one of the marquee names to pass through there from Christy Roche to Ryan Moore, he realised he would have to spread his wings to truly test himself.

"I suppose time waits for nobody," he reflected of his Ballydoyle departure. "It wasn't easy but I had to go for myself, because I wanted to push myself. I always felt I was good enough but I didn't think I was fulfilling what I could do. I wanted to know, and I wasn't getting the rides I had been. That happens and it's just the way it is, but I had to say, 'Now is the time. Go and see if you're good enough.'"

In Alpha Centauri, he had the vehicle he needed to prove himself to the world, and he never missed a beat on her. Indeed, he flourished under his new-found responsibility.

"Alpha has taken me to a different level," O'Donoghue, 37, said in the autumn. "I love to be asked to ride in these big races. That's the thing I want most. Some lads want to be champion jockey but I want to ride in all these big races. That's what drives me.

"Getting on the right horse is what it's all about, and obviously getting on something as special as Alpha Centauri is the sort of opportunity that might only come around once. She's an amazing filly."

Having reached for the stars, O'Donoghue got there with the flying grey.

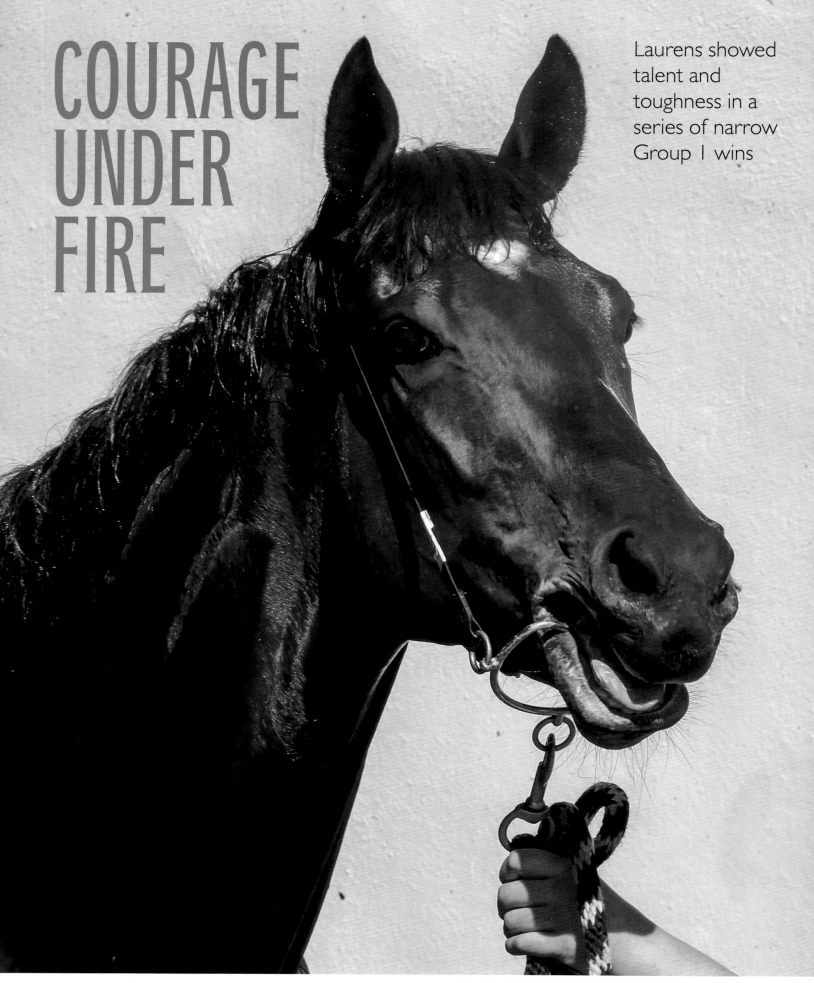

COURAGE UNDER FIRE

Laurens showed talent and toughness in a series of narrow Group 1 wins

By Lee Mottershead

A BIT Yorkshire, a bit French and more than a bit wonderful. That's Laurens, whose multiple major victories and marvellous toughness made her one of the stars of the 2018 Flat season.

Women who hail from the white rose county have a reputation for being strong, no-nonsense individuals. Now, to add to a celebrated list that includes Olympic gold medal-winning athlete Jessica Ennis-Hill, former House of Commons speaker Betty Boothroyd, Oscar-winning actress Judi Dench and broom-waving battleaxe Nora Batty, there is a filly boasting five Group 1 victories, four of them achieved in a glorious three-year-old campaign.

Yet although Laurens lives in a stable in Middleham, she is probably as likely to say bonjour as 'ow do, given she was bred in France and has kept returning to France. It was there she enjoyed her finest hour, the one that most thrilled enthusiastic owner John Dance and underlined her exceptional bravery under pressure.

We did, of course, know the daughter of Siyouni to be an admirably gutsy thoroughbred long before she made her seasonal reappearance. As a juvenile she had netted the May Hill Stakes by a head and then followed up by a nose for trainer Karl Burke in the Fillies' Mile. It was a success that more than earned her a place in

▲ Fighting spirit: Laurens (leading) races to victory in the Matron Stakes

the 1,000 Guineas, which delivered a defeat extremely worthy of praise and a springboard to some super days.

Having led at the halfway stage of the Guineas, she found herself unable to withstand the challenge of outsider Billesdon Brook. It left Burke convinced of one thing. "I think she's crying out for further," he said at Newmarket. Time would show the mile distance and Laurens were actually a perfect match. The northern star was simply not quite good enough on a rather strange day. Her day, four of them in fact, would soon come.

The principal target was the Prix de Diane. First she went back to France, where she had already raced once as a two-year-old, and contested the Prix Saint-Alary. As a trial for a Classic it seems perverse the Saint-Alary holds Group 1 status, but it does, and in terms of commitment to the cause it yielded a Group 1-worthy performance from Laurens. She set out in front, was headed a furlong and a half

from home, regained the lead a furlong later and then resisted the challenge of With You by a short head.

****

SHE was game that day at Longchamp. She was even more so next time at Chantilly in the Prix de Diane. It was early in the home straight that regular partner PJ McDonald, a Scottish Grand National winner when riding over jumps, sent Laurens into the lead. Across every yard that followed she was under assault. At one stage she was in a line of seven horses, five to her left, one to her right. The attacks were sustained but Laurens repelled them all. She was utterly magnificent.

"The crowd at Chantilly made us feel like heroes," said Dance later in the year. At the time he and Burke were pointing towards the Yorkshire Oaks. They were confident Laurens would stay a mile and a half. They were wrong. She could finish only sixth to Sea

Of Class, which almost immediately stimulated thoughts of a new and audacious assignment. Laurens was being directed towards a clash with Alpha Centauri.

"She's in the Matron, so we're seriously considering dropping her back to a mile and taking on Jessie Harrington's filly," Burke said. "She's not slow and she loves to be out there using her stride to its full potential."

Alpha Centauri had won four Group 1 races in her Classic campaign and she went to the Matron having taken the Prix Jacques le Marois by a wide margin. Understandably she was sent off a red-hot odds-on favourite. Anyone who backed her at 30-100 was made to suffer.

With McDonald injured, Laurens was steered by Danny Tudhope. They bonded nicely. It soon emerged Alpha Centauri had chipped a joint in the closing stages. That made her eclipse easier to understand but, equally, it was no disgrace to be beaten by an opponent who once again refused to lie down, making every bit of the running and creating the most stirring of sights.

"They tried to take me on early doors but Laurens wasn't having any of it," said Tudhope, who again had the pleasure of being in the saddle when his new lady friend kept Happily at bay in the Sun Chariot Stakes. It was her fourth Group 1 win of the season. It was achieved by a head. The others had been gained by three-quarters of a length, a neck and a short head. You simply had to feel sorry for those who had been trying in vain to get past her.

Those efforts eventually had to take their toll. By the time Laurens turned up in the Queen Elizabeth II Stakes, they had done and she was only eighth behind Roaring Lion. Dance paid a £70,000 supplementary entry fee in order to participate but would have been quick to admit his filly owed him nothing. Laurens had consistently done her team proud.

There have been better fillies. There have surely been none tougher.

▶ Celebration time: Karl Burke and Danny Tudhope after the Matron Stakes at Leopardstown

IN THE PICTURE

Honours shared as Ayr Gold Cup ends in dead-heat

THE Ayr Gold Cup, established in 1804, had the first dead-heat in its history on September 22 when Son Of Rest, the ante-post gamble of the race, was caught by outsider Baron Bolt in a pulsating finish.

Son Of Rest *(red)* – beaten half a length in a Group 1 six days earlier and 10lb well in – had been backed into 5-1 favourite (from 20-1) and looked every inch a handicap 'good thing' when he went clear a furlong out. However, 28-1 shot Baron Bolt *(blue)* came out of the pack with a strong run and took a narrow lead before his rival fought back at the end, with the pair four lengths clear.

Connections of both horses had to endure an agonising seven-minute wait before the dead-heat was called and there were celebrations all round when it was revealed there would be no loser after an epic battle.

Fozzy Stack, trainer of Son Of Rest, was pleased to clinch Ireland's first win in the historic race and a key victory in his second season with a licence. "I thought we were beat," the 38-year-old admitted. "The other horse got past us and probably went a neck up but we were getting back at the line. I said to Brian [Parker, owner] we'd take a dead-heat. It's a very prestigious race and it's great to be a small part of history."

Baron Bolt's trainer Paul Cole, at 77 more than twice Stack's age, said: "It was a great result in the end. It was a fantastic effort from both horses and it was amazing they drew so far clear."

The result was a notable landmark in the early career of Baron Bolt's jockey Cameron Noble, an apprentice based in Newmarket with Michael Bell and having his first ride not just for Cole but also at Ayr.

"I'd rather share it than take second. This is the biggest win of my career and the biggest opportunity I've had as well," the 20-year-old said.

Son Of Rest's rider Chris Hayes has Classic success on his CV and was delighted to add the Ayr Gold Cup, particularly as he feared he had been overhauled by Baron Bolt. "I thought I was beat, so it's nice to get half of it," he said.

"I was a flared nostril away from getting my P45. He's an out-and-out hold-up horse and as I got there a furlong out I said to myself it was too soon, but he kept going."

Bookmakers were no doubt pleased Son Of Rest was denied outright victory, as the rules on a dead-heat state that all bets are settled at 'half-stake', reducing their substantial liabilities on the gambled-on favourite.

Pictures: **JOHN GROSSICK** (RACINGPOST.COM/PHOTOS)

Tiger Roll added Grand National glory to his three Cheltenham Festival wins with a battling victory at Aintree under Davy Russell

TIGER FEAT

By Alan Sweetman

THERE'S no race quite like it. Year in, year out, the Grand National adds another layer to its legend and mystique, the thrill of the spectacle invariably accompanied by an engaging narrative. It is only with the benefit of hindsight that you see all the angles, all the nuances, all the elements of the human drama involved in how this unique horserace is played out.

This time the plotlines involved a tigerish little Flat-bred horse who had conquered the Cheltenham Festival and would now do the

same at Aintree, a jockey achieving the ultimate redemption with the team that once sacked him, another rider who missed out on the horse he had done so much to nurture and a heavyweight clash between the titans of Irish training, all wrapped up in one of the National's tightest finishes. It was quite a story.

****

THE 2018 Randox Health Grand National is in the closing stages. The leaders have jumped 28 fences, omitting Becher's second time around with a jockey down injured. One fence left, and it is an all-Irish affair with two training giants locked in combat. The

Gordon Elliott-trained Tiger Roll leads Pleasant Company, from the rival camp of Willie Mullins, with the pair clear of Elliott's 13-year-old Bless The Wings and Anibale Fly.

Another of Tiger's Roll stablemates,

▸ *Continues page 56*

Valseur Lido, is fifth but he is beginning to weaken, his race is run. His jockey Keith Donoghue knows all he can do is coax his tiring mount home. He had watched Tiger Roll overtake him, and his dream had died. Donoghue had battled with his weight to get down to 11st 4lb to win on Tiger Roll at the Cheltenham Festival four weeks earlier, but there was never a chance he would do 10lb 13lb in the National. He always knew that.

The story – the biggest that can be written in a jump jockey's life – is about to belong to someone else. Tiger Roll looks strong at the last and by the Elbow his 38-year-old rider Davy Russell has driven him into a six-length lead. Tiger Roll has cruised through most of the race and keeps up the gallop under pressure but then, with not much more than 100 yards to the finish line, his stride starts to shorten. David Mullins is closing fast on Pleasant Company and it is clear that Tiger Roll – once ungraciously described as "a rat of a thing" by owner Michael O'Leary – is going to have to display tigerish qualities if he is to hang on.

Mullins, at 21 years of age, knows about winning this race. Two years ago, on his first National ride, he was half the age Russell is now when he rode Rule The World to win in the same Gigginstown House Stud colours Russell wears on his 14th attempt to win the race.

Gigginstown and Russell, there's history there. Russell rose above all that, put it behind him almost soon as it happened, out of the blue in the dying days of 2013, when O'Leary had a chat over a cup of tea at Punchestown and sacked him. A couple of days before that shock he had ridden Rule The World into second in a Grade 1 hurdle at Leopardstown.

These are anxious moments for some in-running punters, as Pleasant Company whittles down Tiger Roll's lead and £125,000 is matched at the minimum 1.01 on Tiger Roll, Pleasant Company matched for £14 at the maximum.

The line comes just in time for Tiger Roll; a stride beyond it and Pleasant Company is in front. The official margin is a head.

****

WHEN the first microphone was thrust in his face at this crowning moment of his career, Russell took himself out of the story. "This one is for Pat Smullen. I was speaking to him the other morning, and he's as tough as nails, so this one is for Pat," he said.

Only a couple of weeks before, Smullen, the nine-time Irish champion Flat jockey, had revealed his cancer diagnosis. The news left the close-knit world of Irish racing in shock.

As Russell spoke you knew this was his way of putting things in perspective. It was done with directness and dignity. His first thoughts were for a fellow jockey facing a challenge from within his own body. Then, having had a minute or so to let the

▲ Double action: Tiger Roll defeats Pleasant Company in a thriller at Aintree, a month after winning the Cross Country Chase at Cheltenham (right)

▼ Gordon Elliott with his Grand National winner

experience of the past nine minutes and forty seconds sink in, he allowed himself a moment of self-reflection.

"I have won this race a thousand times in my head, in my dreams, as a child," he said. Russell recalled childhood days, building miniature Aintree-style fences with cut grass in the garden of his County Cork home. For a hard man in an unforgiving profession he can be surprisingly lyrical at times.

"I'm thinking of my kids at home, and now they can become part of this wonderful event. I love it so much and I've been coming here for years, hoping, but satisfied just to have taken part in it. Now to have won it, I don't know what to say." Russell has travelled a long road, not always a smooth one. He has seldom been short on self-belief. There was a sense that perhaps he always felt this was his destiny.

****

YOU could hardly say the

same about Tiger Roll. This was not on the agenda when Gerry O'Brien organised the mating of his mare Swiss Roll with Derby winner Authorized in 2009.

O'Brien worked for nearly three decades as a veterinary surgeon at Coolmore Stud. His expertise was in the field of reproduction and it was natural he began to dabble in breeding. One of the mares he bought was On Air, who had won a couple of mile-and-a-quarter races and a novice hurdle for Nick Gaselee.

On Air produced four winners, all trained by Tommy Stack. If that now looks like something of an omen, it is worth mentioning that one of them, named Khachaturian, later won four races for Donald McCain. Stack, McCain – names indelibly linked with Red Rum, the greatest Grand National story of all. Yes, maybe the fates were already conspiring.

The best of On Air's foals was Berenson, a colt by Entrepreneur. He won a maiden first time out at the Curragh in August 2004. The following month he finished second to Dubawi in the Group 1 National

FESTIVAL HAT-TRICK

Tiger Roll prefaced his Grand National triumph by becoming a three-time winner at the Cheltenham Festival – just like his stablemate Cause Of Causes, who completed a festival hat-trick the previous year.

Unlike Cause Of Causes, whose three wins came in chases and in consecutive years, Tiger Roll has scored over hurdles and fences and his festival hat-trick was spread over a four-year span. Remarkably, for a future National winner, his first festival success was as a four-year-old in the Triumph Hurdle and he had to wait another three years – and his conversion to staying chaser – for his second in the 2017 National Hunt Chase over four miles. Two years earlier Cause Of Causes had won the same race to kick off his festival run.

Tiger Roll also followed Cause Of Causes by completing the hat-trick in the Cross Country Chase but another point of difference was that, whereas Jamie Codd rode Cause Of Causes to all three festival wins, Tiger Roll had a different jockey each time.

Having been partnered before by Davy Russell and Lisa O'Neill, Tiger Roll was paired this time with Keith Donoghue, a rider on the way back from the depths of a long struggle with his weight. With Cause Of Causes pulled up in his own latest bid for another festival success, Donoghue and Tiger Roll went on to a two-length win over French challenger Urgent De Gregaine.

Donoghue, 24, who had returned to the saddle the previous May after a break, lost 8lb to take the ride and described winning at the festival as "the best feeling in the world".

He added: "I've given up three or four times because of my weight, but Gordon [Elliott] always pulls me back and gives me rides when I can do the weight. If it wasn't for Gordon I wouldn't be standing here. This day last year I was 12st 7lb; here I'm riding off 11st 2lb."

Stakes and Godolphin bought him. He never ran again.

At that stage Berenson's sister Swiss Roll was still racing. She won a maiden at three and a conditions race at four at the 2004 Galway festival. Continuing in training at five, she achieved black type when second in the Listed Vintage Crop Stakes at Navan in May 2005.

In 2009 Swiss Roll produced a colt foal by Dubawi who was bought for 60,000gns by John Ferguson. He went into training with Godolphin and ended up winning five races, including a narrow defeat of the Willie Mullins-trained Simenon in the Group 2 Lonsdale Cup.

Her next mating was with Authorized, and the resultant foal was bought by Ferguson for 70,000gns at the Tattersalls foal sale in November 2010. He was registered in Sheikh Mohammed's ownership but was unraced when consigned by Darley, now named Tiger Roll, at Doncaster in August 2013.

Nigel Hawke bought Tiger Roll for £10,000 and introduced him in a

▸▸ *Continues page 58*

juvenile hurdle at Market Rasen that November. Starting at 12-1 in a field of five, he took advantage of a poor display by 2-11 favourite Zamoyski to win in promising fashion despite looking a bit green.

Only a month later he was back at the sales. This time it was Brightwells, where Mags O'Toole, the bloodstock agent and daughter of legendary Irish trainer Mick O'Toole, bought him for 80,000gns, bound for Gordon Elliott.

****

TIGER ROLL made his Irish debut in a Grade 1 juvenile hurdle at Leopardstown in February 2014. Bryan Cooper, who had replaced Russell in the Gigginstown hotseat a month earlier, rode him into second place. Cooper was looking forward to riding him in the Triumph Hurdle but on the second day of the festival, in the Fred Winter, he rode Clarcam, another of the Elliott juveniles, and shattered his leg in a last-flight fall. Two days later Russell deputised when Tiger Roll won the Triumph.

A year later Tiger Roll was back at Cheltenham as a 50-1 chance in the Ladbrokes World Hurdle and finished 13th of the 16 runners. Just another Triumph winner who had failed to make the grade.

Another winless season over hurdles followed and then Elliott sent him over fences. He won his first two in the modest surroundings of Ballinrobe and Kilbeggan in the early summer of 2016. Better novices found him out after that, although he picked up the thread again when taking the Munster National at Limerick in October.

A former Triumph winner landing a valuable three-mile handicap chase was unusual. A former Triumph winner landing the four-mile National Hunt Chase was unprecedented, but that was what he did under Lisa O'Neill the following March.

The dual Cheltenham Festival winner started the 2017-18 season well enough with second place at Wexford but struggled when Donoghue rode him in the Clonmel Oil Chase in November. He didn't seem to take to the cross-country course at Cheltenham in December, beaten 42 lengths in fifth behind his Russell-partnered veteran stablemate Bless The Wings.

Elliott gave Tiger Roll a break and Donoghue worked away with him at home. Three months later he came alive again at Cheltenham to give the young jockey his day in the limelight. The little fighter was now a three-time festival winner and soon to be a National hero, albeit without Donoghue in the saddle.

****

BACK in Elliott's yard on the morning after the National, as preparations were being made for Tiger Roll to parade in triumph through the village of Summerhill, the trainer was talking about Donoghue.

"He was Keith's ride. He just couldn't do the weight. He did the work on the horse and he's going to have plenty more days on him. He'll be back on him in the cross-country next season."

Russell, meanwhile, was still in reflective mode as he talked the visiting journalists through his memories of a childhood in which the Grand National was a vivid daydream in an imagined future. National Velvet even got a mention.

But the 2018 race was no National Velvet, just the unlikely romance of Russell and an amazing Flat-bred horse, a leading juvenile hurdler who found his vocation as a staying chaser. Tiger Roll, a hero of Cheltenham and Aintree, was the story.

▲ National heroes: Karen Morgan (left) and Louise Dunne lead Tiger Roll in Summerhill after his Aintree victory, which came 12 days after Gordon Elliott had won the Irish Grand National with General Principle (below)

GENERAL RULE

Tiger Roll completed a Grand National double for Gordon Elliott, 12 days after the trainer had landed the Irish version for the first time on Easter Monday.

General Principle emerged victorious at Fairyhouse from Elliott's 13-strong battalion, which constituted a world record for one stable in a race. Just as at Aintree, the contest came down to a battle between Elliott and his big rival Willie Mullins and once again it was settled by a head as General Principle got up on the line to deny Isleofhopendreams.

Three of the Elliott team were rated more likely winners than General Principle, who had finished fifth to Our Duke the previous year, but the 20-1 shot came out on top to give jockey JJ Slevin the biggest success of his career.

Elliott described the result as "brilliant but a relief as well", adding: "You put yourself under so much pressure. We ran 13 and General Principle wasn't one of our leading candidates, but JJ gave him a smashing ride. It's unbelievable to win an Irish National at last."

The ⬙ vertem
FUTURITY TROPHY
WHERE RECORDS ARE BROKEN

SATURDAY 27 OCTOBER
doncaster-racecourse.co.uk

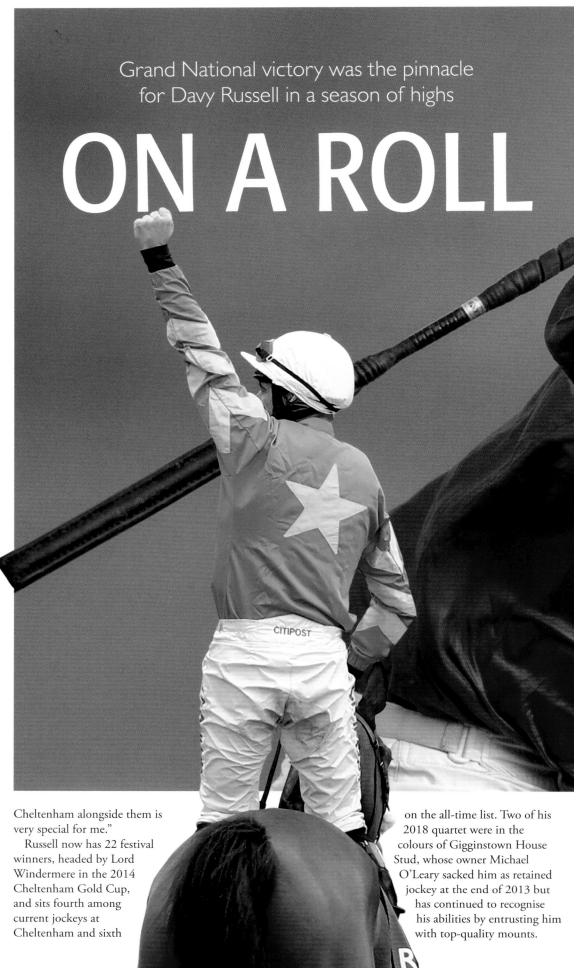

By Alan Sweetman

Grand National victory was the pinnacle for Davy Russell in a season of highs

ON A ROLL

TIGER ROLL'S Grand National triumph was the icing on the cake for Davy Russell in the most successful season of his career. At the big festivals either side of his Aintree triumph, the wily and experienced campaigner was top rider at Cheltenham for the first time with four winners and ended Punchestown week with a third Irish champion jump jockey title.

Before those celebrations, however, there was sadness. In the early days of March, just as anticipation was building towards Cheltenham, Russell suffered a personal blow with the death of his mother Phyllis after a long illness. It was a sad preface to his wonderful spell of successes, which were invariably greeted by the rider pointing to the heavens in memory of his mother.

After the first of his 2018 Cheltenham Festival victories, aboard Presenting Percy in the RSA Chase, Russell said: "Mam was the most outstanding woman. She raised six kids and a business along with my dad. She'd be very, very happy. They'll be in floods of tears at home. She was a great woman."

The following day Russell rode a treble. The centrepiece was Balko Des Flos' defeat of odds-on favourite Un De Sceaux in the Ryanair Chase and there were handicap wins for Gordon Elliott on Delta Work in the Pertemps Final – the rider's third consecutive victory in that competitive handicap hurdle – and The Storyteller in the Brown Advisory & Merriebelle Stable Plate.

At the end of the week he was tied on four winners with Jack Kennedy – at 18 less than half Russell's then 38 years – and what ultimately made the difference on countback was the second place he secured on Midnight Tour in the Mares' Hurdle, with Kennedy third on favourite Apple's Jade.

Russell said: "This is a special place. I've looked up to jockeys like Ruby Walsh, Richard Dunwoody and Charlie Swan all my life and to be crowned leading jockey at Cheltenham alongside them is very special for me."

Russell now has 22 festival winners, headed by Lord Windermere in the 2014 Cheltenham Gold Cup, and sits fourth among current jockeys at Cheltenham and sixth on the all-time list. Two of his 2018 quartet were in the colours of Gigginstown House Stud, whose owner Michael O'Leary sacked him as retained jockey at the end of 2013 but has continued to recognise his abilities by entrusting him with top-quality mounts.

campaign he had compiled 119 wins, 36 clear of his nearest pursuer. Just a couple of months short of his 39th birthday, he became the oldest Irish champion over jumps in the modern era.

Russell's first major success of the season came on the Henry de Bromhead-trained Balko Des Flos, the shortest-priced of six Gigginstown-owned runners in the Galway Plate, his first win in an event that carries greater prestige than any Irish handicap chase bar the Irish Grand National.

In November Russell won another of Ireland's most historic chases, the Troytown at Navan, on the Elliott-trained Mala Beach. A week later Elliott provided him with a first Grade 1 win of the season when the odds-on Death Duty beat the subsequent National Hunt Chase winner Rathvinden in the Drinmore Novice Chase at Fairyhouse.

Just half an hour later he partnered the previous season's Pertemps Final winner Presenting Percy to trounce his rivals under top weight of 11st 10lb in the 3m5f Porterstown Handicap Chase, a key victory on the road to RSA Chase success at Cheltenham.

Leopardstown's big Christmas fixture yielded two Grade 1 wins in tandem with Elliott, Apple's Jade as 4-6 favourite in the three-mile Christmas Hurdle and Mick Jazz at 14-1 in the Ryanair Hurdle over two miles.

After his pair of Grade 1 successes at Cheltenham with Presenting Percy and Balko Des Flos, Russell finished on a high at Punchestown with his final top-level win of the season on The Storyteller in the Growise Champion Novice Chase. It was a most fortuitous success in bizarre circumstances as the spotlight fell not on Russell but on the unfortunate Paul Townend following his dramatic exit on Al Boum Photo.

Yet somehow the episode summed up a campaign when things fell into place for Russell. In grabbing every opportunity with supreme skill and determination, he secured his status as one of the great riders in Irish jump racing history.

▲ Flying high: Davy Russell lands the Ryanair Chase on Balko Des Flos

◄ Another celebration at the Cheltenham Festival after Presenting Percy's win in the RSA Chase

That was most evident with the ride on Tiger Roll in the National, which became available because Keith Donoghue was unable to make the weight. After the Aintree triumph, O'Leary said: "It's well known we parted company over the most legendary cup of tea in racing and it says much about Davy's resilience the way he bounced back. In a group of elite Irish jockeys Davy is right up there – his career has been up and down, with periods of achievement but some lows too, and it's the way he keeps coming back. He could have had a huff and given up, but after a couple of quiet years he has come back. Now he's riding better than ever before."

Russell's quality and consistency was stamped into his title-winning season in Ireland. When Ruby Walsh broke his leg at Punchestown last November, the 2017-18 championship became Russell's to lose. By the end of the

HEAVEN SENT

Samcro lived up to the hype at Cheltenham
and now even more will be expected of him

By David Jennings

MICHAEL O'LEARY wanted to defuse the hype. All he did was add to the hysteria. He wanted to turn us into non-believers, to deny that we were witness to something out of the ordinary, but instead the wonder and the adoration grew.

"The hype with Samcro is rubbish," proclaimed the straight-shooting owner of Gigginstown House Stud. "He has won his maiden hurdle and he won a Graded hurdle reasonably well.

Death Duty did the same last year and he went to Cheltenham and blew up. He has to go to Cheltenham and actually win a race there. It's just hype to delude ante-post punters. He's not as good as the hype would make out. He will never be as good as the hype will make out. If he turns out to be a reasonably good chaser in time then great. But he's not the next coming of Jesus Christ."

Those were O'Leary's words at Fairyhouse on the first Sunday in December, delivered live on At The Races. It is one thing comparing Samcro to Death Duty, it is

another thing entirely when you bring Jesus Christ into the conversation. Even if it was tongue in cheek.

Samcro already had a substantial reputation but now his new nickname was Jesus Christ. A nickname bestowed by his owner. He was going to be crucified for any semblance of a slip-up.

The hype, whether O'Leary liked it or not, had already been there for the best part of 18 months. The strapping son of Germany won a Monksgrange point-to-point on his sole start between the flags for Colin Bowe. He was unbeaten in

bumpers for Gordon Elliott, following a similar path to Death Duty by winning a Listed event at Navan before reappearing at Fairyhouse's Easter festival where he scored by 17 lengths. No Cheltenham, no Aintree, no Punchestown. Baby steps. It was not about now, it was about next season.

After each of his three bumper wins, Elliott finished his post-race interviews with the same sentence: "We will mind him."

The better they are, the more you mind them.

➤ Continues page 64

****

ELLIOTT knew he had something special in Samcro and the rest of us got a glimpse of potential greatness on his first run of the 2017-18 season at Punchestown in mid-October. The two-mile maiden hurdle had 22 runners, one of whom already had a rating of 127, yet 1-5 was the starting price of Samcro for his first try over hurdles. A 15-length demolition of Mind's Eye under a motionless Jack Kennedy was very easy on the eye. Already everybody was wondering what he might do at Cheltenham five months down the line.

The next stop came at Navan the following month. Some high-quality performers had won the Grade 3 Monksfield Novice Hurdle, including Pizarro (2002), Pandorama (2008), Apache Stronghold (2013) and Death Duty (2016), and Samcro added his name to the roll of honour with a smooth success, easing a dozen lengths clear of Jetz after a flawless round of jumping.

The Navan performance had Kennedy purring – "that's definitely the best feel I've ever got from a horse," said the young rider – and it was no longer a case of whether Samcro would be heading to Cheltenham; the only debate was which race to target there. Betfair slashed him to 5-2 favourite from 9-2 for the Ballymore Novices' Hurdle. Paddy Power went 11-4 (from 4-1) for the same race, while he was also made early market leader for the Supreme Novices' Hurdle with BoyleSports going 8-1 for the festival opener and 3-1 for the Ballymore.

Ten weeks passed before we saw Samcro again. It was worth the wait. The inaugural Dublin Racing Festival at Leopardstown was lit up by his dazzling performance in the Deloitte Novice Hurdle as a first Grade 1 triumph was tucked away with the minimum of fuss. Duc Des Genievres, Paloma Blue, Whiskey Sour, Real Steel and Sharjah are not slow horses but they were made to look like they were standing still as Samcro scooted clear off the home turn. This was two miles, not two and a half like Navan, and it was clear there was speed to go with the power.

There was an update on Jesus Christ-gate too. "He's still not Jesus

Christ," O'Leary stressed. "Hopefully he will be when he wins a chase, a proper race. He's going the right way."

The way O'Leary had in mind was, of course, Cheltenham. Samcro was starting to do the talking himself now. At Leopardstown he cleared his throat and shouted that he was the most exciting young horse in training. So exciting that he was now 4-5 with BoyleSports to bag the Ballymore and even shorter with Paddy Power at 8-11.

Elliott did his best to stay grounded in his post-race comments but struggled. "He has opened up a lot of doors and we can go anywhere with him now. We're lucky to have him. Nothing fazes him. He showed a lot of class there today and he could be anything."

Could be anything? Jesus Christ, perhaps?

The Cheltenham preview night circuit was cluttered with Samcro silliness. He was going to win the Ballymore by as far as Cheltenham to Cardiff. The ambulance would be

▲ King of the hill: Samcro powers away from the final flight to win the Ballymore Novices' Hurdle

▼ Jack Kennedy arrives in the Cheltenham winner's enclosure

second. He was the next Arkle. You know what they're like. The recurring theme was that he was without doubt the Irish banker heading to the festival in March. A label that brings with it intense pressure.

Samcro was odds-on for the Ballymore, the chosen race for the chosen one. He had been odds-on for weeks and his starting price was 8-11. The moment of truth had arrived. We were soon to find out whether there was substance to all the silly talk.

Samcro stayed wide, got no cover but laughed hysterically at his rivals coming down the hill and found more than enough to beat Black Op by two and three-quarter lengths. It was more convincing than the winning margin suggests. So much more convincing.

"It's for moments like this we do this," said O'Leary. "He was wider than we wanted and was probably in front soon enough but he's done it."

How did his 18-year-old rider cope with the pressure of being on board the Irish banker? "Pressure comes with riding the best

ones, but I wouldn't change it for anything," Kennedy said. "Samcro is very straightforward to ride – he's just a bit lazy when he hits the front, that's the only thing. But he's a great horse, probably the best I've ridden."

****

THAT great horse now had Punchestown on his schedule. Instead of mopping up the Herald Champion Novice Hurdle, Elliott and O'Leary decided it was time to find out exactly what Samcro was made of and ran him in the Punchestown Champion Hurdle.

Running against more experienced and higher-rated rivals would tell them whether he was a Champion Hurdle contender or needed fences to fulfil his potential.

"The Champion Hurdle at Punchestown was supposed to tell us where we were going. If he'd won that he was staying over hurdles and, if he was beaten, we were going chasing. He fell before we knew what would have happened," Eddie O'Leary admitted.

Samcro departed at the third-last hurdle, almost in tandem with Melon, the Champion Hurdle runner-up behind Buveur D'Air and his main market rival. It was too early to tell

DOUBLE CHAMP

Samcro ranks among the best novice hurdlers since the Anglo-Irish Jumps Classifications started in the 1999-2000 season but he is not quite at the top.

His best rating of 160 came in the 2m3f+ category, achieved in his Ballymore Novices' Hurdle victory at Cheltenham, and has been bettered by three novices in classifications history – Iris's Gift (168), The New One (165) and Black Jack Ketchum (161). Iris's Gift was second to Baracouda in the Stayers' Hurdle as a novice and achieved his biggest victory when he turned the tables the next year, while The New One has gone on to a long and successful career as a senior hurdler, including a Grade 1 win in the Aintree Hurdle. Black Jack Ketchum, however, never reached the same heights after his novice days, with just two Grade 2 wins.

Samcro was rated 158 in the 2m-2m2f category for his Deloitte Novice Hurdle win, putting him below Jezki, Our Conor, Faugheen, Douvan and Labaik (all 161), Altior (160) and Katchit (159). It is an illustrious group, as Katchit, Jezki and Faugheen went on to Champion Hurdle glory, while Douvan and Altior have become top chasers.

With history suggesting a high-performance novice like Samcro – champion in both distance categories – has every chance of making it to the top in the senior ranks, the hype machine is likely to continue in overdrive.

how he would have fared. We were none the wiser.

The unknown makes Samcro all the more intriguing. Had he been tapped for toe and put in his place by Melon, or played second fiddle to eventual winner Supasundae, the truth would have come out. In putting the only blemish in his copybook, just over two years after his first public appearance in the point-to-point field, he had left us all wondering again.

Maybe he could be the next Don Cossack, Elliott's 2016 Cheltenham Gold Cup winner, or even better. But he also seemed to have the potential to be Gigginstown's first Champion Hurdle winner, and Elliott's too. He could be anything.

Each stop along the line tells us a little more, but still the final destination is unclear. Many great novices do not take the next step that guarantees a place in the hall of fame, which explains why early hype is anathema to many, but the latest of their number has been heading in the right direction.

Samcro might not be Jesus Christ but so far all of Michael O'Leary's prayers have been answered.

GALLOP

WITH CONFIDENCE

TRAIN ON THE BEST

Established for 30 years

Fully Synthetic Surfaces

We Specialise In
- Gallops
- Lunge Pens
- Arenas
- Turnout Pens

Free Site Visits
& Quotations

 +44 (0)1282 834970   info@equestriansurfaces.co.uk   www.equestriansurfaces.co.uk

LIONHEART

Roaring Lion emerged as a dominant force along with his jockey Oisin Murphy

By Tom Kerr

THE race had not gone to plan for Oisin Murphy and Roaring Lion. Marooned in a wide draw, the young jockey had been left towards the rear in a slowly run Irish Champion Stakes and now, as the field swung into the straight, he could see Ryan Moore kicking hard on Saxon Warrior ahead of him and quickly opening up a three-length advantage.

The race had been billed as a match between the Murphy and Moore mounts. The pair had met five times previously, Saxon Warrior taking the honours on the first two occasions, Roaring Lion finishing in front on the next three. Now it looked like Saxon Warrior was about to even the score.

In the straight Murphy got lower and lower on his mount, exhorting him to produce his finishing effort. The gap between Roaring Lion and Saxon Warrior closed slowly at first then suddenly, like a lion stalking its prey, and Murphy's horse came sprinting home to nail his old rival once again and triumph by a neck.

By the post Roaring Lion looked well on top, despite the narrowness of the margin, but this was a race that could so easily have gone awry had there been any error of judgement or want of effort from the winning partnership.

"The horse showed a lot of guts," Murphy said. "We thought it might be a tactical race. I got a little further back than I wanted to and had to come wide. But I had the ammunition. My horse showed an unbelievable turn of foot. How good is he? I don't know. He's an exceptional horse."

In outflanking the manoeuvres of the Ballydoyle brigade, which mustered four of the seven runners, Murphy had confirmed himself an exceptional big-race jockey. The establishment of Roaring Lion as a star middle-distance colt of the 2018 season went hand in hand with the emergence of his 23-year-old rider as a leading light of the weighing room. Both entered the season highly regarded, but few observers anticipated they would climb to the pinnacle quite so swiftly or enjoy quite so much success along the way.

****

TRAINED by the all-conquering John Gosden *(below)*, Roaring Lion won three races as a juvenile for his owners Qatar Racing, who had purchased the son of US stallion Kitten's Joy for a mere $160,000 at the 2016 Keeneland September Yearling Sale. He completed his two-year-old season in the Racing Post Trophy at Doncaster, where he had his first tussle with the Aidan O'Brien-trained Saxon Warrior.

As they would so many times the following season, the two colts locked horns in the closing stages, Roaring Lion closing from off the pace to challenge the Irish colt. Murphy's mount edged ahead and looked to have the race sealed, but he hung left and Saxon Warrior rallied strongly against the rail, claiming the race by a neck.

That victory was O'Brien's 26th Group or Grade 1 of the year, a world record, which understandably ensured the lion's share of the attention was paid to the plucky winner rather than the unlucky loser. Gosden, however, was far from discouraged. "He had the race won but then got blown off course – they were quite tough conditions out there," he said. "He's a very nice horse and there's no reason why he won't go for the Guineas."

Roaring Lion's Guineas preparation came in the Craven Stakes, for which he was sent off 8-13 favourite, but he got outpaced by the race-fit Masar, who streaked clear for a wide-margin victory with the market leader more than nine lengths back in third. Gosden said his charge had been only 80 per cent fit for his seasonal debut, but the unexpected reverse was still enough to send his Guineas odds north.

Back at Newmarket two weeks later for the colts' Classic, Roaring Lion again found himself up against Saxon Warrior. Racing nearest to the stand, he once more edged left under pressure and, outpaced in the final furlong, could finish only fifth behind O'Brien's colt.

Roaring Lion was hardly living up to his name at this stage but he looked like he would improve for a step up in trip and duly proved it in the Dante Stakes. Despite being easy to back, he delivered a classy performance under Murphy, scorching clear for a four-and-a-half-length victory.

That marked out Roaring Lion as an obvious Derby candidate and two weeks later at Epsom he was sent off the shortest-priced British contender for a race that was figured to revolve around Guineas winner Saxon Warrior. However, it was Craven star Masar who emerged triumphant, a first winner of the Derby in Godolphin blue. Roaring Lion was a good third, plugging on gamely in the closing stages to finish ahead of fourth-placed Saxon Warrior for the first time but having no answer to the winner.

Roaring Lion's spring campaign had clearly proved this was a colt of high calibre, but it also indicated his preferred trip was an intermediate one, and so it was no surprise that his next target was the Coral-Eclipse over a mile and a quarter.

At Sandown in July he faced Saxon Warrior for a fourth time, the Coolmore colt having also found the mile and a half at Epsom a stamina test too far. Sent off first and second favourite, Roaring Lion and Saxon Warrior served up the duel the betting public expected.

The Coolmore colt got first run, forging ahead with the signature burst of pace that had been blunted at Epsom, but Roaring Lion was closing all the time and

▸ *Continues page 70*

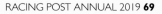

overhauled the leader with 100 yards to run.

It was a well-deserved and perhaps long overdue first Group 1 for Roaring Lion – and also a first British top-tier success for Murphy – but the victory was confirmed only after a stewards' inquiry into possible interference in the closing stages. "Relief," said Murphy when asked for his reaction. "I knew I was on the best horse in the race today, and that's the bottom line. I just had to get it right and not get there too soon."

****

MURPHY, despite his young age, had waited a surprisingly long time to celebrate a first British Group 1 success. Born and raised in Killarney, Ireland, he learned his trade at his uncle Jim Culloty's stable and completed stints with Tommy Stack and Ballydoyle before moving to Britain to join Andrew Balding's apprentice factory in October 2012.

Murphy's progress was swift. He announced himself as a rising star with a four-timer, including the big race, on Ayr Gold Cup day in 2013 and was signed up as number one for Qatar Racing, owner of Roaring Lion, in 2015. Yet a first Group 1 eluded him until he landed the Prix de la Foret on Aclaim in October 2017, more than four years after his big breakthrough at Ayr.

The wait for a British top-tier winner may have been long and frustrating, but once one was in the bag a second quickly followed, Murphy steering Lightning Spear to victory in the Sussex Stakes at Glorious Goodwood less than a month after the Eclipse.

Three weeks after that he was back on board Roaring Lion again, the pair combining in the Juddmonte International. Among his rivals once again was Saxon Warrior, although this time Roaring Lion's stiffest challenge was expected to come from the five-year-old Poet's Word, who had won the King George VI and Queen Elizabeth Stakes and looked a typical late improver for Sir Michael Stoute.

Instead, Roaring Lion delivered his most complete performance at York, cruising to the front and stretching more than three lengths clear of the

chasing pack, led home by Poet's Word. "He has all the attributes of a world-class horse," Murphy said. "He looks the part, he feels the part and now he's doing it on the track." Racing Post Ratings backed up the jockey's view by elevating Roaring Lion to 127, 4lb higher than his previous best in the Eclipse.

While the Juddmonte International was a performance by a brilliant racehorse at the peak of his powers – effectively a steering job for the lucky Murphy – the Irish Champion Stakes the following month at Leopardstown presented a very different challenge for the pair. There, the tactics of the Ballydoyle pack, led by Saxon Warrior, almost defanged Roaring Lion and it was only Murphy's calmness under pressure that ensured he prevailed.

Qatar Racing's manager David Redvers later reflected: "The race could not have panned out any worse for Oisin, but he very quickly worked out what was happening. He stayed calm, then he built up a head of steam in the straight. He didn't immediately throw everything at it. That made all the difference.

"I thought the difference from the Racing Post Trophy to the Irish
⏩ *Continues page 72*

MURPHY'S GROUP 1 HAUL

Date	Horse	Trainer	Race
Mar 31	**Benbatl**	Saeed Bin Suroor	DP World Dubai Turf
Jul 7	**Roaring Lion**	John Gosden	Coral-Eclipse
Jul 29	**Benbatl**	Saeed Bin Suroor	Grosser Dallmayr Preis
Aug 1	**Lightning Spear**	David Simcock	Qatar Sussex Stakes
Aug 22	**Roaring Lion**	John Gosden	Juddmonte International
Sep 8	**The Tin Man**	James Fanshawe	32Red Sprint Cup
Sep 15	**Roaring Lion**	John Gosden	Qipco Irish Champion Stakes
Oct 7	**Royal Marine**	Saeed Bin Suroor	Qatar Prix Jean-Luc Lagardere
Oct 20	**Roaring Lion**	John Gosden	Queen Elizabeth II Stakes

▲ United in victory: Oisin Murphy acknowledges the crowd after winning the Juddmonte International at York on Roaring Lion

◀ Murphy and owner Sheikh Fahad Al Thani after the Irish Champion Stakes

Champion Stakes was really noticeable. Oisin has brought added energy and confidence to his riding this season. The difference between winning and losing can be down to milliseconds and millimetres. The reasons for it are not always obvious to the naked eye."

****

MURPHY'S growing confidence went in tandem with Roaring Lion's progress on the track. The colt's next target was Qipco British Champions Day at Ascot, so important to his owner Sheikh Fahad Al Thani in his role with the flagship sponsor, but soft ground in October was a stumbling block. All his wins in 2018 had been on good to firm and, in a bid to counteract the numbing effect of wet ground, the decision was made to drop Roaring Lion back to a mile in the Queen Elizabeth II Stakes.

Gosden was confident the 2-1 favourite was ready for his sixth Group 1 run of the year – "Roaring Lion goes there in good form and I've never had a horse progress physically and mentally as he has through this year" – but concerned that he was coming out of stall 15. "I'm not in love with his draw out on the wing as the low numbers could well be the place to be but we'll get on with it," he said.

The trainer's reading of the race looked spot on when four of the first six home came from stalls two to five, but Roaring Lion managed to make his class count and score by a neck even if he was far from his best. His RPR of 121 was the lowest of his winning spree through four of the most prestigious contests in Britain and Ireland.

The victory showed another facet of Murphy's skill as he nursed his mount into contention and had just enough in reserve to see off outsiders I Can Fly and Century Dream. "He hated the ground and was never on the bridle but he wanted it," the jockey said. "It was nip and tuck in the final furlong and my horse had no petrol left, but he stuck his head out. If he'd gone ten furlongs today we'd have been in trouble."

It was a fittingly hard-fought victory in an exceptional season for Roaring Lion and Murphy.

'HE HAS SEIZED EVERY OPPORTUNITY'

THE flowering of Oisin Murphy's talent began in the autumn of 2017, with his first top-tier wins on Aclaim in the Prix de la Foret and Blond Me in Canada's EP Taylor Stakes, and reached full bloom in a magnificent 2018 campaign.

Murphy was quick to strike again at Group 1 level on Benbatl in the Dubai Turf on World Cup night at Meydan in March and took his 2018 score to nine when Roaring Lion won the Queen Elizabeth II Stakes on Champions Day at Ascot in October, confirming the 23-year-old's coming of age as a big-race rider.

Andrew Balding, the trainer of Blond Me and Murphy's boss during his apprentice days, has not been surprised to see the rider take his place among the elite. "His rise has been very quick; he's now the go-to man every bit as much as Ryan Moore and James Doyle. He's now getting on better horses but there's a reason for it," he says. "His professionalism, preparation and homework have always been outstanding but he's proving he has an excellent big-match temperament."

Murphy has slotted seamlessly into Sheikh Fahad Al Thani's Qatar Racing outfit since taking over as retained jockey from Andrea Atzeni towards the end of 2015. Atzeni lasted a solitary season in the job; Jamie Spencer just two before him. The role places particular demands on its incumbent, as Spencer highlights.

"It's one of the hardest positions, especially if the owner has a lot of trainers," he says. "Most of the time you'll ride for a trainer even though you wouldn't be that trainer's choice of jockey. Some trainers will like you, some won't. It's a hard balance."

That Murphy has risen to the challenge may be down in part to a moment of happenstance. In May 2014 he was still a 3lb claimer when he rode Qatar Racing's Hot Streak to win the

Temple Stakes, in the process registering his first Pattern-race triumph. By the year's end he was champion apprentice and second jockey to Sheikh Fahad. One year on and he was the sheikh's main man.

"We had the discussion when Andrea left but it was quickly obvious there was no need to replace him with an outside appointment," recalls David Redvers, who manages Qatar Racing for the sheikh. "We knew by then that Oisin had serious talent. On a personal level Oisin and Sheikh Fahad hit it off straight away. Oisin is seen as part of the family."

Appreciation of Murphy extends way beyond his direct employers. He has ridden a spate of big-race winners for other concerns, including Godolphin. "He has seized every opportunity with both hands," Redvers says. "He has great self-belief; I don't think any jockey is riding better. He's now at the stage where you watch him ride and you almost expect him to make things happen, even on a rank outsider."

RACESAFE | PRORACE

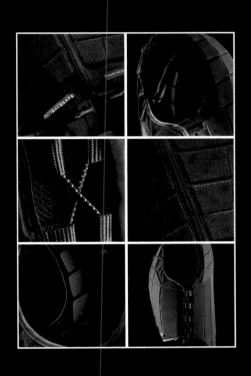

Available in 3 levels of protection, complying to EN13158:2018 (Level 1, 2 or 3):

PRORACE 1.0

PRORACE 2.0

PRORACE 3.0

Bringing new levels of comfort & performance to the Racing body protector range.

Incoporating a new elasticated adjustment system for movement & comfort.

- LATEST PROTECTION STANDARDS
- ULTRA LIGHTWEIGHT
- DUAL BREATHABILITY
- INCREASED FLEXIBILITY
- IMPROVED SIZE RANGE
- NEW ELASTIC ADJUSTMENT

+44 (0)1536 771051
WWW.RACESAFE.CO.UK

Cracksman gave the top-rated performance of the Flat season once again with a repeat triumph in the Champion Stakes

DOUBLE TAKE

By David Carr

FOR the second year in a row, Cracksman showed some things are worth waiting for as he put the 'champion' into the Qipco Champion Stakes. And once again he showed how John Gosden is a master at getting a horse ready for the autumn – as if that needed restating of the trainer who coaxed a second Arc win out of Enable on the back of one all-weather run.

Cracksman was hailed as the 'brilliant Champion Stakes winner' in the index of big stories in last year's Racing Post Annual and, while the b-word can be overused in racing, it seems apt again this time. How else can you describe another awesome performance from a colt who could be argued to be the best horse in the world?

On Champions Day 2017 he had emerged from the shadow of stablemate Enable with an astonishing display, making his Group 1 breakthrough with a

stunning seven-length victory. "Roll on next year" was the concluding thought of our breathless feature in this annual, reflecting the huge expectations that his performance created.

Those prepared to wait a full 12 months, perhaps the once-a-year racegoers that Champions Day is designed to attract, were handsomely rewarded. For Cracksman was just as impressive a winner of the feature event second time around on the richest card ever staged in Britain.

Maybe, just maybe, Frankie Dettori grabbed a crucial advantage as he dashed for home after the field levelled up, catching main rival Crystal Ocean ever so slightly flat-footed.

But this was a victory for blistering horsepower rather than canny jockeyship. The way that Cracksman surged clear in the last furlong and a half, passing the post six lengths in front of Crystal Ocean despite Dettori's whip-waving celebration late on, suggested few horses in the world

– perhaps none – would have lived with him on the day.

****

THE more observant among those making their annual visit to Ascot may have spotted one important difference from 2017: Cracksman was wearing blinkers. He became the third British Group 1 winner of the season, after Merchant Navy (Diamond Jubilee Stakes) and US Navy Flag (July Cup), to sport the headgear once dismissed as the 'rogue's badge'.

Gosden started his training career in California and has more of the American view of such aids. "I can tell you the great Secretariat and Northern Dancer raced in blinkers," he said after the Champion Stakes. "I don't have a prejudice against them. Sometimes you need to focus their minds."

But the fact that he reached for something to focus the four-year-old's mind was an indication that things hadn't quite gone to plan between Cracksman's two Ascot highs.

The new season could not have started any better as Anthony Oppenheimer's homebred colt lit up the official reopening of Paris Longchamp after two years of redevelopment with a sparkling success in the Prix Ganay in April.

A zesty four-length victory looked a thorough vindication of the handicapping team who had rated him officially the best horse in Europe – and third best in the world – in 2017, not to mention Gosden's view that "the boy has grown into a man", expressed after

a racecourse gallop during the Craven meeting.

Oppenheimer, who had opted to keep him in training rather than follow Golden Horn to stud at the end of his three-year-old career, admitted: "It took my breath away. I was so excited. It was what we dreamed about but I wasn't sure."

The dream almost turned to nightmare at Epsom, where Cracksman was sent off 2-7 favourite for the Investec Coronation Cup but made
▶▶ Continues page 76

peculiarly heavy weather of things behind an enterprisingly and brilliantly ridden Salouen – champion jockey Silvestre de Sousa gets so few Group 1 chances that he tends to make the most of those that do come his way.

Having apparently banged his head on the stalls, Cracksman missed the break and took almost all of the race's mile-and-a-half distance to scramble past the 33-1 outsider and win by a head.

Epsom may not be his place – he had finished only third in the Derby there 12 months earlier and subsequent events make it hard to argue that he is not a better horse than his two conquerors, Wings Of Eagles and Cliffs Of Moher.

Yet there was no blaming the track for his defeat in the Prince of Wales's Stakes at Royal Ascot, where the 2-5 favourite was readily brushed aside by Poet's Word – who had been the distant runner-up in the Champion over course and distance eight months earlier.

Gosden felt Cracksman had been distracted by the fillies returning from the previous race and it is true that the colt – who could have just finished his first season's stallion duties, had his owner valued stud fees more than racing prize-money and prestige – was sweating notably and never travelled with any of his usual enthusiasm.

But the trainer's words were all that punters had to go on in the four months leading up to Champions Day, a period when running plans were governed more by the weather forecast than the programme book. The driest summer in more than 40 years was not good news for a horse reckoned to need give underfoot, and a succession of big races went by without him.

He was pulled out on the day of the King George VI and Queen Elizabeth Stakes at Ascot – in which old rival Poet's Word narrowly beat future Champion Stakes second Crystal Ocean – and also bypassed a clash with stablemate Roaring Lion in the Juddmonte International at York.

Nor did the autumn start any better when he was pulled out of the Arc – for the second year in a row – as conditions at Longchamp were not deemed soft enough. "It's so

▼ Flying high: Frankie Dettori leaps from Cracksman after another stunning show in the Champion Stakes

▲ Scenes of joy: fist pumps and smiles as Cracksman doubles up

disappointing when you know how good he is, and he really is brilliant, and he's right back to his very best," Oppenheimer said at the time. "It's driving us all round the bend."

****

EVERYTHING came good in the end but assessing just how brilliant Cracksman is, or was, has now become a question for the international handicapping panel once again as he was retired straight after his Ascot triumph.

That denied him the chance to become just the second three-time Champion Stakes winner in history, matching the feat of the remarkable Tristan in the 1880s. Racing was rather different in the 19th century

CHAMPION STAKES WINNERS BY RPR

Year	Horse	RPR
2018	**Cracksman**	131
2017	**Cracksman**	131
2016	**Almanzor**	129
2015	**Fascinating Rock**	125
2014	**Noble Mission**	123
2013	**Farhh**	127
2012	**Frankel**	136
2011	**Cirrus Des Aigles**	130
2010	**Twice Over**	126
2009	**Twice Over**	123

but it was still some feat for a horse renowned as "a very vile-tempered animal" to land three Champions in a career during which he also won both the six-furlong July Cup and the Gold Cup over two and a half miles.

Cracksman was not quite so versatile and after his winning debut over a mile as a two-year-old he did all his racing at a mile and a quarter or a mile and a half. Yet he was undeniably talented and his Racing Post Rating of 131 in the Champion Stakes, matching his 2017 mark, was the highest by any European-trained horse during the core turf season.

He can justly be hailed as 'Frankel's best son', which is quite a tagline with which to woo mare owners as he begins his own career at stud.

A FUN, SOCIAL & AFFORDABLE FORM OF RACEHORSE OWNERSHIP

JOIN THE CLUB

The British Racing Club is an exciting new membership club that brings the thrill of racehorse ownership to everyone for just £25 a month. Experience the buzz of being part of this friendly and fun team supporting your horses at the races, visiting all the trainers' yards and receiving daily tips and racing articles from the 4 professional sport journalists.

VISIT WWW.BRITISHRACINGCLUB.CO.UK TODAY!

THE BRITISH RACING CLUB

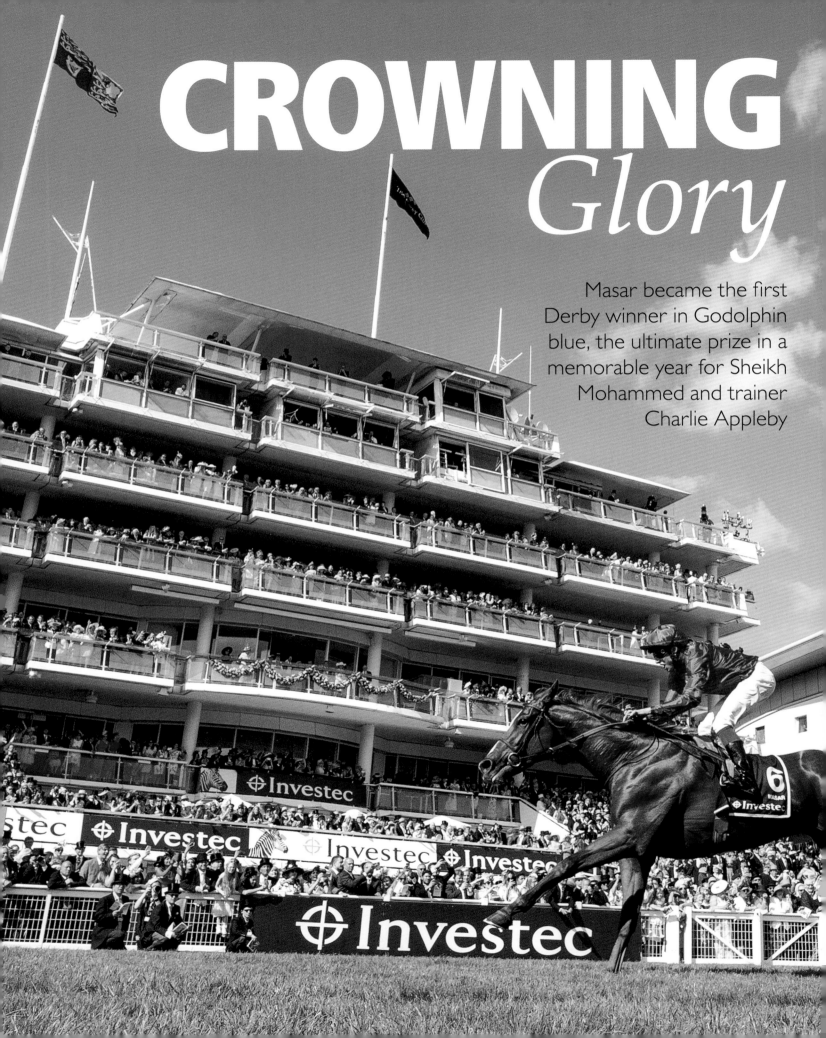

CROWNING
Glory

Masar became the first Derby winner in Godolphin blue, the ultimate prize in a memorable year for Sheikh Mohammed and trainer Charlie Appleby

By Peter Thomas

IT was the year in which Godolphin, the global racing vision of Sheikh Mohammed, racked up its 5,000th winner worldwide, and a year could hardly be more special than that. Unless, of course, it was the year that ended the Sheikh's 41-year wait for his colours to land the biggest prize of them all, the Derby. That it proved to be both made 2018 an annus mirabilis.

At the heart of the success was Charlie Appleby, a former West Country work rider who had grafted his way diligently up the Godolphin ladder, travelling horses around the globe before becoming an assistant trainer and then in 2013 taking charge of both Moulton Paddocks in Newmarket and Marmoom Stables in Dubai.

His appointment to one of the most coveted and prestigious positions in world racing was viewed variously as unorthodox, unprecedented and refreshing by people who would surely now agree that the 43-year-old, who started as "one of the lads", has proved himself as indisputably the

right man for the job. With Godolphin seemingly emerging from the shadows after many years of being eclipsed by Coolmore, it is the one-time amateur rider who is leading the charge and, while it may be true that he is being given a high calibre of ammunition with which to go to war, the case of Epsom hero Masar showed how true Appleby's aim has become.

After four Derby wins in the previous six years, Aidan O'Brien and the Coolmore partners were widely expected to strike again with odds-on favourite Saxon Warrior but Appleby achieved a dramatic turnaround of the 2,000 Guineas form to come out on top with Masar, a 16-1 chance.

"Obviously I've been congratulating them more than they've been congratulating us," he said of the recent years of competition with Godolphin's Irish rivals, "but I feel we're getting to where we need to be now and being competitive with them far more. We're turning up not just as a number but to be respected in these races and we've turned out on top during the course of the year."

Few could dispute that assertion after the royal blue silks had been carried to victory in the second colts' Classic, but the year began with Masar, a homebred by New Approach out of UAE Derby winner Khawlah, hardly setting pulses racing as a Classic contender. The impressive Solario Stakes winner had been well beaten in the Breeders' Cup Juvenile Turf and his stay in the Middle East had been marked by a March flop in Listed company at Meydan – but Appleby was happy, then as now, to tell the full story to anybody who was prepared to listen.

"The Breeders' Cup was a messy race that didn't pan out for us and he was always on the cards to winter in Dubai," he recalls, "but coming into February I had to say to Sheikh Mohammed that the horse was doing a bit too well, he was climbing the walls and I didn't want him to go the wrong way, so we decided to give him a run on the dirt there. It was a win-win: if he won he'd be heading for the Derby and if he didn't he'd at least have a run under his belt to put the manners back on him. He was drawn ten and we were up against

it, so when it didn't happen for him it wasn't a shock, but more importantly it put him where we wanted to be for the year."

It wasn't textbook stuff, but it showed Appleby as a man able to think outside the racing box – as long as the rest of the year panned out as he hoped. It panned out just fine, as we now know, with Masar destroying his field in the Craven – with Roaring Lion more than nine lengths back in third – and leaping to favouritism for the 2,000 Guineas. That he could finish only third at Newmarket behind Saxon Warrior and Tip Two Win may have been a disappointment, but the team quickly turned it into a statement of intent.

"He put up a decent performance in the Guineas and William [Buick] got off and said he felt like a ten-furlong horse in a mile race," recalls the trainer, "so within five minutes we'd decided to go straight for the Derby. His Highness was very keen for it, we thought he had the pedigree, and although it was a big step up in trip we knew we had to have a crack at it."

If it was a relatively simple decision for Sheikh Mohammed, it was one that carried with it a weight of hope and expectation that hardly diminished after
▸▸ *Continues page 80*

Godolphin's Wild Illusion, also trained by Appleby, finished second in the Oaks at Epsom. The Sheikh had been waiting a long time for his Derby and it was one of the two races that had been put on Appleby's 'to do' list when he took the job (along with the Melbourne Cup); he knew his employer was a patient and reasonable man, but still it would be a great way to cement a relationship.

"Having had the favourite in the Oaks finish second, it was at the back of my mind, what did we need to do to win a Classic?" Appleby remembers. "As it turned out, the Derby was one of those comfortable races to watch where you always felt you were in control and it was a special moment I'll never forget, with the whole royal family there to enjoy it. To see everybody's enjoyment meant a lot, to stand back and watch it all happen."

Masar was a commanding winner, seeing off Dee Ex Bee and Roaring Lion, as well as comprehensively turning the tables on Saxon Warrior, who had started the 4-5 favourite.

That it turned out to be his final run of the season was a blow to all concerned – not least the racing public, who were denied further clashes between Masar and Roaring Lion – but his owner was happy to look on the bright side.

"Sheikh Mohammed always emphasises positivity and the positive thing about the injury was that it came after the Derby rather than before it," Appleby says gratefully. "It was a disappointment but we wanted to do what was best for the horse and his future. We're keen to keep him in training as a four-year-old, so what was best for him was to give him all the time he needed as a three-year-old.

"All being well, he'll winter in Dubai and come back for next season. With a horse of that profile, you'd be hoping to target the Coronation Cup, the King George and, dare I say it, on to the Arc. It would be lovely to be able to race-plan like that, but they're the kind of races he deserves to be going for."

▲ Blue-blooded: from left, Masar streaks home in the Craven Stakes; in the winner's enclosure at Epsom; Godolphin's hot summer continues with Blue Point winning the King's Stand Stakes and Old Persian landing the King Edward VII Stakes for Charlie Appleby (below)

****

THE Masar story marked the most conspicuous success of a significant change of tack for Godolphin, that of wintering horses in the sunshine to give them a theoretical edge over those wrapped up against the cold in Britain for the duration. The jury is out for some but Appleby is a believer, and why wouldn't he be?

"We made a point of taking what we thought were the right horses over there and bringing them back in the condition we felt was to our advantage for the rest of the European season," he explains.

"To be honest, if you've got the horse you could probably take them anywhere in the world, but in my mind a bit of heat through the winter doesn't do them any harm, particularly bearing in mind that we never quite know what the British winter is going to throw at us.

"Perhaps it did give us an advantage in the spring over

'SOMETHING REALLY SPECIAL'

Masar was a first Derby winner for William Buick on his eighth ride in the race.

Buick, 29, in his fourth season as a Godolphin retained jockey, had finished second on two occasions – with Libertarian in 2013 and Jack Hobbs in 2015 – and said: "I've dreamed of this since I wanted to be a jockey. This is everything. It's something really special. It's the pinnacle of our sport, the holy grail, the be-all and end-all.

"To do it for His Highness Sheikh Mohammed and his family in the famous royal blue – they are very loyal supporters of me and I'm very happy to be part of it."

Reliving his winning ride shortly afterwards in a Racing Post interview, Buick said: "He was by far the most comfortable Derby ride I've had. He's an incredibly well-balanced horse, very athletic, and he relaxes well. And he's intelligent. He gets the messages a jockey delivers. I'd say the first four furlongs are the most important part of the Derby and Masar jumped into exactly the position I wanted from the start. When we got to the top of the hill he was close up, one off the rail, without having wasted energy to get there. And he was relaxed.

"I didn't think [Saxon Warrior] looked comfortable coming around Tattenham Corner, but I was too focused on riding my own race to really know how he was going. I was aware of where he was, of course, but when you come down that hill it's such an intense part of the race that you're only thinking about what you're doing."

His mount was doing just fine as the field levelled for home. "That's when the race starts to develop; you see the separation of the field three out. The good horses quicken and the rest get left behind." At that point Buick was on the horns of a dilemma. "He'd come alive underneath me as we came down the hill. I was just containing him a little bit. He was going so well he felt like he'd just jumped into the race. I wanted to make sure we had one run up to the line, and that we would last out."

Masar did, by a length and a half, to put himself and Buick on that famous roll of honour.

here. It certainly felt like it. It's just been one of those very special years."

If reflecting on the exploits of Masar makes it sound as though Appleby had a one-horse 2018, then nothing could be further from the truth. By the time the Derby winner had got his British campaign under way, the master of Moulton Paddocks had already won two Group 1s on Dubai World Cup night, his first ever, courtesy of Hawkbill and Jungle Cat, and was clearly in charge of a squad in rude health.

If the spring was hot, flaming June was a veritable blaze of glory, which started, but didn't finish, at Epsom. Having delivered a first Derby to Sheikh Mohammed, Appleby was told by his boss to relax and enjoy himself. With the burden of expectation lifted, he flew ever higher, starting with a King's Stand win from Blue Point and later a King Edward VII for Old Persian.

The run seemed as though it would never end, and the trainer was glad to be seen to advantage in all the right places. "For me it couldn't have gone any better," he remembers, allowing himself one final bask in the glory. "We got started on the right foot with six winners at the Craven meeting, five winners at the Guineas meeting, trundled on to Goodwood with Wild Illusion, Old Persian at York, then to Deauville, where I didn't expect it to go quite as well as it did. We had the right horses and they were all well and we ended up with seven winners from 15 runners.

"If you didn't feel some kind of pressure, if you didn't get excited or revved up for these meetings then you wouldn't be human, but they are where, in my mind, we need to be focusing and having winners. That's why historically Godolphin was set up and where the team needs to be competing, wherever in the world.

"We've got a great team behind us, my Group 1 winners apart from Blue Point have all been homebreds, so from the breeding sheds to the training yards we've got our confidence up and it's great to see Sheikh Mohammed enjoying his sport and getting the results he deserves."

MIGHTY MOUSE

Stradivarius belied his size with a colossal feat as he landed a £1m bonus with an unstoppable run in the big staying races

By Nick Pulford

HE was the mouse that roared. Stradivarius, the little horse with the big heart, claimed the biggest prize available in British Flat racing with four wins that unlocked the treasure chest of the Weatherbys Hamilton Stayers' Million bonus. In less than 100 days he turned what had seemed a huge task at the outset, with bookmakers offering 20-1 about any horse winning the bonus, into thrilling reality with his run for the riches.

When he completed his winning sequence at York on August 24, the John Gosden-trained four-year-old was the year's fourth-highest earner in British and Irish racing but with the addition of the £1m bonus he leaped above Poet's Word, Roaring Lion and Masar to the top of the money tree at that stage. In winning the Yorkshire Cup, Gold

Cup, Goodwood Cup and Lonsdale Cup, plus the bonus, he accumulated the grand sum of £1,788,269. Having raced a total of eight and a quarter miles in those four contests, he earned £27,095 per furlong – or, to put it another way, £125,276 for each minute of racing.

It was some total, and some journey.

****

THE bonus had been announced in January, forming part of British racing's drive to strengthen the programme for long-distance horses. The backer was Weatherbys Hamilton – the insurance arm of the historic family firm – and chief executive Charles Hamilton later explained: "We all remember these great stayers, like Persian Punch and Double Trigger, and anything we can do to make sure we retain the variety in the programme has got to be a good thing. We don't want breeding to become one-dimensional and cards with just six- and seven-furlong races."

If the bonus was won, the £1m would be split between the connections of the successful horse, with 70 per cent awarded to the owner and 30 per cent divided equally between the trainer, stable staff, breeder and jockey. Among those who welcomed the prize was Michael Bell, trainer of 2017 Gold Cup winner Big Orange, although he was quick to say: "It may be mission impossible. It will be incredibly difficult to win because horses have to give so much to win these top-class staying races."

Although the final three legs – the Gold Cup, Goodwood Cup and Lonsdale Cup, which is sponsored by Weatherbys Hamilton – were compulsory, there were four potential starting points for bonus hunters. That meant a quartet of horses could be in contention heading to the Gold Cup, giving the sponsor added exposure. Big Orange would not be one of them, however, being ruled out for the season just before his intended reappearance in the Henry II Stakes, one of those starting points.

Stradivarius, rated a 50-1 chance for the bonus at the outset, collected his golden ticket in the Yorkshire Cup with an impressive victory as 4-6 favourite under Frankie Dettori. "He's a star – it's very rare you get a stayer with a turn of foot, but that's what he's got. It's a deadly combination," Dettori said after scoring by three lengths from Desert Skyline.

The others who had a potential shot at the million were Torcedor, winner of the Sagaro Stakes, Ormonde Stakes scorer Idaho and Magic Circle, who took the Henry II. Idaho, however, went to the Coronation Cup and then the Hardwicke Stakes at Royal Ascot, while Magic Circle's connections opted not to supplement him for the Gold Cup.

Already the bonus race was down to two horses and they faced strong opposition in the Gold Cup from Order Of St George, the 2016 winner, and crack French stayer Vazirabad. Stradivarius was joint-favourite with Order Of St George and it was his combination of pace and power that won the day in one of the races of the year, with Dettori's mount coming home by three-quarters of a length from Vazirabad. Torcedor performed valiantly, just a head back in third in a driving finish.

That was the end of Torcedor's bonus challenge but Stradivarius had moved one step closer, and the sponsor's offer seemed to be adding an extra element to the staying division. "You would have a heart of stone not to be moved by the finish, with three outstanding horses battling it out after two and

▸▸ *Continues page 84*

a half miles. It encapsulated everything that is so fantastic about the stayers," Hamilton said.

It was a 60th Royal Ascot winner for Dettori and a sixth Gold Cup. "It was thrilling to win a Gold Cup in that manner," he said after his flying dismount. "That's what the public wanted to see and that's what they got. This was a nailbiter to the end. To have the three best horses in the last furlong battling it out, you can't beat it. Full credit to the horse, he was as brave as a lion."

Gosden, winning his first Gold Cup, heaped praise on Stradivarius. "He's a proper little staying horse," he said. "He's a dear horse – we call him Mighty Mouse because he's not very big and he's got these lovely little white legs and face, he looks like a mini-Trigger. He's a gorgeous little horse – I could see Wyatt Earp riding into town on him."

****

IF the bonus road looked open now, there was a reminder of the possible potholes with the news that Stradivarius was found to be lame after a routine post-race examination, having lost his right-hind shoe. And if anyone was in any doubt about what a battle the Gold Cup had been, Vazirabad was soon ruled out of a rematch in the Goodwood Cup with trainer Alain de Royer-Dupre reporting the battle-hardened stayer had returned "pretty weary" from Ascot.

Vazirabad would miss the whole of the summer but to keep the bonus alive Stradivarius had to back up from the Gold Cup just 40 days later in the Qatar Goodwood Cup – the race where he had announced himself as a staying force the previous year when he beat Big Orange by a length and three-quarters.

As a three-year-old he had the advantage of a 13lb weight-for-age allowance then, but this time he was on level weights with his rivals and would meet Torcedor 1lb worse than in the Gold Cup. He also had a change of rider, with Andrea Atzeni deputising for the suspended Dettori. Stradivarius was 4-5 favourite but Gosden was taking nothing for granted. "I don't think it's a one-sided

⏵ Continues page 86

▾ Ascot thriller: Stradivarius (right) and Frankie Dettori win the Gold Cup from Vazirabad: previous page, the first step on the bonus road in the Yorkshire Cup

'HE'S A ONCE-IN-A-LIFETIME HORSE'

"All my horses are bred or bought with the Derby in mind. To wind up in the St Leger means I'm doing something wrong." So said Bjorn Nielsen, owner-breeder of Stradivarius, before his colt finished third in the world's oldest Classic in 2017.

Even then, however, Nielsen (below) was looking forward to 2018, although he could have had no idea about the riches it would bring. "I hope he'll make up into a proper Cup horse next year. It doesn't do you any favours commercially but the thrill of watching them is more than enough."

Born in South Africa and raised in Epsom, Nielsen lives in America but indulges his passion for British racing thanks to a fortune made in commodities trading. He keeps around 15 broodmares and has roughly as many horses in training each year, although he offers some yearlings for sale to mitigate costs.

Stradivarius narrowly failed to make his reserve at Tattersalls as a yearling, where he was retained for 330,000gns and sent into training with John Gosden. The initial signs were not that promising but he came into his own over staying distances as a three-year-old.

"He came on a lot from what we thought he was early on," Nielsen said. "When he beat Big Orange in the Goodwood Cup [in 2017] I knew he was going to be able to compete with the best stayers. He's got a turn of foot, which is quite rare for a stayer, and he has a big heart.

"He's very chilled, if you watch him in the pre-parade ring nothing seems to bother him, which is probably why he's a good horse. Just like a sportsman, the good ones can relax under pressure. He does that and seems to know when he has to pass something late in the race – he knows he has to get there."

The owner revelled in every win on the bonus road but was always careful to say it was one step at a time. "I'm aware how hard it is to get these horses ready for a single Group 1, to get a horse to peak time after time, and John Gosden is a master at it.

"With staying horses, you're not really under pressure to retire them and stand them at stud. If you look after them, they go round for two or three years. In that sense he's a once-in-a-lifetime horse."

NOVEMBER HANDICAP

SAT 10TH NOV

FINAL OF THE BRITISH FLAT SEASON

BOOK TICKETS NOW
doncaster-racecourse.co.uk

doncaster
racing & events

race – on the book it isn't – and Torcedor looks a real threat to us," the trainer said, and he was right to be wary.

On the run downhill towards the finish, Colm O'Donoghue took Torcedor three lengths clear. Briefly it looked as if Stradivarius might not respond but then he kicked into gear and battled hard for a half-length victory. Idaho, returning to staying races after not taking the bonus route, was left six lengths behind in third.

"When Colm quickened it may have looked like he put the race to bed, but I was on the best horse and I wasn't really panicking," said Atzeni, winning a second Goodwood Cup on Stradivarius. "Colm rode a very clever race but Stradivarius was always going to get on top. I didn't want to give him a hard race; I kept him fresh for Frankie."

****

THE bonus was really on now, with the Lonsdale Cup 24 days away, and Hamilton said: "We've taken defensive action. Part of our marketing budget is to spend money but not necessarily £1m. But I very much want him to do

it: the whole purpose is to promote the stayer and there's nothing like getting the £1m won to do that."

If it seemed plain sailing now, with Stradivarius 4-11 favourite for the York race and Idaho the highest-rated of his rivals, it would be anything but. Reunited with Dettori, Stradivarius struggled to find his usual rhythm and had to be forced past Count Octave – officially rated 13lb inferior – before scoring by a length and a half.

"He didn't give me the same feel as at Ascot," Dettori said. "He was lethargic. He's run in every

▼ Extra dividend: staff at John Gosden's Clarehaven Stables are presented with a £100,000 cheque as their share of the Stayers' Million bonus, with the sponsor's £75,000 boosted by an additional £25,000 from Stradivarius's owner Bjorn Nielsen

championship race and they take their toll. Even if they look like they win easily, they still have to run the distance. Class and courage got him through. It wasn't his best performance but, hey, we're millionaires."

Gosden had similar sentiments. "I wouldn't say he was at his sparkling best but we're not going to complain because he won," he said, before emphasising the tough task Stradivarius had tackled and conquered. "He has managed to get over every hurdle and he must feel

▲ Money trail: Stradivarius wins the Yorkshire Cup (left) under Frankie Dettori and the Goodwood Cup (centre) with Andrea Atzeni; Dettori celebrates Lonsdale Cup success (right) as the Stayers' Million is secured (inset)

like he has gone 12 rounds with Muhammad Ali."

Small in stature he may be, but Stradivarius has a huge heart and had pulled off a gigantic feat. Since 1980 – when the Lonsdale Cup started – no horse had completed the Gold Cup, Goodwood Cup and Lonsdale Cup treble, let alone added one more to the run with the Yorkshire Cup.

"There were many who thought the WH Stayers' Million would be nearly impossible to win," Hamilton said, "but they were reckoning without a horse who encapsulates everything that is great about a stayer – soundness, longevity, versatility and real quality."

The bonus had done its job in bringing out a star with those attributes, and Stradivarius had done his with true staying power.

HOUDINI ACT PROVIDES A FITTING FINALE

STRADIVARIUS confirmed himself the top stayer with victory in the Group 2 Long Distance Cup at Ascot on British Champions Day – but he needed a lucky break to get himself out of trouble.

Order Of St George and Torcedor, the pair who had beaten him in the two-mile race the previous year, were no longer around and the way looked clear for Stradivarius to record his fifth win of an unbeaten campaign.

Even a six-runner field can be problematic, however, and Frankie Dettori found himself trapped on the rail on the turn for home, desperately looking for a gap with the even-money favourite. Fortunately, a chink of light opened when Ryan Moore, leading on Flag Of Honour, swung a little wide out of the turn and Dettori was quick to seize the opportunity.

That was the decisive moment and Stradivarius went on to score by a length and a half from Thomas Hobson. Dettori said: "I thought if I don't get this gap I won't

get out. I had half a chance to take it and I took it. I think he took Ryan by surprise. It was instantaneous – but you can only do that when you have plenty of horse left."

Trainer John Gosden paid tribute to Dettori's daring and skill. "I said he'd need to be Houdini to get out of the box – well, he did. He saw that glimpse on the bend and dived for it. Then Ryan tried to shut it but, thank goodness, it was too late. What a clever ride from Frankie. That was jockeyship at its highest level."

◄ Winning move: Frankie Dettori after his escape act on Stradivarius

IN THE
PICTURE

Baker a rider no more – but a writer, pundit, agent and family man

IT'S the picture those close to George Baker thought they might never see. A picture of family contentment and bright-eyed good health, far removed from the turmoil of the previous year, when a thudding crash in a race on the packed snow of St Moritz had seen the jockey airlifted to hospital with a head injury that threatened all manner of horrors.

As George lay in an induced coma, doctors guessed at the severity of the trauma. George's wife Nicola sat by his bedside and four-month-old Isabella stayed at home with her grandmother, oblivious then as now to the knife-edge her father was on.

"I watched a TV programme about brain injuries, with a doctor saying he'd take an amputation of both his legs over a brain injury any day," said Nicola, "because to lose your character must be the worst thing. If you lose a leg you're still you, but if you lose your character you're not you anymore. Luckily, enough of George is still there that he's still George."

The patient had narrowly avoided a spinal injury but did have a brain injury, and a significant one at that, so he had to start relearning many of life's simplest functions from scratch. It soon became apparent to friends and family that the road back to the saddle would be a long one, possibly even a dead end.

George – who rode 1,364 winners, racked up six centuries, landed a British Classic on Harbour Law in the 2016 St Leger and Group 1s on Seal Of Approval, Thistle Bird and Quest For More – was stubborn and resolute in his belief that he would return to race-riding, right until the day he watched a film – about an American champion snowboarder who had suffered a similar injury – that made him realise his limitations.

"To watch him struggle, from being the best in the world to looking literally as though he'd never been on a snowboard before, to hear his specialist say he couldn't take another knock to the head, made me realise what was happening to me."

George, thankful for the ultimately fruitless obsession that had driven him to get out of his hospital bed every day, recalibrated his career, wrote an autobiography, worked a few days a week for Lambourn trainer Ed Walker, launched himself into his role as an insightful TV pundit and then leapt at the chance to become agent to jockeys William Buick and James Doyle.

The popular 36-year-old was back in racing, not in the saddle perhaps – "my balance is still horrific" – but walking well, talking well and looking, to all intents and purposes, like a happy husband and a loving father.

Picture: EDWARD WHITAKER (RACINGPOST.COM/PHOTOS)

AGAINST ALL ODDS

Three incredible stories of survival — and triumph on the big stage

miracle *n,* an event or act which breaks a law of nature, *esp* one attributed to a deity or supernatural force

EDWULF
Irish Gold Cup, Leopardstown

Some sort of divine intervention certainly seemed to be at work at Leopardstown in February when Edwulf inflicted a shock defeat on his Unibet Irish Gold Cup rivals. The race itself was remarkable enough, with the 33-1 shot scoring by a neck from Outlander after narrow leader Killultagh Vic had fallen at the final fence, but Edwulf's journey there was extraordinary.

Less than a year earlier the JP McManus-owned chaser's life hung in the balance after he had a seizure in the closing stages of the National Hunt Chase at the Cheltenham Festival as a result of oxygen starvation to the brain. As Tiger Roll was hailed the winner, Edwulf was behind the green screens in front of the stands with the vets battling hard to save him.

Liam Kearns led the veterinary team on the day and, speaking to the Racing Post after Edwulf had won the Irish Gold Cup, he recalled the incident. "Most of the horses we deal with in recumbency for a long time are down due to falling or being brought down, so there's a physical trauma involved and you're trying to assess what

physical injury might be affecting a horse's nervous system," he said.

"This horse hadn't got the fall, hadn't got the direct trauma, so we were dealing with exertion, oxygen deprivation, heat stress, all the factors that could come in with any endurance athlete under pressure. That's what we were dealing with and treating clinical signs we had that just didn't fit into the normal recumbency situation we would more routinely see."

After the final race of the day was delayed while Edwulf continued to be treated on the track, the stricken chaser was eventually loaded into the equine ambulance. "He was down for a bit longer than 40 minutes and when he got up he was still quite uncoordinated. To have him up and fit to walk in and support himself in the ambulance meant a delay," Kearns said.

"It was an exceptionally long time. Once you go on beyond that 40-minute stage it's a rare occurrence for a horse to get up."

The worst was over but Edwulf was only in the

first stage of recovery and a long period of recuperation lay ahead, as trainer Joseph O'Brien explained later. "He's very lucky to be alive. He actually went blind for a couple of days after the race. He was in Cheltenham for two weeks before he came home and I can't stress enough the job the vets did and how well he was looked after at [McManus's] Martinstown Stud over the summer. My own staff also deserve a lot of credit."

At the age of 25, and so early in his training career, O'Brien had the far from easy job of seeing whether he could bring Edwulf back to the racecourse. "The vets all said there was no higher risk of what happened to him [at Cheltenham] happening again than to any other horse on any other day. When I heard that I had the confidence to come back with him," he said.

"We went slowly and took it day by day and he was going to tell us. But that was only possible because of the care he got at the track and after he left the

track. We wanted to bring him along slowly and give him every opportunity to do something on the track. The horse was in very good form and very sound.

"Edwulf loves his racing and it wouldn't have been fair to just throw him out in the field. It wouldn't have made sense. To get him back to the racecourse was going to be a big achievement. But you couldn't have expected him to come back and win an Irish Gold Cup."

Nine and a half months after the Cheltenham horror, the first step back was in the Leopardstown Christmas Chase. Edwulf, having his first run in Grade 1 company, went off at 66-1 and was pulled up before the third-last by Derek O'Connor. Just over five weeks later, he was half those odds for another Grade 1 attempt in the Irish Gold Cup over the same course and distance.

Nobody could have envisaged what would happen this time. Edwulf, the rank outsider of the ten-runner field, was at the back for most of the way but took closer order two out and was involved in a four-way battle going to the final fence. Killultagh Vic was just in
▶▶ *Continues page 92*

◀ Life affirming: Edwulf on his way to Irish Gold Cup victory and with trainer Joseph O'Brien (left) in the winner's enclosure

front but came down at the last, leaving Outlander in the lead from Edwulf and a tiring Djakadam.

Under a tremendous drive from O'Connor, scoring his first Grade 1 win, it was Edwulf who proved the stronger by a neck from the gallant Outlander. The great comeback was complete.

"We just wanted to save him for a happy retirement," McManus admitted afterwards. "That day at Cheltenham was about saving the horse's life and it was a huge team effort. It wasn't about coming back and winning Grade 1 races, so I'm lost for words."

McManus wasn't the only one.

ARTHUR KITT
Chesham Stakes, Royal Ascot

Arthur Kitt was bred for Royal Ascot success – expressly so by owner Andrew Black – and he fulfilled his destiny with victory in the Chesham Stakes, but the happy ending in the summer heat could not have been further removed from the cold, dark February night in 2016 on which the colt was born. That, by contrast, presented a scene of utter heartbreak and a desperate struggle for life.

Arthur Kitt was the third foal of 2012 Queen Mary Stakes winner Ceiling Kitty but he was also her

last. Arriving home after a night out in London, Black, co-founder of Betfair and owner of Chasemore Stud, received a call from his stud manager Paul Coombe to tell him the foaling had gone tragically wrong. Ceiling Kitty had lost her life and her Camelot foal had a slim chance of surviving the night.

Writing in his blog a few days after the foal was born, Black said: "He had a heartbeat but was not breathing – Paul managed to get him to breathe but it was a battle and he had to be resuscitated four times. It was probably an hour before he turned the corner and

settled down; we fed him milk from one of the other mares.

"It was eerily silent as I entered the foaling unit; then came a little whinny from one of the boxes. Opening the top door I saw a foal sat up in the middle of the stable, wearing a blanket. Four stable staff – Paul, Pat, our vet, Laura and Jamie – were sitting in the four corners of the stable box looking quietly at their prize; the foal they had salvaged from the wreckage."

A day and a half later Arthur Kitt was out with his new nanny, a black-and-white mare who had arrived from Ireland to look after the miracle foal, and the long

▼ Destiny's child: Arthur Kitt (left, green) holds off Nate The Great by a neck in the Chesham Stakes

ROYAL ASCOT

process of getting him to the racecourse had begun. Eventually he moved from spending lazy days in Surrey to Manor House Stables in Cheshire, the purpose-built facility in which Black is a partner alongside former footballer Michael Owen.

Under the careful hand of resident trainer Tom Dascombe, Arthur Kitt showed promise at home – more than the average equine athlete – and all those around this extraordinary character started to think maybe the horse bred for the Chesham Stakes at Royal Ascot might have what it takes to get there after all.

His racecourse debut came at the end of May in a six-furlong novice stakes at Haydock and it was a successful one. Now came the biggest day – the Royal Ascot date that had been in the calendar even before he was born.

Smartly away from the stalls in the seven-furlong Chesham Stakes, Arthur Kitt initially raced handily before losing his position with just under half the race to go. Responding valiantly to rider Richard Kingscote, however, he surged to the front on the final climb and held off Nate The Great in the closing stages, triumphing by a neck and sending those connected with him into emotional overdrive.

"This is the most special [victory]. I have more emotion attached to this horse than any other I have owned," Black said. "The night he was born was such an incredibly difficult, painful night. I always hoped he would be special and we always thought this was the race, being by Camelot out of a speedy mare. I just thought we would win the Chesham and make it right somehow.

"We put the mare down within seconds of having the problem. Then you have all the problems of getting the foal out. There were lots of complications there. He had a twisted leg at that point and it took a long, long time for that to heal.

"We put the call out for a foster mare and managed to get one, and we still have her today. Arthur Kitt was brought up by her, and when they are brought up by a foster mare, they are kind of different. He was much more friendly than your average horse. He would come over to you whereas the rest of them wouldn't."

For Black, this was a special kind of horse, and a special kind of victory.

▸▸ *Continues page 94*

THE TIN MAN
Sprint Cup, Haydock

When The Tin Man landed the 32Red Sprint Cup at Haydock in September to become a Group 1 winner for the third year in a row, the half-length margin of victory could not tell the tale of the battle he had fought and won simply to be there. Just nine months earlier his career – and maybe even his life – had hung in the balance.

Christmas 2017 was not a happy time for The Tin Man. Comfort and joy were in short supply after the James Fanshawe-trained speedster was struck down with pnuemonia on his journey to the Hong Kong Sprint in December, causing him to miss the race and then the flight home with the rest of the British travellers as vets tried to nurse him back to health.

It was a long process. The Tin Man had a temperature of 105F on arrival in Hong Kong and, while some horses can start to recover within 24 hours, he was still running a high fever five days later, necessitating an extended stay in the territory. "There was also a danger in flying him back," Fanshawe said. "Another flare-up could have killed him."

Thankfully the six-year-old made it back safely to Newmarket but the prognosis was unclear for a return to racing, let alone to the Group 1 level where he was used to competing. Time would be the healer and he was kept out of training for three months until tests on his lungs showed no sign of fluid. Only then could he be subjected to the stress of training and eventually racing.

The Tin Man's return to the racecourse could not have been more encouraging as he took a Listed race at Windsor in late May, five months after his illness, but frustration followed when he returned to Group 1 company. Although he handled the high intensity as well as ever, he came up a little short – perhaps unluckily so – with fourth place in the Diamond Jubilee Stakes at Royal Ascot and third in the Prix Maurice de Gheest at Deauville.

Those runs had been on The Tin Man's supposedly favoured good or fast ground and it seemed maybe his best chance had passed him by when

the going at Haydock came up heavy. In the previous two runnings of the Sprint Cup, Fanshawe's flyer had been second to Quiet Reflection on soft and third to Harry Angel on heavy, and punters again fancied Harry Angel as they made him 6-4 favourite with Tasleet 6-1 and The Tin Man 7-1 along with Sir Dancealot.

Those other fancied runners disappointed, however, and it was The Tin Man who roared into the lead a furlong out under jockey-of-the-moment Oisin Murphy, riding him for the first time. Brando and Gustav Klimt tried to challenge but could not close the gap to the deserving winner.

"He's a wonderful horse and so consistent," Fanshawe said. "You

▲ Man alive: The Tin Man roars back to Group 1-winning form in the Sprint Cup at Haydock

could argue he'd been unlucky this year. Everyone is biased towards their own horses but I felt he'd run really good races at Ascot and Deauville. I was concerned about the ground but the rest of the family love it."

Reflecting on the long journey back from adversity, the trainer added: "It's amazing. He nearly died in Hong Kong. The vets have done a great job getting him back again. We couldn't do it without our staff as well. They've done a wonderful job to get the horse to run in this race."

Fanshawe might allow himself some of the credit too. All round, this was a victory to be proud of.

Reporting by Brian Sheerin, Peter Scargill and Nick Pulford

THE
BIGGER
PICTURE

Starter Simon McNeill sets the 14 runners on their way in the 2m5f handicap hurdle at Kempton on February 24. Kings Walk (blue and pink) won by a neck from The Mighty Don (brown and yellow), with the pair already prominent in the early stages
EDWARD WHITAKER
(RACINGPOST.COM/PHOTOS)

ROYAL ASCENT

Sir Michael Stoute took the outright record as top trainer
at Royal Ascot in grand style with four winners in 2018

By Lewis Porteous

IN 2017 Sir Michael Stoute had been long odds-on to stand alone as the most successful trainer of all time at Royal Ascot. A single success would have taken him clear of Sir Henry Cecil on to 76 winners and he had five favourites among a formidable team for the week. Yet, one by one, his runners came up short and the champagne remained on ice.

That was only the second time since 1995 he had failed to register a single Royal Ascot success and the timing was most inopportune for a trainer who, like the late Sir Henry, is synonymous with Ascot success in June. It still seemed inevitable that Stoute would move ahead of Cecil at some point, but there was the feeling that he might limp over the line rather than flash home in a blaze of glory.

What a difference a year makes. Stoute did not go to Royal Ascot 2018 with a team of market leaders but he returned to Freemason Lodge in Newmarket with a top-hatful of big prizes. Not only was the outright record his, he had done it in style thanks to Group 1 triumphs with Poet's Word in the Prince of Wales's Stakes and Eqtidaar in the Commonwealth Cup, plus impressive wins for Crystal Ocean in the Group 2 Hardwicke Stakes and Expert Eye in the Group 3 Jersey Stakes.

The royal flush of success was emblematic of a revival in Stoute's fortunes on the big days that was sparked by Ulysses in 2017 and continued throughout 2018 as he enjoyed his most high-profile campaign in years. Even if numbers and quality at his famous yard have waned over the past decade, what has never changed is his ability to wring the best from his horses, nor the competitive spirit that drives him to produce his runners at their peak for Royal Ascot. And never was that more evident than at the 2018 meeting.

****

SINCE Etienne Gerard opened Stoute's account at the most famous Flat festival in the world by winning the 1977 Jersey Stakes, the master of Freemason Lodge has been on the Ascot scoresheet in all but seven of the subsequent years, his victors including champions like Marwell, Shareef Dancer, Sonic Lady, Zilzal, Kalanisi and Estimate. He told the official Royal Ascot magazine in 2017 that planning starts early, saying: "I think it starts to happen when you get them moving again at the start of the Flat season. You are looking at the team from early on in the season, looking at potential Royal Ascot runners – like Cheltenham with the jumps boys. When you finalise it, the staff really love it. They love taking a horse there." With such an attachment to the meeting, failing to score in 2017 was a significant setback.

Fast forward 12 months and Stoute's squad – on paper at least – looked competitive rather than formidable. That did not dampen expectations when it came to setting a new record for Royal Ascot winners, although any attempt to get the cricket-loving Barbadian to entertain the possibility of moving clear of Cecil was expertly rebuffed to the boundary.

Stoute's main hope on day one was Mirage Dancer in the Wolferton, but there were shades of the previous year as the 7-2 favourite met some trouble in running and ended up one place behind stablemate Autocratic in fifth.

Day two and Stoute had just two bullets to fire. Both had definite chances but they also had better-fancied rivals and were not screaming out as potential record-breakers for their trainer.

Poet's Word in the Prince of Wales's Stakes was the epitome of the improving older horse on which Stoute's lofty reputation has been built – think Pilsudski, Singspiel or Islington, champions who got better with age under Stoute's patient handling.

The five-year-old Poet's Word had climbed through handicaps to establish himself as a Group 1 performer, finishing runner-up at the highest level three times before Ascot. The latest of those seconds had been in the Dubai Sheema Classic in March, before a

▸▸*Continues page 100*

▲ Record breaker: Poet's Word wins the Prince of Wales's Stakes
▼ Expert Eye cruises home in the Jersey Stakes

confidence-boosting Group 3 success at Sandown, and he would have been a worthy Prince of Wales's favourite in most years. The problem was he had to face Cracksman, who had been seven lengths too strong for him over course and distance the previous October and was coming off victory – albeit not so impressive – in the Coronation Cup at Epsom.

Running scared from one horse is not in Stoute's nature, however, and Poet's Word was ridden to track the favourite before seeing if he was good enough to pounce in the straight. He was more than up to the task, running 7lb better than ever before according to official ratings as he registered a first top-level win by a comfortable two and a quarter lengths from odds-on favourite Cracksman.

As well as pride, there must have been relief for Stoute to move one clear of Cecil with a record 76 Royal Ascot winners, although there was no fanfare from the trainer himself, rather recognition of the friend he had just surpassed.

"Henry's record was formidable, because he accumulated those numbers when there were four days of Royal Ascot for most of his career and the five-day meeting hasn't been implemented for that long," said Stoute. "We're very glad it has happened and it's a great reflection on the staff. I love the game and we have great staff and very supportive owners, so I'd like to keep going for a little while more."

****

IF WINNER number 76 had taken an age to arrive, 77 was little more than an hour away as Expert Eye recaptured his juvenile form to rocket away with the Jersey Stakes. Whereas Poet's Word's career graph had charted a smooth gradient, Expert Eye had shot to 2,000 Guineas favouritism when winning the Vintage Stakes at two before slumping to three subsequent defeats, including a lacklustre tenth in the Guineas on his previous start before Ascot.

In moving Expert Eye back to seven furlongs and down in grade, Stoute worked his magic once more, the explosiveness from Goodwood back in evidence as the colt burst from the

pack to register one of the most convincing wins of the entire week.

That return to form was not by fluke, with Stoute lifting the lid soon after on what goes on behind the scenes to bring a horse like Expert Eye back from the brink. "A lot of work has gone into this horse at home," he said. "My staff deserve a lot of credit – James Savage, my head man who rides him out every morning, and I'd like to mention Gary Witheford and his son Craig for the stalls work they did with him, and also Ted Durcan who played his part too."

Stoute is the skipper but his shipmates are among the very best and he can trust others to help rebuild a

▲ Speed machine: Eqtidaar gives Stoute a second Group 1 success at the meeting by landing the Commonwealth Cup under Jim Crowley

horse like Expert Eye when things go wrong. The best working with the best is clearly a winning combination.

Whereas Expert Eye was dropping in grade to get back on track, Stoute's third winner of the meeting was pitched in at the deep end.

Eqtidaar's sole win in four starts had come on his debut in maiden company as a two-year-old but, despite a defeat at Listed level on his previous run before Royal Ascot, Stoute trusted what the colt was telling him at home in the build-up and took aim at the Group 1 Commonwealth Cup.

Eqtidaar's homework was starting to stand out for the right reasons and when big-race rider Jim Crowley confirmed that impression in a gallop the weekend before Ascot, Stoute was happy to go for the big pot with a three-year-old who had plenty to prove.

That conviction, to trust his instinct, proved inspired as Eqtidaar had too much speed for his 21 rivals and gave Stoute his third win of the week and 78th success at the meeting.

Stoute might be best associated with older horses, the majority of them middle-distance performers who have been handled patiently to shine over time, yet the truth is he can excel with
▶▶ *Continues page 102*

STOUTE AT ROYAL ASCOT

Winners 79

First winner Etienne Gerard (Jersey Stakes 1977)

Top trainer Six times (1991, 1998, 2000, 2005, 2006, 2014)

Most winners in one year Four (1991, 1998, 2005, 2014, 2018)

Gold Cup winners Shangamuzo 1978, Estimate 2013

Triple winner Cover Up (Ascot Stakes 2001, Queen Alexandra Stakes 2002 & 2003)

Dual winners Hard Fought, Rock Hopper, Maraahel, Estimate

Winners for the Queen Four

Most successful race Hardwicke Stakes (11 winners)

Longest-odds winners 25-1 Etienne Gerard (Jersey Stakes 1977), Imperial Stride (Wolferton Handicap 2005)

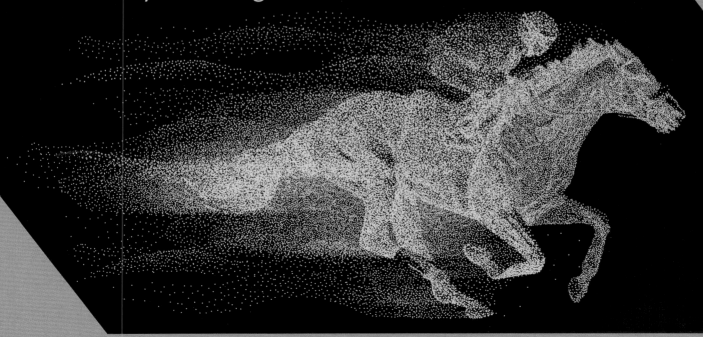

any horse. Marwell, Ajdal and Green Desert, three of the best sprinters of any generation, were all handled by Stoute and there can be no pigeon-holing one of the greatest Flat trainers of all time.

****

WITH winners over a mile and a quarter, seven furlongs and six furlongs in the bag, Stoute still had his banker at the beginning of the week, Crystal Ocean, to come in the Hardwicke Stakes. This Group 2 contest over a mile and a half is firmly established as a Stoute favourite, having fallen his way ten times before, and Crystal Ocean was trying to join the likes of Harbinger, Telescope and Dartmouth on the roll of honour.

Crystal Ocean, owned by one of Stoute's loyal owner-breeders, Sir Evelyn de Rothschild, was the quality horse in the field, reflected in his 4-7 starting price, and there was never any cause for concern under Ryan Moore.

Like the majority of those who run under Stoute's name, Crystal Ocean

settled beautifully before landing the knockout blow with a powerful surge from over two furlongs out.

Only stablemate Poet's Word would deny Crystal Ocean a first Group 1 win in the King George back at Ascot the following month, the duo separated by just a neck with nine lengths back to the third, both horses showing further progression to register career-best ratings.

****

BY the conclusion of Royal Ascot, Stoute had four winners and three thirds, but more significantly had saddled more winners than any other trainer at the meeting with 79 and had reaffirmed his position as the meeting's master trainer.

Although he lost out on the top trainer award due to a lack of second-place finishers, Stoute had matched Aidan O'Brien and John Gosden when it came to winners, a phenomenal achievement considering the immense firepower at his rivals' disposal.

'Crystal Ocean settled beautifully before landing the knockout blow with a powerful surge from over two furlongs out'

▾ Final flourish: Crystal Ocean storms home under Ryan Moore in the Hardwicke Stakes to become Stoute's fourth winner of the meeting

Before the brilliant Ulysses fulfilled his potential to win the Coral-Eclipse and Juddmonte International in 2017, Integral back in 2014 had been Stoute's last domestic Group 1 winner.

Yet, above the waterline at least, there was never any panic or self-pity from the master of Freemason Lodge, who has weathered the storm and emerged with a clutch of Group 1 performers. Indeed, this was the first time since 2006 he had landed two of Royal Ascot's Group 1 races in the same week, his current team collectively looking as strong as any he has had this decade.

While bloodstock superpowers like the Weinstocks may no longer be on Stoute's books, the biggest owner-breeders continue to back him to get the results. Cheveley Park, the Niarchos family and the Rothschilds have horses dotted across different yards but, due to his outstanding record, Stoute still gets his share of the breeders' brightest prospects.

Perhaps they are not the most precocious horses in training, but they all have the potential to be something special and this year Stoute unlocked their very best.

A well-worn cliche it may be, but Stoute's resurgence is proof that while form is temporary, class is permanent. Just look at his Royal Ascot record for the ultimate confirmation.

By Scott Burton

Poet's Word outbattled stablemate Crystal Ocean in a dramatic King George to continue Sir Michael Stoute's memorable year

MAG|C WORD

SIR MICHAEL STOUTE has often in his long and successful training career appeared to follow the dictum of Kutuzov, the Russian general who observed to Tolstoy's dashing Prince Bolkonsky in War and Peace that "the two most powerful warriors are patience and time".

Neither of those commodities is in plentiful supply in modern-day racing but Stoute has deep reservoirs of both, allied to a sporting nature shared by owners Saeed Suhail and Sir Evelyn de Rothschild, and those elements combined to produce a thrilling King George VI and Queen Elizabeth Stakes as stablemates Poet's Word and Crystal Ocean

▶ Fight to the finish: Poet's Word (right) gets up to beat Crystal Ocean in a thrilling King George

fought out their own private battle with the rest of the field nowhere.

The Stoute pair were typical late bloomers for the stable. The four-year-old Crystal Ocean, the 6-4 favourite, had finished the previous season with a half-length second to Capri in the St Leger, his first crack at a Group 1, and had started the current one with three straight wins, most recently in the Hardwicke Stakes at Royal Ascot. The King George was only his second attempt at a Group 1, on the tenth start of his career.

Poet's Word, a year older and close behind his stablemate in the betting at 7-4, had already graduated to the top level – albeit at his fifth attempt – when running away from Cracksman in a Prince of Wales's Stakes that had steadfastly refused to follow the script. So recently proven over ten furlongs, Poet's Word was supposed to be the rapier with the finishing kick to match Crystal Ocean's relentless gallop over a mile and a half in the King George. That was about to be put to the test in the most dramatic fashion.

"That day in the Prince of Wales's they went a hell of a pace," says James Doyle, whose growing reputation as a big-race jockey saw him handed the ride on Poet's Word at Royal Ascot. "Beforehand I could see it unfolding that I might be in front of Cracksman. But they went a hell of a pace and Frankie [Dettori] rode Cracksman quite aggressively to keep tabs on the leaders and it just worked out great.

"It was one of those satisfying races to ride where you're following your main danger, almost man-marking him. He seemed to be in trouble from a fair way out and Poet's Word was well within his comfort zone and travelled fantastically."

****

ARMED with the confidence that such a success brings, Doyle felt he knew exactly how to get the best out of Poet's Word as he retained the ride for the King George. But as Kutuzov would no doubt attest, a battle plan rarely survives the opening skirmishes. Doyle had to abandon his preconceptions about how any potential duel with Crystal Ocean and his jockey William Buick

▸▸ *Continues*
page 106

might play out within 30 seconds of the stalls opening.

"Tactically I thought the race would be quite straightforward. I had a plan to follow Crystal Ocean because I knew William would be quite positive as his horse stays the trip well.

"I was drawn widest of all and when we left the stalls, there were four or five in a line for the first couple of furlongs and I didn't want to be five wide and pressuring to get in. You have to save ground at Ascot and I elected to come back and get across so I wasn't too deep off the rail.

"I found myself following Coronet, which I wasn't too concerned about early on. But when we went through Swinley Bottom and started to climb up towards the home turn, she started to lose ground on Crystal Ocean. She ended up dropping two, three, four lengths off him climbing up to the

bend, which was a concern. You're on the turn for quite a while at Ascot, so I was very conscious not to pull out too early and lose a lot of ground on the bend. I decided to bide my time a bit and believe in the horse that he could quicken up in the straight. I had to be patient, which was difficult because I wanted to pop out and get going."

The pace-setting Rostropovich and Salouen began to beat a retreat a fraction earlier than Buick might have anticipated and, as Crystal Ocean hit the sweet note of a thrumming vintage Bentley, he burst three lengths clear approaching the two-furlong marker.

The first thought from the stands was that Buick had outsmarted Doyle, his longtime friend and Godolphin ally, and it did not feel too different in the midst

▲ Word association: trainer Sir Michael Stoute, owner Saeed Suhail and jockey James Doyle with Poet's Word

▼ Doyle with the trophy

of the battle. "Coming out of the turn when I pulled out around Coronet and started to wind Poet's Word up, I could see Crystal Ocean had a bit of a break on me and I was a bit concerned," Doyle admits.

Poet's Word responded with purpose to Doyle's urgings but delicious uncertainty hung over the outcome for what seemed a lot longer than the 24.75 seconds the pair officially clocked for the final quarter-mile. Buick had the rail on Crystal Ocean with Doyle challenging wider out on the track.

Doyle recalls: "A furlong out I felt I was going to get there. Having ridden Poet's Word a few times I know he's a grinder who loves a battle and I thought that, once I could get within reach of Crystal Ocean, I would have every chance of running him down. But I was concerned until the furlong marker, definitely."

▸▸ *Continues page 108*

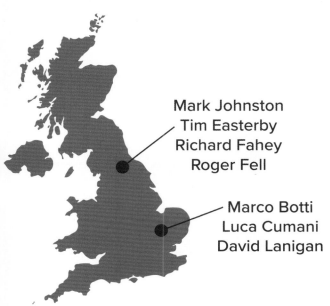

Poet's Word had pulled almost level with Crystal Ocean by that point but still Buick's mount would not yield and it was not until deep inside the final half-furlong that Doyle managed to edge in front and settle the issue.

****

UNMISTAKABLE joy was wreathed across Doyle's face as he allowed Poet's Word to unwind after the line, a single cry of joy from the saddle audible above the sea of noise as those present attempted to process what they had just witnessed – an instant classic. It didn't take long for the sense of occasion – banished from both jockeys' minds in the build-up – to come crashing in on Doyle.

"From the media myself and William were asked quite a bit about being the two Godolphin retained jockeys up against each other with the two fancied horses in the King George.

"I have to be honest, neither of us thought too much about it because we ride competitively against each other almost every day. We didn't see it as any different and we both had a job to do.

"But I watched the race back a few times in the car on the way home and I really appreciated being part of what was a great duel between two fantastic horses. I think everyone really enjoyed watching the race."

As for Stoute, he could bask in the satisfaction of a job well done with both horses and a sixth King George, extending his own record in the midsummer showpiece. "It's lovely to win a King George," he said. "It's a race we always love to come and compete in and win. It's a great mid-season race and we've been lucky enough to do very well in it.

"There was nothing between them really. I felt Poet's Word wouldn't get there until the last 100 yards or so. It's a pity there was a loser. They're two admirable horses, delightful to train."

Two horses who could have been kept apart to preserve their reputations, brought to perfect pitch by a master trainer and joined in enthralling battle for one of the showpiece prizes of the British racing summer.

Without doubt it was one of the races of the year.

SIX UP

James Doyle became the sixth different jockey to win the King George for Sir Michael Stoute (right), joining an illustrious list

Stoute's King George winners

1981 **Shergar**
Walter Swinburn

1993 **Opera House**
Michael Roberts

2002 **Golan**
Kieren Fallon

2009 **Conduit**
Ryan Moore

2010 **Harbinger**
Olivier Peslier

2018 **Poet's Word**
James Doyle

THE
BIGGER
PICTURE

The Amy Murphy-trained Mercian Prince has the leaders in his sights in the 2m4f handicap chase at Kempton on January 13 as he takes the fourth-last fence behind Breath Of Blighty (right) and Rothman before going on to score by three and a half lengths
EDWARD WHITAKER (RACINGPOST.COM/PHOTOS)

FALLING STAR

By Alan Sweetman

AFTER Saxon Warrior had extended his unbeaten juvenile record to three with a neck defeat of Roaring Lion in the 2017 Racing Post Trophy, Aidan O'Brien said: "He's a very special horse, we think."

O'Brien is essentially cautious and reserved by nature. At the same time, he is prone to invoke the odd superlative in moments of post-race euphoria, good copy for Coolmore's in-house marketing team. Unbeaten Classic prospect Saxon Warrior was a marketing dream in progress, the product of a mating between brilliant Japanese stallion Deep Impact and a Group 1-winning mare by Galileo, a blend of east and west

with the makings of a global superstar.

The attraction of the pedigree was obvious, although it was possible to question Saxon Warrior's stamina credentials with reference to his dam Maybe, out of the money behind stablemate Was in the 2012 Oaks on her only run beyond a mile. Maybe's background involves an amalgam of speed and stamina, her dam a five-furlong Listed winner closely related to Oaks winner Dancing Rain.

While such considerations may seem merely academic when reviewing the hard evidence of Saxon Warrior's flawed career, they belong as an intrinsic part of the story, informing the narrative that prefaced his reappearance in the Qipco 2,000 Guineas and assuming more lasting significance

in its aftermath, when the implication was that he could only get better.

Slightly muted expectations surrounded Saxon Warrior's Newmarket bid, reflected by his position as second favourite, half a point longer than the front-running Craven Stakes winner Masar. Oddly, he was only a point shorter than his stablemate Gustav Klimt. Admittedly, Gustav Klimt had the merit of a first run of the season under his belt, having won a four-runner trial in deep ground at Leopardstown, but if Saxon Warrior was still a "special horse" as billed the previous autumn, how come his status as the stable's first string was not more pronounced?

A possible answer emerged when the rug came off to reveal a colt carrying plenty of condition, a hint

that this was a starting point more than anything else, a stepping stone to the Derby and beyond.

Anyone prejudging the race in those terms would have had to be impressed by the way in which Saxon Warrior surged to the front under 19-year-old Donnacha O'Brien a furlong out, took command and then idled with the race firmly in the bag. Roger Teal's Tip Two Win, a dual winner in Qatar during the winter, was a 50-1 anomaly in second. Just behind him the key horses gave the form a solid framework – Masar, the well-fancied Tattersalls Stakes winner

▸▸ *Continues page 114*

▾ Classic first: Donnacha O'Brien and Saxon Warrior after the 2,000 Guineas

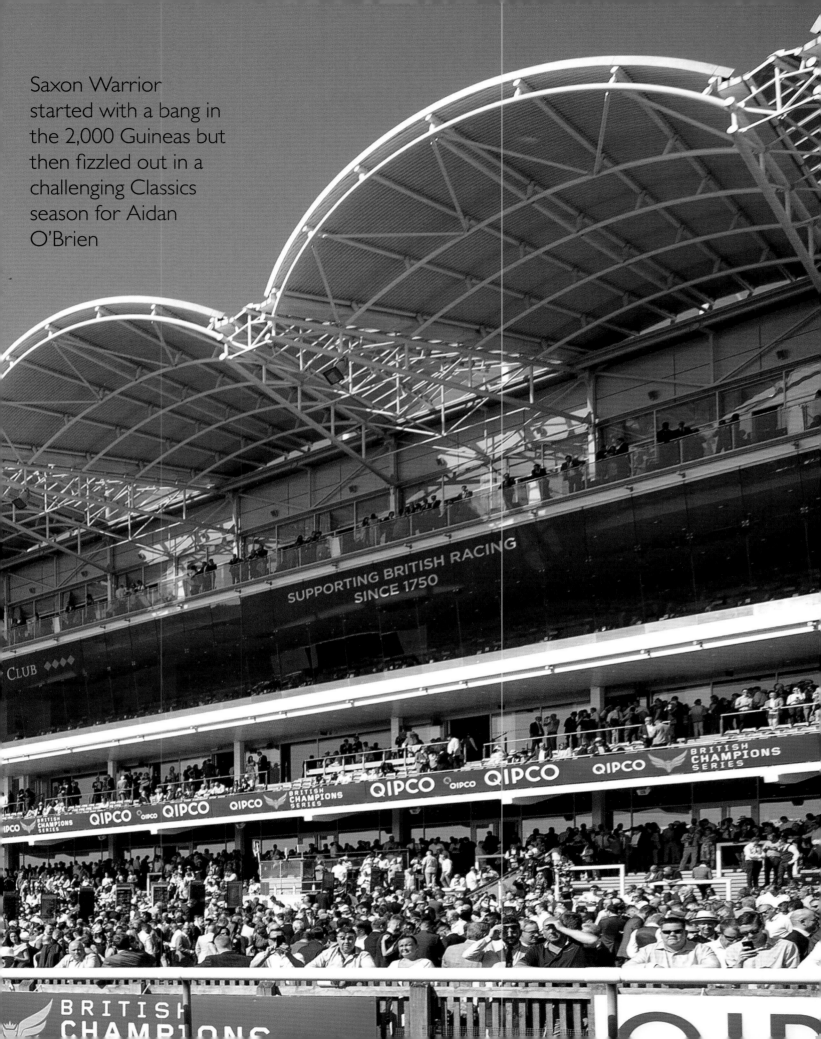

Saxon Warrior started with a bang in the 2,000 Guineas but then fizzled out in a challenging Classics season for Aidan O'Brien

Elarqam and Roaring Lion, with Gustav Klimt back in sixth.

Michael Tabor's perspective on the winner made sense at the time: "Obviously a mile is not his trip, but with the speed and class Saxon Warrior has we were always hopeful that the mile would be fine, which it proved to be . . . Aidan has said he will improve, although he still thought he could win or run a very big race. That's how he special he thinks he is."

That word again, "special". Now it seemed he might be, since the broad thrust of the analysis was that we would see a better horse up in trip with the benefit of the run. There was heady talk of a Triple Crown, a daring suggestion that the most problematic leg was out of the way.

****

SAXON WARRIOR was 4-5 favourite in the Derby, with his rivals again including Masar at 16-1 and Roaring Lion at 6-1. Ridden this time by Ryan Moore, he stumbled slightly coming out of the stalls, which had no discernible impact on his performance but serves as a metaphor for his career and for the nature of O'Brien's 2018 Classics campaign. There was to be only partial recovery for Saxon Warrior's reputation after his tame fourth behind Masar, and it took time to materialise.

Four weeks later Saxon Warrior was expected to redeem himself in the Irish Derby. Home advantage and the memory of his Newmarket triumph were enough to make him a strong favourite to reverse form with the Epsom second Dee Ex Bee.

However, the spark was not there and he was only third behind Latrobe, whose course-and-distance maiden win had been achieved in a weak race only three weeks previously, and Rostropovich, one of his stable's lesser lights, reappearing only eight days after finishing second in the King Edward VII Stakes at Royal Ascot.

It looked like an act of desperation when O'Brien sent Saxon Warrior on a quick retrieval mission in the Coral-Eclipse only a week after the Irish Derby, accompanied in a field of seven by two stablemates, the 2017 Derby runner-up Cliffs Of Moher and the dual 1,000 Guineas third Happily.

▸▸ *Continues page 116*

▾ Easy does it: Forever Together scores an emphatic win in the Oaks under Donnacha O'Brien

CLASSIC HEROINE

Forever Together was the shining light among Ballydoyle's three-year-old fillies

In 2017 a quartet of three-year-old fillies, comprising Hydrangea, Rhododendron, Roly Poly and Winter, were terrific contributors to Aidan O'Brien's record-breaking season.

In contrast, 2018 was a story of unfulfilled promise for several high-profile Ballydoyle fillies. Great things were expected of Cheveley Park winner Clemmie. There were Classic aspirations for Happily, who accounted for Group 2-winning stablemate Magical in the Moyglare Stud Stakes and beat the colts in the Prix Jean-Luc Lagardere. Moyglare third September, runner-up in the Fillies' Mile at Newmarket and a fine third in the Breeders' Cup Juvenile Fillies Turf, was high in the pecking order too.

Alas, Magical was the only one from that group to make a significant mark and that did not come until late in the campaign when she landed the Qipco British Champions Fillies and Mares Stakes at Ascot.

Three days after Happily finished third behind shock winner Billesdon Brook and Laurens in the 1,000 Guineas, her twice-raced maiden stablemates Magic Wand and Forever Together emerged as Investec Oaks candidates by taking the first two places in the Cheshire Oaks.

Both fillies duly went to Epsom, where O'Brien supplied five of the nine runners, and Ryan Moore's mount Magic Wand was the shortest-priced of them, 4-1 second favourite behind Godolphin's 1,000 Guineas fourth Wild Illusion.

Many potential contenders had fallen by the wayside. Forever Together, a late-May foal whose two juvenile outings were in October, took advantage, joining the select club of horses who have lost maiden status in a Classic by stretching away on the favoured stands' rail to an emphatic win from Wild Illusion. Bye Bye Baby, Magic Wand and Flattering took the next three places for O'Brien.

If this hinted at a wholesale revival for the squad, it was not maintained. Magic Wand played her part by trouncing Wild Illusion in the Ribblesdale Stakes and later finished a close runner-up in the Prix Vermeille. In between, she was well beaten in fifth when favourite for the Irish Oaks in which Sea Of Class outpointed Forever Together. It was a similar story in the Yorkshire Oaks.

The general tenor of the season was illustrated when Clemmie, Magical and dual 1,000 Guineas third Happily, who had not managed to impose her presence when going up in trip in the Prix de Diane and the Coral-Eclipse, were confirmed as bit-part players on the Group 1 fillies' scene in third, fourth and fifth respectively behind Laurens and Alpha Centauri in the Matron Stakes at Leopardstown on Irish Champion Stakes day.

ESTABLISHED LEADER IN THE DISTRIBUTION OF INTERNATIONAL HORSE RACING

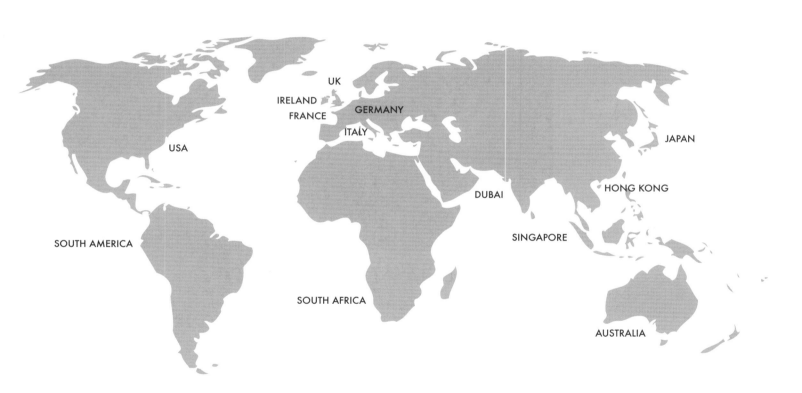

UK

IRELAND
FRANCE   GERMANY

ITALY

USA

JAPAN

HONG KONG

DUBAI

SINGAPORE

SOUTH AMERICA

SOUTH AFRICA

AUSTRALIA

 MELBOURNE CUP CARNIVAL 2018

To be fair to connections, the gamble very nearly paid off. Donnacha O'Brien, aboard for the first time since Newmarket, got first run before the Derby third Roaring Lion and Oisin Murphy wore him down inside the last 100 yards to score by a neck.

It was an honourable defeat, though it dampened any major optimism for a brilliant reinvention as a mile-and-a-quarter specialist. By the time of his next appearance, in the Juddmonte International, the stable had gone through a definite slump, acknowledged by the trainer as one of the most serious bouts of sickness in his two decades at Ballydoyle.

The team would not be long in getting back into top gear on the domestic circuit. However, with Roaring Lion now firmly in the ascendant and the King George winner Poet's Word also ranged against him, the Group 1 York test proved too demanding for Saxon Warrior. A further fall from grace was underlined by his fourth place, a length and a quarter behind the 109-rated five-year-old Thundering Blue.

****

NOW 2-3 down in his individual battle with Roaring Lion, Saxon Warrior was given the chance to level the score in the Irish Champion Stakes, scene of many great head-to-head battles in the past.

O'Brien's team did its best to exploit Murphy's relative unfamiliarity with the Leopardstown track, Wayne Lordan riding an intelligent race on outsider Deauville in an attempt to set up the race for Saxon Warrior. It very nearly worked. Saxon Warrior got to the front two furlongs out and stole an advantage, but Murphy held his nerve and Roaring Lion got up to win by a neck.

There was a sense of rehabilitation about Saxon Warrior's spirited performance, serving only to deepen the sadness provoked by the news of his retirement with a tendon injury.

O'Brien's summary of Saxon Warrior's career paid tribute to "a very talented horse, top class". Not the "special" one then, though there was perhaps a hint of what might have been when the trainer ruefully admitted, "it's possible a mile was his best trip".

DONNACHA IN DREAMLAND

Saxon Warrior's victory in the Qipco 2,000 Guineas was the 300th top-flight Flat triumph of Aidan O'Brien's illustrious career but greater significance for the trainer lay in the fact that it was the first Classic winner ridden by his 19-year-old son Donnacha. It was not going to be the last.

In emulating his elder brother Joseph, who steered Camelot in the same Derrick Smith silks to teenage Guineas glory six years earlier, the youngest man in the O'Brien family achieved a major personal milestone that was greeted with excitement by his father, who was in the States to saddle Mendelssohn in the Kentucky Derby.

O'Brien snr watched on a computer screen in a hotel room as Donnacha coolly guided Saxon Warrior to victory and later said: "We got an unbelievable kick from it. Donnacha had ridden Saxon Warrior in all his work and he was the first horse [daughter] Ana was preparing every day for a Classic with me. It was a massive thing for us."

That was a ninth 2,000 Guineas for the trainer and his seventh Oaks followed in June at Epsom, where Donnacha was again in the saddle as Forever Together scored by four and a half lengths. "It's absolutely incredible," the rider said. "Since I was a kid, this was what it was about – all I wanted."

The dream season continued later that month when Donnacha teamed up with elder brother Joseph – himself a ten-time Classic winner on his father's horses – to land the Irish Derby with Latrobe. Their father had the next four home but was delighted for his sons. "It's one of those special days," he said. "It's so tough and competitive and the two lads [Donnacha and Joseph] work so hard day in, day out. I was hoping all the way up the straight we wouldn't chin them."

The winners continued to flow for Donnacha, who turned 20 on July 22, and he reached a first century in Ireland in the last week of September as he powered towards the senior crown, having won the apprentice title in 2016. That was a milestone week too, as he notched a Group 1 double with two of his father's most promising juveniles by taking the Middle Park Stakes on Ten Sovereigns *(top left)* and the Cheveley Park Stakes with Fairyland *(top right)*.

All in all, the 2018 season was quite some ride for this talented young man.

By Alan Sweetman

AN important afterthought for a stable seldom short on stamina-endowed pedigrees. That seems a fair summary of Ballydoyle's perspective on the St Leger.

Since Coolmore Stud's main strategic concern lies in establishing reputations within the 1m-1m4f range, the St Leger has low priority on the annual wish-list for Aidan O'Brien and his team. In an ideal world, the significance of the Doncaster Classic for the County Tipperary operation would be limited to its status as the culmination of a Triple Crown, an elusive target since 1970.

Yet the Ballydoyle outfit headed to St Leger weekend in mid-September with more riding on the double-header at Doncaster and the Curragh than usual. In marked contrast to the stable's annus mirabilis of 2017, when a total of eight British and Irish Classic wins contributed to a record-breaking achievement in Group/Grade 1 races worldwide, O'Brien had won 'only' two Classics from the first four available in Britain and none at all in Ireland.

O'Brien's challenge for the 2018 St Leger began to take shape when Kew Gardens trounced his stablemates Southern France and Nelson in the Queen's Vase at Royal Ascot.

Chelsea Rose, the dam of Kew Gardens, achieved Group 1 honours over seven furlongs in the Moyglare Stud Stakes. She also won at Listed level over a mile and a half at three, and Kew Gardens demonstrated stamina at two, becoming O'Brien's first winner of the 1m2f Zetland Stakes at Newmarket with a clear-cut success over subsequent Derby runner-up Dee Ex Bee.

The furlong-shorter trip at the same venue looked inadequate when he finished third

WEEKEND WARRIORS

▲ On the run: Ryan Moore hotfoots it from his helicopter after travelling from Doncaster to Leopardstown following his St Leger win on Kew Gardens

in the bet365 Feilden Stakes on his seasonal debut. There followed a comprehensive defeat inflicted by Knight To Behold in the Betfred Derby Trial at Lingfield and a rapid capitulation in the final quarter-mile in the Derby.

His campaign was heading towards anonymity. Against this run of play he displayed a strong constitution and growing maturity by shaking off the effects of his Epsom run to triumph at Royal Ascot only 18 days later.

O'Brien had more immediate Group 1 plans ahead of a Doncaster bid, sending Kew Gardens for the Grand Prix de Paris at Longchamp in which the

opposition was headed by Dee Ex Bee on a recovery mission following a disappointing run in the Irish Derby. Showing an ability to accelerate that had previously been absent, he mastered Dee Ex Bee quite readily, pulling clear to beat local hope Neufbosc.

As so often, the Ebor meeting at York helped to clarify the St Leger picture. Burdened with a 5lb penalty for his Group 1 win in France, Kew Gardens came from off the pace to finish third in the Great Voltigeur Stakes behind Old Persian, who had beaten the O'Brien pair Rostropovich and Giuseppe Garibaldi in the King Edward VII Stakes at Royal Ascot.

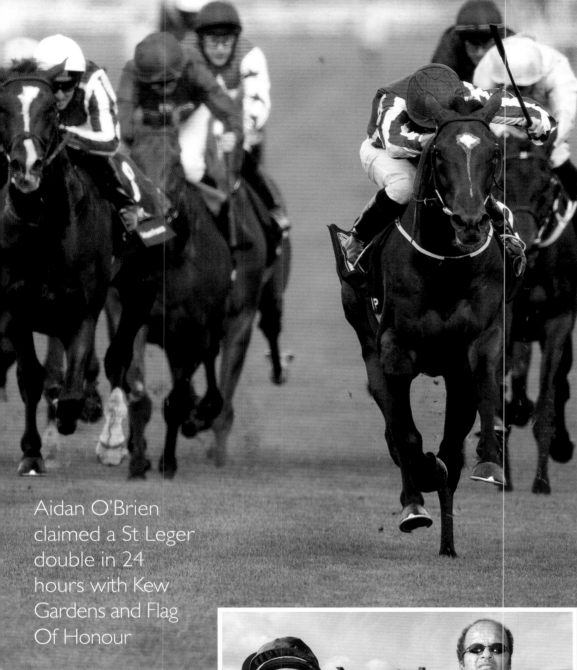

Aidan O'Brien claimed a St Leger double in 24 hours with Kew Gardens and Flag Of Honour

It was a satisfactory trial, though nothing like as visually striking as the victory of the John Gosden-trained filly Lah Ti Dar in the 1m4f Galtres Stakes the following day. The one-time Oaks favourite was back in business after an interrupted campaign.

As August drew to an end Old Persian's stablemate Loxley emerged as a strong candidate by winning the Group 2 Grand Prix de Deauville. With Dee Ex Bee also in the field, the 242nd St Leger had ample depth and the chance of an unbeaten winner in Lah Ti Dar, a warm 7-4 favourite to complete a quick double for her dam Dar Re Mi after her 2016 foal

▲ Double first: Kew Gardens (top right) scores at Doncaster; a day later Ryan Moore in the winner's enclosure at the Curragh with Flag Of Honour

Too Darn Hot had underlined long-range Classic prospects with victory in the Champagne Stakes 35 minutes earlier.

The pace was supplied by Nelson, one of three O'Brien-trained outsiders, and Kew Gardens got first run on Lah Ti Dar when taken into the lead by Ryan Moore two furlongs out. Frankie Dettori sent the filly in pursuit but she never looked like making up the deficit. She saw out the trip certainly and had plenty to spare over third-placed Southern France, with Dee Ex Bee one-paced in fourth and Old Persian performing like a non-stayer in fifth.

On the following day O'Brien's Flag Of Honour was sent off the 2-1 favourite in a field of six for the Irish St Leger. Here was another colt whose early-season form had given little or no sign of Group 1 potential. However, following nondescript performances in the Chester Vase and the Prix du Jockey Club, he proved a different proposition when stepped up to 1m6f, winning the Group 2 Curragh Cup and a Group 3 trial at the Curragh in late August.

Even so, his promotion to the stable's first-string came about only with the retirement, announced early in the week leading up to the event, of Order Of St George, who had won the race in 2015 and 2017, either side of a sensational defeat by Wicklow Brave in 2016.

Moore stuck with the forcing tactics employed for the two previous course-and-distance wins and the Galileo colt kept up the gallop to defeat Irish Derby winner Latrobe and the Gosden-trained Ebor runner-up Weekender.

O'Brien's 2018 three-year-old crop will not be remembered as one of his best. Yet the winning of three British Classics in a season amounts to a significant demonstration of strength by any standard, and there is further potential. Kew Gardens is sufficiently versatile to make his presence felt in major 1m4f races at four and Flag Of Honour looks a tailor-made replacement for Order Of St George in the Cup ranks, where Doncaster third Southern France could also flourish.

RISING SON

Joseph O'Brien thwarted his father to land a first Classic with Latrobe in the Irish Derby

By Alan Sweetman

THE Irish Derby may not be the race it once was, but the 2018 edition is likely to be remembered as a significant moment in the training career of Joseph O'Brien. Even if he is not the best, Latrobe could be the first of many Classic winners for the young man who is rapidly compiling an impressive roll of honour.

Eight months after capturing the Melbourne Cup with Rekindling, and in the year when he brought Edwulf back from a near-death experience to win the Irish Gold Cup over jumps, O'Brien reached another landmark with Latrobe's half-length Classic victory. In what is becoming a habit, O'Brien's success came at the chief expense of a challenger from his father Aidan's stable.

It is a pity for O'Brien, perhaps, that his breakthrough Classic should come amid the low-key atmosphere that has afflicted the Irish Derby during the redevelopment work at the Curragh. It will be a major challenge for the track and the Irish racing authorities to restore the popular appeal of the race when the new facilities are up and running in 2019.

As for prestige, the race has lost the appeal it had for much of a 21-year spell under Budweiser sponsorship between 1986 and 2007. A strong and dynamic French influence waned after the Prix du Jockey Club was reduced in distance in 2005, and the race was done no favours in the international context by a seven-year period of domination by Aidan O'Brien, culminating in a 1-5 victory for Camelot under Joseph O'Brien against only four opponents in 2012.

Two years later things reached an even lower ebb when the same trainer/rider combination prevailed at 1-8 with Australia, another Epsom winner in another five-runner field.

Following odds-on wins for Derby second Jack Hobbs in 2015 and for Epsom hero Harzand in 2016, Derby sixth Capri gave O'Brien snr a 12th win in the race in 2017 by turning the Epsom tables on Cracksman and Wings Of Eagles.

In 2018 the Ballydoyle trainer attempted another reversal of Derby form by giving 2,000 Guineas winner Saxon Warrior a second shot at a mile and a half in a rematch with the Mark Johnston-trained Dee Ex Bee, who had finished three lengths in front of him at Epsom. O'Brien snr ran three others, including Rostropovich, whom his son Donnacha had partnered into second behind Charlie Appleby's runner Old Persian in the King Edward VII Stakes at Royal Ascot.

The 19-year-old jockey, however, deserted Rostropovich to team up with Latrobe for brother Joseph.

▲ Family tree: Joseph O'Brien with parents Aidan and Annemarie after winning the Irish Derby
▸ Joseph and brother Donnacha in the winner's enclosure with Latrobe

A son of Camelot out of a six-furlong winner by Shamardal, Latrobe was a January 2015 foal. Even so, he was slow to mature, racing only once at the back-end of his juvenile season, when second to Ballydoyle-trained odds-on chance James Cook in a mile maiden at Leopardstown. On the strength of that he was made a warm favourite for his seasonal debut in a mile-and-a-quarter maiden at the Curragh. This time he finished second behind Ballydoyle's subsequent Hampton Court Stakes winner Hunting Horn.

Latrobe continued to enjoy a good home reputation through the spring. Despite his maiden status he again started favourite for the Group 3 Gallinule Stakes at the Curragh towards the end of May. In what looked a substandard affair he finished well for second behind Platinum Warrior, who had been fourth in the Derrinstown Stud Derby Trial.

At the beginning of June, O'Brien found one of the weakest maidens of the season at the Curragh for Latrobe. He duly made all to win unchallenged at 1-7 from nine-year-old handicap hurdler Tornado Watch. As a prep run for a Classic just three weeks away, it would hardly have registered on the radar but for the growing respect for his young trainer.

Some observers latched on to the potential significance of the trainer's brother being on Latrobe, who attracted good each-way support on the day and was sent off at 14-1, with Saxon Warrior the even-money favourite in a 12-strong field.

Rostropovich, the mount of 2017 Derby-winning jockey Padraig Beggy, was in front after about a furlong and maintained a fairly steady gallop, tracked by Latrobe, with Saxon Warrior third and Dee Ex Bee settled in fourth. As Beggy raised the tempo in the straight, O'Brien made his move on Latrobe over two furlongs out and got to the front. Rostropovich rallied along the far rail as Saxon Warrior failed to pick up significantly on the outside, but Latrobe pulled out enough to win by half a length and a neck.

Just as with Intricately, his first Group 1 winner in the 2016 Moyglare Stud Stakes, and with Rekindling at Flemington, the 25-year-old former champion jockey had won his first Classic as a trainer by thwarting his father, who this time supplied the next four home. O'Brien jnr's next Group 1 win would come in the same fashion too when Iridessa denied his father's Hermosa in the Fillies' Mile at Newmarket.

The boot was on the other foot, however, when Latrobe attempted another Classic victory in the Irish St Leger. This time it was the son who had to settle for second as Ballydoyle's Flag Of Honour scored by two and three-quarter lengths.

Before that Latrobe's limitations had been exposed in elite company when he was seventh of eight in the Juddmonte International at York, beaten more than ten lengths behind Roaring Lion.

Clearly he was not an Irish Derby winner who would set about restoring the race's wider standing in the European Group 1 calendar, but for O'Brien jnr he had played his part.

THE BIGGER PICTURE

Frankel, who has completed six breeding seasons at Banstead Manor Stud, with stallion man Rob Bowley in September. The sire's star performers in 2018 included Cracksman, sensational winner of the Champion Stakes for the second year in a row, and St James's Palace Stakes scorer Without Parole
EDWARD WHITAKER (RACINGPOST.COM/PHOTOS)

Four of the biggest Flat prizes had major upsets with winners ranging from 25-1 to 66-1. Here are their stories, starting with Billesdon Brook's record-priced victory in the 1,000 Guineas

SHOCKWAVES

BILLESDON BROOK 66-1
1,000 Guineas, Newmarket

Today's bloodstock industry is ruled by fashion but the late Bob McCreery was a breeder with the confidence to take an alternative approach and his methods, which have yielded consistent success down the years, hit the heights again in May with Billesdon

Brook's shock win in the Qipco 1,000 Guineas.

The Richard Hannon-trained filly and her talented half-sister Billesdon Bess in many ways typify McCreery's approach. Neither is by a fashionable stallion: Billesdon Brook is from the fifth crop of Champs Elysees, who had been relegated to the ranks of jumps sires by the time his 1,000

Guineas-winning daughter came to prominence, while Listed winner Billesdon Bess is the sole black-type winner by Dick Turpin.

All the more fitting is that Billesdon Brook is a granddaughter of Anna Oleanda, a mare by dual Classic winner Old Vic, himself the product of McCreery's great Camanae family that was also responsible for 1972 2,000

Guineas winner High Top. Old Vic and High Top were the pinnacle of the breeder's achievements during his lifetime – he died in December 2016, aged 86 – and Billesdon Brook has ensured his legacy lives on.

Millions and more are spent trying to breed the 'perfect' racehorse and nowhere measures the results better than the Classic

▾ Billesdon Brook (red cap) springs a huge surprise in the 1,000 Guineas

battlefield. Group 1s are one thing but victory in a Guineas, Oaks, Derby or St Leger has a special cachet.

Breeding superpowers like Darley and Coolmore are geared to producing those Classic winners, but once in a while the best bloodlines meet an unlikely match, proving anything is possible regardless of breeding and budget.

On 1,000 Guineas day, the giant killer was unheralded 66-1 shot Billesdon Brook. She was bred by McCreery at Stowell Hill Stud in Somerset and the breeder was also the mastermind behind owners Pall Mall Partners, a syndicate of "like-minded people" in the later throes of life, brought together to enjoy some of the horses bred at Stowell Hill on the racecourse.

Thanks to the Billesdon sisters among others, their journey has been spectacular and, best of all, it has not cost the 20-strong syndicate millions or even thousands to get all the way to the top.

McCreery's widow Jeanette, who still runs the stud as a business, recalled: "I think they all put about £500 in to race Piping Rock. They got a dividend when he was sold after winning the Horris Hill and have never had to put a penny in since. It's all Bob's work, though.

"We've been running for five years now and have had some marvellous fun. We lease 50 per cent to the partners and they pay half the training bills and keep half the prize-money, while we own the animals. They're all friends and it's been great."

Billesdon Brook showed she had the capacity for the unexpected when rescuing a seemingly hopeless cause to snatch a last-gasp win in a Glorious Goodwood nursery as a juvenile.

Yet what was to come at Newmarket was almost beyond comprehension.

Well held in Group 2 company at Doncaster on her eighth and final run at two, she had returned at three with a respectable fourth in her Group 3 trial at Newmarket. However, facing her conquerors from both Doncaster and Newmarket, along with the front rank from Ballydoyle and Godolphin, she was up against it in the Guineas and bookmakers made her the complete outsider of the field. It mattered not to her.

Anchored towards the rear early on under Sean Levey, seeking his own breakthrough at the highest level, Billesdon Brook steamed her way to the leaders passing the Bushes on the Rowley Mile. With battle about to commence, Levey did little more than loosen his grip on the reins and his partner unleashed a searing turn of foot that sent her bounding clear.

Subsequent French Oaks winner Laurens, dual Group 1-winning two-year-old and favourite Happily and Wild Illusion, a top-level winner at two and three, chased hard in the final furlong but Billesdon Brook had flown, eventually running out a comprehensive winner by a length and three-quarters.

At 66-1 she had become the biggest-priced winner in 1,000 Guineas history, trumping Ferry's success at 50-1 in 1918. Jacqueline Quest was also 66-1 when first past the post in 2010, but she was demoted to second.

Victory was greeted with elation in the winner's enclosure and, as the wealth of Coolmore and Godolphin was relegated to third and fourth spots, the Pall Mall pensioners and Jeanette McCreery celebrated their Classic fairytale.

"You can't get to the top of Formula 1 or football without
▶ Continues page 126

spending hundreds of millions, but in this sport it's possible," Hannon later reflected.

"I had so many people coming up to me to tell me how pleased they were. It got quite emotional in the winner's enclosure and results like that are good for racing."

Among the golden oldies in the winner's circle was the trainer's father Richard Hannon snr, not only celebrating Classic success for his son but also himself, as one of the Pall Mall Partners. "He's fluky like that," quipped his son.

While Billesdon Brook failed to frank the form at Royal Ascot and Glorious Goodwood, she was by far the best on the day that mattered most. A surprise result for sure but one that gives hope to all those racehorse owners with shallow pockets and big dreams.

ALPHA DELPHINI 40-1
Nunthorpe Stakes, York

"Today's the day. I need all of it. All your heart – everything." Those were the words of trainer Bryan Smart to Alpha Delphini as he tacked up the 40-1 chance before the Coolmore Nunthorpe Stakes at York's Ebor festival.

His gutsy seven-year-old duly obliged, fighting 14-1 shot Mabs Cross for every single yard on the Knavesmire straight as the surprise front pair exchanged the lead multiple times right up to the line and passed the post virtually as one.

Then there was an agonising five-minute wait before discovering Alpha Delphini had beaten his Michael Dods-trained rival by the narrowest of margins – a single pixel on a photo print.

Dods had won the Nunthorpe twice with Mecca's Angel and to many at first glance it looked as if Mabs Cross had given him a third victory in four years.

"I spoke to Michael briefly on the track," Smart said. "Mabs Cross had already beaten us at Newmarket and to the naked eye it looked like she'd got up and caught him. But the longer the wait for the photo went on, the more I thought we hadn't been beaten and it would go to a dead-heat.

"I'll always remember waiting

around with Graham [Lee] and walking around with the horse. I went through all the emotions in the world and as soon as they announced the result my daughter ran towards me – it was amazing to have her and my wife Vicky there. And I was so proud of my horse sticking his neck out to win."

Somebody had forgotten to read the script. The Group 1 sprint was supposed to be the race in which Battaash, the odds-on favourite with the golden shoes who was rated 19lb higher than Alpha Delphini, cemented his position as the world's fastest thoroughbred.

But the headline act failed to perform at York for the second year in a row, allowing Alpha Delphini to take centre stage. It was the third big upset in the Nunthorpe in the current decade, following Sole Power's 100-1 triumph in 2010 and Jwala's win at 40-1, like Alpha Delphini, in 2013.

It was a special moment for Smart, a proud Yorkshireman, as he

welcomed back his first British Group 1 winner. His two previous top-level victories came in France with Sil Sila in the 1996 Prix de Diane and with Alpha Delphini's half-brother Tangerine Trees in the 2011 Prix de l'Abbaye.

Smart returned to his native county in 2002 to train at the historic Hambleton House on the edge of the North York Moors, following a successful spell in Lambourn, and winning his first Group 1 on home soil meant everything.

"My mum was a factory worker and my dad was a miner. They used to go on club trips to the Ebor festival and dump me by the paddock, because all I wanted to see was the horses and jockeys," he recalled. "I'm a Yorkshire lad who moved down south for my career. I remember Julie Cecil telling me how pleased she would be to see Group winners back at Hambleton House again after I bought it. We've had top winners there, but to win a Group 1 at York with a horse we

bought in for 20,000gns was a fantastic feeling."

Alpha Delphini, whose syndicate owners are also from the surrounding area, has a bit of a back problem and is kept supple by regular massages and special exercises. Before the Nunthorpe, his trainer knew the hard work had paid off.

"I told Vicky over breakfast six weeks before that this horse would win the Nunthorpe," Smart said. "It was an eerie feeling on the day because I knew I'd never had the horse better. He was the first in the preliminary paddock because he walked so fast. He pricked his ears and had the look of eagles about him."

The trainer also valued the advice of winning jockey Graham Lee, who showed the unprecedented scope of his talents by following up his 2004 Grand National victory on Amberleigh House over the longest trip in British racing with a Group 1 win over the shortest.

"Graham suggested taking the cheekpieces off him, which really helped. My horse could see the other one coming, so he stuck his nose out and said 'you're not getting past me'."

Smart fondly remembers every detail from the day and will never forget going straight to Alpha Delphini when he got back from the track, letting him rest his head in his arms and sharing a few minutes with his new stable star. A 40-1 shot in the books but a true favourite at Hambleton House.

ACCIDENTAL AGENT 33-1
Queen Anne Stakes, Royal Ascot
"It's unbelievable, un-be-lieve-able." Eve Johnson Houghton emphasised every syllable as she made her first visit to the Royal Ascot winner's enclosure after Accidental Agent's 33-1 triumph in the Queen Anne Stakes.

"I haven't slept properly for two nights. I dreamed he would be third. Then I was watching it and I thought, no, he's going to be second, and then . . ."

And then . . . Accidental Agent, trained by Johnson Houghton at her family's famous Woodway stables in Oxfordshire and bred and owned by her mother Gaie, surged to the front

▶ Continues page 128

◀ Pride and joy: Alpha Delphini in the York winner's enclosure with Graham Lee after landing the Nunthorpe for a delighted Bryan Smart (bottom)

▼ Accidental Agent with trainer Eve Johnson Houghton

under Charlie Bishop to score by half a length from Lord Glitters, a 20-1 shot. Benbatl, Rhododendron and Recoletos, the first three in the betting, were all outside the top six, while Accidental Agent equalled the record for the longest-priced winner of the Queen Anne. Berrilldon was also 33-1 in 1912, when the race was known by its original name, the Trial Stakes.

"A Group 1 winner!" Johnson Houghton exclaimed. "I've never trained a Group 2 winner, let alone a Group 1 winner. I've never trained a Royal Ascot winner, let alone a Group 1 winner at Royal Ascot. It's great, unbelievable, ridiculous, something I just cannot believe has happened, and for it to have happened to my mother, who bred him, is wonderful. What a legend she is. I'm so proud of her."

This was a family triumph in so many ways. Johnson Houghton was assistant to her father, Fulke, before taking over the licence in 2007 and now the roles are reversed, while the Queen Anne winner is named after Eve's grandfather, John Goldsmith, a World War II special operations executive who wrote a book titled Accidental Agent about his escape from the Gestapo.

Ascot runs deep in the bloodline. Eve's grandmother Helen guided Nucleus to a pioneering Royal Ascot success in the 1955 King Edward VII Stakes but was denied her place in the record books by the Jockey Club's refusal to acknowledge

women trainers, instead crediting her assistant Charles Jerdein, while her father sent out ten winners at the royal meeting and in 1978 landed the King George VI and Queen Elizabeth Stakes with Ile De Bourbon.

Accidental Agent's success may have caused a disbelieving rustle of racecards in the crowd but it was not such a surprise to the trainer. He had won a Newmarket sales race as a juvenile – showing enough speed and promise to be entered for the 2017 Commonwealth Cup – and a valuable Ascot handicap (beating Lord Glitters) as a three-year-old.

Unfortunately he had a habit of banging and bruising himself, which hampered his progress, and in 2018 he started pulling off his shoes, which meant his preparation for his first run of the year was less than ideal and his third in that Ascot Listed race a shade underwhelming.

He pulled off another shoe and was back in his box for three days in the run-up to his second outing in the Group 1 Lockinge Stakes.

"It was a blow but at least it meant I was confident he was a lot better than his sixth place at Newbury," Johnson Houghton said. "We had a clear run with him from the Lockinge to Ascot and he was bucking and kicking round the box – our physio wouldn't go near him, he was so full of himself – so I was confident I'd got

'This day meant so much for me and for all the family. All my friends were there and I gave him a good shout home'

him ready to peak when he needed to."

On Queen Anne day, Johnson Houghton had to be helped to put her badges on, "because I was shaking so much". She explained that "it was more excitement than nerves, because I really believed we had a shot at it," and added: "This day meant so much for me and for all the family. All my friends were there and I gave him a good shout home. I'm very emotional, maybe too emotional, but I think a good shout helps them, or at least it helps me."

Victory was vindication of her belief in both the horse and her rising-star rider, as well as repayment of the faith shown by her 77-year-old mother, who had bought back Accidental Agent as a yearling for just 8,000gns and turned down tempting offers once he showed his ability on the racecourse.

"Mum was offered a lot of money for Accidental Agent to go to Hong Kong, and as she has the mare it means so much for him to win a Group 1, but she said 'if he's any good then you should have him'. When it got to stupid money, properly life-changing money, I told her she should take it, but she just said 'what am I going to do with it?' I told her I could easily spend it for her, but she stood firm, and thank God she did."

▸▸ *Continues page 130*

▸ Special Agent: Eve Johnson Houghton (left) with Accidental Agent and jockey Charlie Bishop

ROMANISED 25-1

Irish 2,000 Guineas, Curragh

When a Guineas hopeful beats only two home in a Listed race at Naas on his first start at three, it is almost inevitable that he will become blurry in the Classic picture.

Ken Condon, however, warned not to be too presumptuous about Romanised. "If he relaxes early on I think he'll run a big race at a big price. His Solario Stakes run last year was good and he met with some interference on his first start of the season at Naas. He came out of that race well," said the softly spoken Curragh-based trainer in the Racing Post on the day of the Tattersalls Irish 2,000 Guineas.

If you listened, you were soon loaded. The clues were there but you had to delve deep. There was the debut win at Navan when Declarationofpeace – later a Listed winner on the Breeders' Cup card at Del Mar – was only third. There was the Solario Stakes second to runaway Craven winner Masar. There wasn't much else to make most punters think he was overpriced at 25-1.

If Romanised rocked up to the Curragh on the last Saturday in May with plenty to prove, so too did his trainer. Condon had never trained a Group 1 winner before but, more worryingly, he had not sent out a winner all year. Those two facts were soon to become history.

There had been even fancier prices available about Romanised in the lead-up to the first Irish Classic of the season. Some snapped up 50-1 and 33-1 was freely available on the morning of the race and even in the betting ring beforehand.

Those big odds looked justified when Shane Foley sat last at halfway and began to push and shove long before most of the other ten riders. US Navy Flag was setting a ferocious pace out in front, however, and those who sat too close to him paid the price.

The highly regarded Elarqam, the 2-1 favourite who had finished fourth to Saxon Warrior in the 2,000 Guineas at Newmarket, seemed perfectly poised under Jim Crowley turning for home but his effort petered out tamely from the two-furlong pole, as did Gustav Klimt's.

Romanised was the one rolling from the rear. He had never tried a mile before but stamina questions were soon answered as he swept by US Navy Flag and stormed to a two-and-a-quarter-length success. He did not just win a Classic, he commanded a Classic. It was as emphatic as the winning margin suggests.

Cue an outpouring of emotion for one of the most popular trainers around. Condon is universally liked and handshakes ran into the hundreds, as did hugs. This was a victory for one of the good guys. There were no begrudgers.

"It's magic and I'm in a bit of shock

> 'To win a Classic is all I wanted to do when I entered racing. It's a very select club and to step into that club feels like you're walking through special doors'

but, to be perfectly honest, Romanised has always been a nice horse and we've kept faith with him. He was a big price but we always thought there was a big race in him," Condon said in the aftermath of the biggest win of his career. He did try to tell us in the Racing Post that morning, remember.

Condon added: "He did the nicest piece of work he had done all spring last Tuesday and we felt he was going to run a big race. He has only come to himself in the last few weeks. It's just amazing to win a Classic like this."

Amazing indeed. Aidan O'Brien was bidding for his 12th Irish 2,000 Guineas and the Classic club in Ireland is quite exclusive.

"It's all I wanted to do when I entered racing, to win a Classic," Condon said. "It's a very select club and to step into that club feels like you're walking through special doors to be considered one of those. I knew I was never going to be training a huge amount of winners, but we aimed to have a few nice horses through our hands."

Romanised is the nicest of the lot and, even if he went back to being an also-ran in later Group 1 races through the summer, he ensured Condon gained access to the Classic club. It is where he always wanted to be.

Reporting by Lewis Porteous, Jonathan Harding, Nick Pulford and David Jennings

▶ In command: an elated Shane Foley lets out a shout as Romanised crosses the line in the Irish 2,000 Guineas at the Curragh

THE
BIGGER
PICTURE

The snow starts to recede on the Curragh
training grounds as the gallops slowly become
usable in early March following a week of bad
weather in Ireland and Britain brought in by
the Beast from the East
PATRICK McCANN (RACINGPOST.COM/PHOTOS)

THRILLS &SPILLS

Battaash and Harry Angel produced two of the season's most explosive performances but bombed out on the biggest occasions

By Nick Pulford

TOP-LEVEL sprinting is a game of fine margins. With races lasting only 60 or 70 seconds, or even less, nearly everything has to go right if there is to be a successful outcome. When the stars align the results can be dazzling but even the brightest lights can be extinguished in a flash. Between these two extremes of light and shade hurtled Battaash and Harry Angel, who produced two of the standout performances of 2018 but also a series of spectacular failures in a sprint season that featured superlatives, shocks, new stars and old favourites.

The season started with apparent confirmation that Battaash and

Harry Angel – the joint world champion sprinters of 2017 having established themselves as the best at their respective distances of five and six furlongs – would be two of the year's biggest stars and that at least one of them might shoot even higher into the rarefied atmosphere of 130-plus ratings.

That was particularly the case with Harry Angel when he opened his campaign with an electrifying two-length victory over Brando in the Group 2 Duke of York Stakes, earning him a Racing Post Rating of 128 that matched his best of the previous year in the Haydock Sprint Cup.

If he could do that on his first start as a four-year-old – with trainer Clive Cox saying his colt was physically and mentally stronger – what might he achieve

once he stepped back into Group 1 company?

Battaash's return was less impressive – a head success over Washington DC in the Temple Stakes at Haydock, worth an RPR of 121 – but nonetheless a solid prep for his first big target, the Group 1 King's Stand Stakes at Royal Ascot, and with trainer Charlie Hills reporting the four-year-old was "a head and a half taller and about 30kg heavier".

The previous year Battaash was still working his way up the ladder in June, winning a Listed race at Sandown the week before Royal Ascot, and this would be a big test in the Queen's playground. He had boiled over before the Nunthorpe at York as a three-year-old and, even with another winter under his belt, many doubted whether he

would handle the Ascot atmosphere. Hills put plans in place to keep the lid on Battaash but admitted he wasn't sure they would work, saying: "You never know about him, he's like a coiled spring."

Lady Aurelia, the 2017 King's Stand winner, went off 2-1 favourite for a repeat success, with Battaash next in the market at 9-4, but the race didn't go as expected. The American filly was unable to dominate as usual from the front and instead it was Battaash, breaking faster than expected, who set the fractions. Unfortunately they didn't quite add up and the Charlie Appleby-trained Blue Point, the 6-1 third favourite, picked him off inside the final furlong to score by a length and three-quarters. The Michael

Dods-trained filly Mabs Cross, having her first start in a Group 1, was quick to show she belonged by finishing third, while Lady Aurelia trailed home a disappointing seventh.

Battaash had run his race, having come through the preliminaries well, but there was still a hint of over-keenness. "I didn't expect him to jump so fast," said jockey Jim Crowley. "I got two lengths from the stalls and you can't mess around with him, so I sat against him from there and he just got tired in the last 50 yards. It's a hard track to make the running and you're always there to be shot at. He's still a very good horse, it just didn't go his way."

Harry Angel took his turn in the spotlight on the final day of Royal Ascot in the Diamond Jubilee

Stakes and, as with Battaash, questions swirled around him. This time the focus was on his record at the track, as he arrived at Ascot without a win from four previous visits while he was a perfect five out of five elsewhere. Cox said the figures were "purely coincidence" and punters made Harry Angel the 5-2 favourite ahead of Australian Group 1 winners Merchant Navy and Redkirk Warrior at 4-1.

If there is an Ascot hoodoo around Harry Angel, it struck early this time. Just before the stalls opened, his hind leg got stuck on the gate and, with no time to recover, he set off lengths adrift with his chance already gone.

Merchant Navy, trained by Aidan O'Brien for this one start in Europe before going to stud, took the prize by a short head from

French raider City Light, with Harry Angel trailing home 11th of the 12 runners under Adam Kirby. He was found to have cuts on his near-hind fetlock and on a joint, and he would not appear again until the autumn.

Cox was more concerned with his star's wellbeing than dwelling on the misfortune at the start, saying: "It was nobody's fault – just one of those things. When the stalls opened he was on three legs like a dog with his leg up. We have a wonderful stalls team, and I would say the starter was unaware his leg was up. Adam couldn't see it either."

****

HARRY ANGEL'S summer absence left the door open for others and the one to burst

▲ Blue flash: Battaash produces the sprint performance of the year as he rockets clear in the King George Stakes at Goodwood

through in the July Cup was the three-year-old US Navy Flag, a second top-level sprint winner of the year for O'Brien. The race brought together Diamond Jubilee winner Blue Point and the Commonwealth Cup one-two Eqtidaar and Sands Of Mali but it was the 2017 Middle Park and Dewhurst winner who prevailed, having dropped back from a fruitless spring campaign at a mile.

US Navy Flag now departed the scene too, earmarked for a crack at The Everest – the world's richest turf race – in Sydney in October. When he turned up there, the

▶▶ *Continues page 136*

ground was heavy – in contrast to good to firm at Newmarket – and he was soundly beaten in ninth behind Redzel.

On the European scene, nothing was getting near the same level as Battaash and Harry Angel at their best. Something special was needed to light up the sprint season, and at Goodwood we got the most glorious demonstration of pure speed.

That it came from Battaash was not surprising, given that he was the fastest horse in training at his peak, but he went to new heights in the Group 2 King George Stakes. This time Crowley got a lead from Take Cover and Kachy, two of the fastest starters around, and he was able to settle Battaash just behind the pace before taking over in front around halfway.

From there it was a one-horse race. Battaash, carrying a 3lb penalty as a Group 1 winner, went smoothly through the gears and seemed to have at least a couple more than his opponents as he poured on the power across the slick ground of a baking-hot summer. He stopped the clock at a blistering 56.50sec, finishing four lengths clear of Take Cover.

Battaash's performance took his Racing Post Rating to a new high of 129, making him one of the joint-top European-trained sprinters since 2000 alongside Mozart (2001) and Oasis Dream (2003). Only Cracksman recorded a higher RPR in the European Flat season across all distances.

"Nothing was fast enough to give him a lead and I think today he was back to his best," Hills said. "I always thought the faster the ground the better he would be – he's got the most amazing action and is so light on his feet."

Clearly Battaash was going to waltz away with the champion sprinter title on that performance but still he had not won a Group 1 in 2018. His next chance to put that right came in the Nunthorpe in August but again he slipped up on the York stage, repeating his 2017 showing by finishing fourth. Ahead of him there was a thrilling battle as 40-1 shot Alpha Delphini denied Mabs Cross, taking another step up in Group 1

company. "She'll be a proper Group 1 horse next year," trainer Michael Dods had said after Mabs Cross finished third at Royal Ascot, but now he knew she already was. The ultimate confirmation lay ahead.

Just three weeks after his Goodwood demolition, Battaash had slumped to an RPR of 108 and Crowley was mystified. "I don't know what to make of it," he said. "I was upsides the winner and he just had no kick, I don't know why. I'm gutted. He obviously doesn't like it up here."

****

THE five British Group 1 sprints for three-year-olds or older run to that point had brought five different winners and there was a sixth when the caravan moved to Haydock for the Sprint Cup in September. This marked the return to action of Harry Angel, a stunning four-length winner the previous year, but he disappointed again in sixth place.

Victory went to a familiar name as

▲ Trouble with Harry: Having started the season with a bang, Harry Angel did not manage to win again after his stalls mishap at Royal Ascot

BEST SPRINT RPRS IN EUROPE IN 2018

Battaash	129
Harry Angel	128
Blue Point	123
Merchant Navy	122
US Navy Flag	122
City Light	121
Sands Of Mali	121
The Tin Man	121
Gifted Master	120
Bound For Nowhere	119
Brando	119
James Garfield	119
Polydream	119

The Tin Man – twice a Group 1 winner at Ascot – scored at the top level for the third year in a row. July Cup runner-up Brando was second again, giving the form a solid if rather unspectacular feel in comparison to the fireworks Harry Angel at his best might have produced.

A real damp squib followed at the Curragh the next weekend when the Flying Five, promoted to Group 1, did not seem worthy of its new status. The Karl Burke-trained Havana Grey grabbed the opportunity ahead of Ayr Gold Cup dead-heater Son Of Rest, but it was a mark of the lower quality that the winner had finished sixth behind Battaash at Goodwood and fifth in the Nunthorpe.

A more worthy Group 1 winner was Mabs Cross, who completed her progress from third to second to first in top-level sprints with victory in the Prix de l'Abbaye at Longchamp, where Battaash fell below his own high standard once again. He was in

▸ *Continues page 138*

contention most of the way but did not have his Goodwood zip, nor the same power he had shown in winning the previous year's race at Chantilly by four lengths.

Instead the honours went to Mabs Cross, who went from excruciating defeat at York to exhilarating victory at Longchamp with a late surge that got her home by a head from Gold Vibe. A short head further back was Soldier's Call, Archie Watson's Royal Ascot-winning two-year-old. Havana Grey, incidentally, was eighth.

Dods, who has been quick to turn up another top sprint filly soon after the retirement of dual Nunthorpe winner Mecca's Angel, was delighted with Mabs Cross at Longchamp. "Every time she has run she has improved. In the middle of the season we thought she might want stepping up to six but, as you've just seen, she's an out-and-out five-furlong horse. She's very talented and we'll be aiming her at all the top sprints next year."

The final act in the Group 1 speed season was the British Champions Sprint at Ascot in October and again it produced a different name in the number-one spot – and another major turn-up as Sands Of Mali scored at 28-1. Harry Angel, back at Ascot for the first time since his stalls mishap, was beaten a length in second – his sixth defeat at the course, and the fourth time he had been runner-up.

Sands Of Mali, the Gimcrack winner as a juvenile, had started the season looking as if he would make the top grade as a three-year-old, winning a Group 3 in France and a Group 2 at Haydock before going down by half a length to Eqtidaar in the Commonwealth Cup, but a slump in form in high summer left trainer Richard Fahey stumped.

"We just got nailed in the Commonwealth and then it all went pear-shaped," he said at Ascot. "As a trainer, when you believe in a horse and it doesn't happen it's frustrating. We were scratching our heads – we did scopes and checked his heart and couldn't find anything – but luckily it all went to plan today."

Fahey's mixed emotions of frustration and elation would have been familiar to many in a topsy-turvy sprint campaign.

▲ Leading players (clockwise from top): The Tin Man, Havana Grey, Mabs Cross and US Navy Flag

Merchant Navy arrived from Australia with the single aim of winning the Diamond Jubilee Stakes and he did it, under the handling of Aidan O'Brien

ONE-HIT WONDER

By Julian Muscat

THE 2018 renewal of the Diamond Jubilee Stakes at Royal Ascot wasn't short of incident. It was the race in which Harry Angel got a hind leg trapped on the side of his stall, causing the 5-2 favourite to miss the break before trailing throughout. Up ahead of him, a barnstorming finish unfolded in which City Light conjured dramatic acceleration to hit the line in one blurred image with Merchant Navy. The pair were inseparable to the naked eye, but it was Merchant Navy who had prevailed by the scantest of short heads.

While sympathy extended to the runner-up, who had ventured from France, Merchant Navy had journeyed from another continent and his story was quite remarkable, one that illustrated the intertwining of internationalism and commercialism in the modern racing world.

A Group 1 winner over six furlongs in his native Australia, Merchant Navy had joined Aidan O'Brien's string on March 30 after a two-day journey from his homeland. From that day the

Ballydoyle brains trust pondered how to get the best from a horse who would be there only until Royal Ascot. They had 12 short weeks in which to produce him at his best for the most important race of his life, which would take place 10,500 miles from home.

There were pros and cons with this audacious attempt to make Merchant Navy a more attractive stallion prospect. Plans to stand him at Coolmore's southern-hemisphere home, in Sydney's Hunter Valley, had already been announced before Merchant Navy boarded the plane that would take him to Ireland.

Victory at Royal Ascot would undoubtedly enhance his appeal to northern-hemisphere breeders. For it to be gained, however, the son of Fastnet Rock would have to override a biological clock that was telling him he was just about to enter the winter recess after a season of racing. And of course, there was that arduous journey to contend with. Any minor mishap had the potential to scupper the venture.

In one respect, it helped that Merchant Navy was race-fit when he reached Ireland. On March 10 he had run an excellent race in the Group 1 Newmarket Handicap at Flemington, an all-aged six-furlong sprint. Carrying 5lb more than the other two sophomores in the 15-runner field, he had closed late and hard from an unfavourable draw to get within a short head and a neck of Redkirk Warrior.

Against that fitness edge, however, the Newmarket came towards the end of the regular season in Australia. Merchant Navy had been on the go for six months, during which he contested a series of top-class sprints. His breeding rights had been purchased by Coolmore after he had won the Group 1 Coolmore Stud Stakes, a six-furlong sprint for three-year-olds at Flemington on November 4.

"He'd had a whole season in Australia before he arrived here," O'Brien recalled. "By the time he came to us, his coat was turning. He was changing inside with the seasons; he was preparing for winter when it was springtime here. We took it as a sign that we had to be careful with him. Right the way through we treated him as if he was a baby three-year-old."

But that wasn't all. "He looked tired," O'Brien continued. "He looked a bit like he was trained out, as though he was ready for a break. He looked like he needed time to be built up again, but we didn't have time. We knew we only had him until Royal Ascot."

****

THERE were other logistical challenges facing O'Brien. When Merchant Navy arrived at Ballydoyle the trainer was reluctant to amalgamate him with the rest of the string.

"We put him in a yard away from the other horses," he said. "We didn't ask him to deal with too much at once. He was coming into a different environment as it was, and I think being on his own allowed him to rest rather than become interested in a lot of new things going on around him."

O'Brien couldn't help but notice how much time Merchant Navy spent lying down asleep in his box. It was an encouraging sign: it showed that the horse was relaxed. "He was recharging, if you like," the trainer said. "It was also a big plus that he was very straightforward; a good-natured horse to deal with. He never got fresh, so he helped us a lot in that way. He helped himself too."

For the first five weeks O'Brien gave Merchant Navy as easy a time as he dared. He spoke at length to the horse's former trainer, Ciaron Maher, cross-checking Maher's way of training the horse with the early impressions Merchant Navy had made on him.

When horses move from one trainer to another, their behavioural traits can change for no tangible reason. So it was with Merchant Navy. O'Brien noted that the horse had raced in blinkers and a tongue-tie at home. Maher explained that Merchant Navy was a lazy galloper, yet O'Brien's brief experience was that his new charge was a willing work horse.

"What Ciaron told me was fair enough," O'Brien said, "but in the short time the horse was here we never understood why he needed either, to be honest. He was a super-clean horse in his wind, he

▸ Continues page 142

behaved more like a gelding than a colt, and he put his head down in his races. But when it came to racing him, we were afraid to try anything different because we had so little time. We had to take everything we heard about the horse on trust."

When it came to daily exercise, O'Brien entrusted the Aussie import to his son, Donnacha. Merchant Navy had settled well into his new surroundings but the clock was ticking: O'Brien wanted to run him in the Group 2 Weatherbys Ireland Greenlands Stakes at the Curragh on May 26. That race was just three weeks away when the trainer eased Merchant Navy back into his faster paces.

"After a break, we like to have our horses in full work for a minimum of six to eight weeks before they run," O'Brien said. "This horse had only had five strong canters before he went to the Curragh, so we were concerned."

The schedule was far from ideal, and the horse would carry a 3lb penalty for his Group 1 triumph in Australia. But O'Brien wanted jockey Ryan Moore to get a critical first feel of the horse at racing pace. He was also anxious to discover for himself where Merchant Navy stood in terms of his Royal Ascot preparation.

"Honestly, we'd have been pleased if he'd finished fourth or fifth at the Curragh," O'Brien said. "Everyone here was prepared for him to get beaten but hopefully improve between then and Royal Ascot. That's how we saw it anyway."

As it turned out, Merchant Navy's competitive instincts kicked in at the sight of the starting stalls. He was unsurprisingly a shade sluggish early on. As the race unfolded, however, he got stronger and stronger under Moore, who drove him past stablemate Spirit Of Valor to prevail, going away, by one length.

"We were surprised and delighted," O'Brien said, "especially because Spirit Of Valor is plenty fast enough himself."

The race answered several key questions about Merchant Navy. He was plainly on track for Ascot, despite his minimal workload, so O'Brien resolved to keep it simple.

"We went very gently with him all

the way to Ascot," the trainer said. "We'd seen positive signs but all the while we had it in the back of our minds that he'd been a busy horse. We integrated him into the rest of the string soon after he ran at the Curragh and kept things as natural as possible.

"We never worked him with any of our sprinters," O'Brien continued. "He paired up with one of our modest mile-and-a-half horses because we didn't want him going too fast or overtaxing himself.

"Just before Ascot his coat started changing back [to a summer coat], which pleased us. It told us he was acclimatising internally, so we knew his body had reacted to being here. It gave us confidence going into Ascot – and he was very good there, wasn't he? He travelled stronger in the Diamond Jubilee than at the Curragh."

****

IT was a case of mission accomplished, even though Merchant Navy competed on unfavourable weight-for-age terms. Foaled in Australia on November 14, 2014, the colt was only three years and seven months old when he won at Ascot, yet he raced at level weights against horses who had passed their actual fourth birthdays.

That was down to the different

▲ Delivering the goods: Merchant Navy (Ryan Moore, purple cap) beats City Light (Christophe Soumillon, left) in a tight finish to the Diamond Jubilee Stakes

'official' birthdays for thoroughbreds in the northern and southern hemispheres. All horses in Europe become one year older on January 1; in Australia it is August 1. Yet this couldn't stop Merchant Navy from making the most attractive statement about himself on British racing's biggest stage.

He is a son of one of Australia's most potent stallions in Fastnet Rock. Ironically, Fastnet Rock suffered from acute travel sickness when he was dispatched from Australia to contest the Royal Ascot sprints in 2005. He could not run, but he has gone on to become champion sire in Australia twice.

Fastnet Rock also made an impact during his stallion stints at Coolmore's Irish division. His best progeny in Europe have included Group 1 winners Fascinating Rock, Intricately, Rivet and Zhukova in addition to the O'Brien-trained Diamondsandrubies, Qualify and now Merchant Navy.

The Coolmore clan will be hoping Merchant Navy conforms to an old adage: like father, like son. Certainly O'Brien would like to have seen more of him.

"The decision to stand him at stud had already been taken before he came to us," he said. "We felt there was a lot more he could have shown us. It was tough for him but he impressed us with his attitude, his mind, his movement, his open stride. Everything was in the right place."

Including, as it turned out, his 12-week stay at Ballydoyle.

'We integrated him into the rest of the string soon after he ran at the Curragh and kept things as natural as possible'

RoR
Retraining of Racehorses

Racing to a new career at ror.org.uk

RoR Source a Horse
Retraining of Racehorses

sourceahorse.ror.org.uk

A new website for selling or loaning a horse directly out of a trainer's yard and for all former racehorses.

Owner/Trainer Helpline

A dedicated helpline to assist in the placement of horses coming out of training.

Rehoming Direct

RoR has compiled a checklist to safeguard your horse's future when moved directly into the sport horse market.

Retrainers

RoR has a list of retrainers recommended by trainers who can start the retraining process and assess each horse.

Visit
ror.org.uk
for rehoming options and advice

Equine Charities

Retrain former racehorses for a donation, as well as care for vulnerable horses with the help of RoR funding.

RoR is British horseracing's official charity for the welfare of horses retired from racing.

T: 01488 648998

By Peter Scargill

FAMOUSLY his horses are always trying and in August more than three decades of toil had taken Mark Johnston to the brink of standing alone as the most prolific winning trainer of all time in Britain. So it was not for lack of effort that, after drawing level with Richard Hannon snr and with the racing public and national media watching every move, the finishing post in this longest of races remained stubbornly out of reach for a further five days.

Fittingly the barrier-breaking moment came in Yorkshire – the Scot's adopted home – when Poet's Society fended off 19 rivals under Frankie Dettori in the Clipper Logistics Handicap at the York Ebor festival. It was winner number 4,194 for Johnston. The record had finally tumbled.

Pride mingled with relief as the trainer stood alongside Poet's Society, in many ways the archetypal Johnston horse. This was the hardy four-year-old's 26th run, and sixth victory, of a campaign that started on the all-weather at Southwell in January and he made all the running, holding on gamely by a neck.

"It's a relief to get it out of the way and on to the next one. I've been wishing we could switch it all off and pretend it never happened," Johnston said. "It's great it has happened with a horse like this and it hadn't even occurred to me he was carrying my own colours. If we could have written the result we would have had Joe Fanning on the horse, and of course it would have been great if it had been one of our regular jockeys, but I did say before the race that at least if it was Frankie no-one would forget it."

Dettori said: "When Mark got the saddle I asked him if he had broken the record yet. 'No,' he said, 'I'm waiting on you!' It's great, as he has shown amazing consistency over so many years. I've been riding for him since the early days. I'm delighted as perhaps I might now be on a picture in the Johnstons' downstairs loo forever."

The York victory was a major

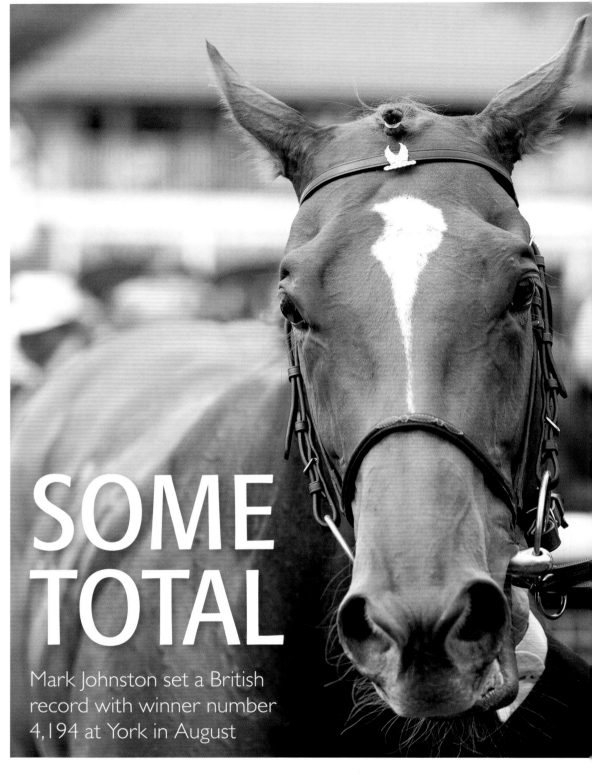

SOME TOTAL

Mark Johnston set a British record with winner number 4,194 at York in August

milestone on a road that started in 1987 with what Johnston called "three and a half paying horses" at a Lincolnshire yard whose gallops were part of an RAF practice range. Along the way Johnston has trained horses with the class of Attraction and Shamardal and the popularity of Double Trigger, as well as hundreds and even thousands more whose names will

not be remembered but in their own small way contributed to a remarkable total.

Instrumental to Johnston's success was his move to Middleham in 1988. He has built up Kingsley House Stables into one of the elite training establishments in Britain, handling approximately 250 horses and more than 1,200 runners annually.

Furthermore, he has been a central figure in the North Yorkshire town's revival as a major training centre. When Mister Baileys gave Johnston a first Classic success in the 1994 2,000 Guineas, he was also the first Classic winner trained in Middleham since 1945 Derby victor Dante.

Johnston's best Classic performer was Attraction, the filly with the

▼ Mark of success: Mark Johnston at York with Poet's Society, his 4,194th winner

to Saeed Bin Suroor and became a dual French Classic victor in 2005.

His best-known horse remains Double Trigger, who scored a record seven victories in Cup races at Ascot, Goodwood and Doncaster, winning all three in 1995. He is the only horse to win the Goodwood Cup three times. Johnston also won back-to-back Gold Cups at Ascot with Royal Rebel in 2001 and 2002.

Yet Johnston has not achieved what he has by himself. Standing alongside him has been his wife Deirdre, his childhood sweetheart and an accomplished rider and assistant to the trainer. She handled Attraction at home for much of her career and supported her husband with a teaching job in the early days to help pay the bills. They have been joined in recent years by eldest son Charlie, who plays an increasingly prominent role in the operation.

Johnston has inspired great loyalty from many others, with jockeys Kevin Darley and Joe Fanning working in tandem with him for years and Jock Bennett always there as a steadfast right-hand man.

Unlike jumps legend Martin Pipe, a previous holder of the record as winningmost trainer in Britain and an inspiration to Johnston in his approach to racing, the proud Scot seems likely never to be champion trainer, a title decided on prize-money won in a calendar year. If winners determined where the accolade went, Johnston would have collected no fewer than 11 titles.

Reflecting on his record mark, Johnston, who turned 59 in October, said: "People keep saying, what does it mean? I don't think anyone has tried to belittle it, but sometimes I think, how important is it? At the same time I do have to pinch myself and ask how I could get to 4,194 from where we started. It's unimaginable.

"The ambition to train top-class Flat horses was there from the outset and it's the same now. One of the things about me is that I'm always looking at new ideas and always looking to change things."

And always trying.

wonky forelegs who won the 1,000 Guineas and Irish 1,000 Guineas in 2004 and three more Group 1s. In that vintage 2004 campaign he also had Europe's champion two-year-old, Shamardal, nominated by Johnston as "the best I've trained". Having capped an unbeaten season with Johnston by winning the Group 1 Dewhurst Stakes, Shamardal was transferred

TOP FIVE TRAINERS IN BRITAIN

Wins	Trainer	First-last win	Flat	Jumps
4,194	Mark Johnston	1987-	4,189	5
4,193	Richard Hannon snr	1970-2013	4,145	48
4,183	Martin Pipe	1975-2006	253	3,930
3,853	Sir Michael Stoute	1972-	3,841	12
3,377	Sir Henry Cecil	1969-2013	3,377	0

Figures up to and including Mark Johnston's record winner on August 23, 2018

IN THE PICTURE

Remarkable Ralph still going strong – and still going racing

THERE has been talk of adding a veterans' chase to the Cheltenham Festival. It seems unlikely to happen, but in its absence a veteran of extreme proportions graced the meeting in 2018. At 109 years old Ralph Hoare became almost certainly the oldest racegoer ever to attend the festival and perhaps the oldest person ever to go racing.

It was a visit he had been looking forward to for some time, as he explained before the meeting when visited by the Racing Post at the Gloucester house he has called home since 1956.

"I think I saw all of Arkle's Gold Cups and I went two or three times after that," said Ralph *(pictured with his daughter Kate Hughes)*. "I suppose the first time I went racing was around the time World War II started. I've enjoyed the sport since I was about 30. I was always interested in who would win the Guineas and Derby."

Ralph liked a bet then and has continued to do so, placing regular ten-pence wagers, particularly on horses trained by John Gosden. He has a good memory for form – and much more besides.

"I remember the day the First World War was declared," he said. "I was a six-year-old in Devonport at the time. I was in a room with my grandfather and four aunts. Someone walked in and said war had been declared. Someone else said it would be over in a few weeks. Of course, it wasn't.

"There was another day I recall when I was in exactly the same room. My grandparents and aunts always had a glass of ale for supper. Auntie Bessie used to take a jug to the local pub and get it filled. She came back from one of those trips crying her eyes out. I asked her what was the matter? 'Terrible news,' she said. 'Kitchener has drowned. Worse than that, I've dropped the jug and we haven't got any ale for supper.' I've told that story more than once."

When you get to Ralph's age – he turned 110 in July – you have likely done everything more than once. He has been a special guest at the Cheltenham Festival, where on Gold Cup day, flat cap on his head and a rug across his knees, he made a very welcome return. He also gave us all some advice for living a long – extraordinarily long in Ralph's case – and happy life.

"I would always say to people that they should look forward to the future," he said. "Don't look backwards. You're bound to remember a lot of bad things and you'll end up wishing you could have done things differently."

Wise words from a wise old racing fan.

Picture: EDWARD WHITAKER (RACINGPOST.COM/PHOTOS)

By Tony O'Hehir

FLYING FINISH

NINA CARBERRY and Katie Walsh, sisters-in-law, both from famous racing families, spurred each other on and shared many notable moments over the years as the outstanding female riders in jump racing. At the 2018 Punchestown festival they stood in the spotlight for one last time before heading off into retirement.

Their departures, which came within 24 hours of each other on the last two days of the festival, had not been widely heralded, nor were they co-ordinated, and the scenes that followed their final rides showed the regard in which these two fine jockeys – amateurs in name but professionals by nature – were held.

Walsh, 33, was first to go and she did it in style – and in tears – after getting up on Antey to beat Barry Geraghty on Shrewd Operator by a nose in a two-mile novice hurdle. The strength and determination she showed to beat one of the top professionals was emblematic of a 17-year career that saw her succeed on the biggest stages in jump racing.

"I wanted to go out on a winner and I said to myself that I'd retire whenever I rode my next winner," she said. "I wanted to go out on my own terms and everyone is here, my husband Ross [O'Sullivan] and my family. I couldn't have picked a better place."

Only a month earlier Walsh had won the Champion Bumper at the Cheltenham Festival on Relegate, her third success at the meeting following a double in 2010 on Poker De Sivola in the National Hunt Chase and Thousand Stars in the County Hurdle. Victory in the 2015 Irish Grand National on Thunder And Roses was her career highlight, having gone close in the Grand National at Aintree three years earlier when third on Seabass, trained by her father Ted.

The following day Carberry, also 33, announced her retirement immediately after winning a cross-country chase on Josies Orders for Enda Bolger and JP McManus, the duo who provided her with many notable successes during her career.

Carberry was cheered into the winner's enclosure, where among those waiting to greet her were husband Ted Walsh jnr – Katie's brother – and their year-old daughter Rosie, her brother Paul and mother Pamela.

"It's sweet to finish off on a winner," she said. "I'm delighted to have won on Josies Orders for JP and Enda as I've enjoyed many great days with them. I'm sad it's finished and I'll miss the banter in the weighing room, but it's time to move on."

Carberry's biggest victory also came in the Irish Grand National, on Organisedconfusion in 2011, and she was a seven-time Cheltenham Festival winner aboard Dabiroun (2005 Fred Winter Juvenile Hurdle), Heads Onthe Ground (2007 Cross Country Chase), Garde Champetre (2008 and 2009 Cross Country Chase), On The Fringe (2015 and 2016 Foxhunter Chase) and Josies Orders (2016 Cross Country Chase).

Twice Ireland's champion amateur in her 18-year career, she also conquered the big fences at Aintree to win the 2015 Fox

Pioneeering women jockeys Katie Walsh and Nina Carberry both bowed out on a winner at the Punchestown festival

◀ Final curtain: Katie Walsh (left) and Nina Carberry at Punchestown

Hunters' Chase with On The Fringe.

Going into Punchestown both riders were of one mind without giving much away in terms of specifics, even to each other. In Carberry's case Punchestown was going to be the end regardless of whether she rode a winner. For Walsh it needed a winner for the curtain to come down. What united them was that retirement came on their own terms and wasn't forced upon them.

Carberry, who continues to ride out regularly for Aidan O'Brien at Ballydoyle, recalls: "Myself and Katie were walking the course on the first day of the festival and I told her it was going to be my last Punchestown. She told me she was thinking along similar lines.

"I'd been thinking of retiring for a couple of months and had decided I was going to go at the end of Punchestown regardless of results. I found it fine during the winter months, going to ride at Thurles or Clonmel on a Thursday and riding at the weekends. But all the evening meetings during the summer made things difficult, especially with a young child, and I decided that if I wasn't prepared to give race-riding 110 per cent it was time to go.

"To finish up by winning over the banks course on Josies Orders, a horse I had won on a few times at Cheltenham, for Enda and JP, was the perfect way to end. You miss the buzz of riding winners but I had a great time and enjoyed it all. That Saturday at Punchestown was very emotional, with family and so many friends and colleagues there. They made it a wonderful occasion."

For Walsh her farewell victory on the Willie Mullins-trained Antey came about literally by accident. "It was a spare ride. Danny Mullins was due to ride Antey but he got injured in a fall early in the day and I got the call-up from Willie," she says.

"I'd been thinking of retiring for some time. I thought it was time for me to end one chapter of my life and to move on to the next one. The way it all worked out was unbelievable. All the family were there to lead the cheering when I came into the winner's enclosure. The reaction was fantastic once word got out that I was retiring. It was a day I'll never forget and bowing out on a horse trained by Willie was very appropriate in view of our association over the years."

Reflecting on her career, Walsh, who assists her husband with his training operation and is actively involved in buying and selling horses, says: "Riding three Cheltenham Festival winners, finishing third on Seabass in the Aintree Grand National and winning the Irish Grand National on Thunder And Roses were all huge. I also enjoyed success in France and Australia, so I have a lot to look back on and be grateful for."

Her Grand National third on Seabass is the best finishing position achieved by a female rider in the history of the famous race. "That was a fantastic experience," she says. "He jumped from fence to fence and gave me a huge thrill. I don't know that I ever thought he was going to win but we were going as well as anything else with two fences to jump. It wasn't to be but it was a day I'll never forget."

There were so many unforgettable days down the years, for Katie and for Nina, and for us.

NEW WAVE

Young, gifted and female – the jump jockeys breaking barriers

By Nick Pulford

KATIE WALSH was part of a landmark achievement, six weeks before her retirement, when she was one of four female jockeys to taste success at the 2018 Cheltenham Festival. The new record went one better than the previous year as women increasingly make their mark over jumps.

First to strike at Cheltenham was Lizzie Kelly, who took the Ultima Handicap Chase on the opening day with Coo Star Sivola, trained by her stepfather Nick Williams.

The 24-year-old sent the 5-1 favourite into the lead after three out and held on by a neck from Shantou Flyer and James Bowen, a fellow 3lb conditional, to create history by becoming the first female professional to score at the festival.

The previous year Kelly had suffered bitter disappointment when picking the wrong horse in the Fred Winter, missing out on a winner, and falling on Tea For Two in the Gold Cup, and she said: "I couldn't stop thinking about how it went wrong last year and thankfully everything has fallen into place. I'd made my peace with

never being a Cheltenham Festival winner and now I am."

The second win for a female professional followed before the week was out when Bridget Andrews, 24, won the Randox Health County Handicap Hurdle on Mohaayed on Gold Cup day. Andrews' sister Gina, a leading amateur, had won the Fulke Walwyn Kim Muir Handicap Chase on Domesday Book at the 2017 festival.

Trainer Dan Skelton's confidence in Mohaayed's chance had dwindled when the rain came and his brother Harry, the stable jockey, chose to ride

Spiritofthegames, leaving Andrews on the 33-1 shot. There were emotional scenes at the finish as Harry pulled up beside Bridget, his partner, for a congratulatory hug and kiss. "Going down the hill Harry shouted, 'Steady Bridge' because I was going so well," said Andrews, who also revealed that for luck she had hung her kit on the peg where her sister signed her name 12 months earlier.

The 3lb conditional, who had taken a brave decision to step out of the amateur ranks, added: "When I started riding I always said I'd never go conditional because it's so hard, but when Dan

◀ Making waves: clockwise from far left, Grade 1 winner Bryony Frost; Cheltenham scorers Bridget Andrews with Mohaayed, Lizzie Kelly on Coo Star Sivola and Harriet Tucker with the Foxhunter trophy

offered me the job I couldn't turn it down. I might be biased, but I think I have the best conditionals job in the country."

Walsh struck on the Wednesday with the Willie Mullins-trained Relegate in the Weatherbys Champion Bumper, eight years after her double on Poker De Sivola and Thousand Stars at the 2010 festival.

A second amateur success for a woman rider came on Gold Cup day when Harriet Tucker landed the St James's Place Foxhunter Chase on Pacha Du Polder. This was just the 22-year-old's second ride under rules and, even more

remarkably, she took victory despite a "half-dislocated" shoulder that prevented her from using her whip.

Having collared gallant front-runner Top Wood to score by a neck, Tucker explained: "My shoulder sometimes half-dislocates when I reach it too high and it did it when I was

coming to the second-last. I couldn't push it back in, so I couldn't slap him down the shoulder. I was just pushing and screaming and praying that nobody would come and beat me because of the shoulder."

The Paul Nicholls-trained Pacha Du Polder has become quite a friend to women jockeys, having carried Bryony Frost to a first festival win in the

same race 12 months earlier and famously gone close with Victoria Pendleton in 2016.

****

FROST used her festival success on Pacha Du Polder as a springboard into the professional ranks and she enjoyed a standout 2017-18 with a string of high-profile victories. When she won on her first ride as a 5lb conditional in July 2017 in a Worcester novice chase aboard the Nicholls-trained Black Corton, there was little indication of how success would snowball for both horse and rider.
▸▸ *Continues page 152*

They ended up winning seven races together, including the Grade 1 Kauto Star Novices' Chase at Kempton's Christmas meeting and the Grade 2 Reynoldstown Novices' Chase at Ascot in February, with the hardy seven-year-old having improved more than a stone since his Worcester victory.

After the Kempton success, which put Frost alongside Kelly as the only women to win a Grade 1 over jumps, Nicholls said: "Bryony works hard on her fitness, works hard at home. Horses run and jump for her and this is a great example. She's as good as any girl that's ever ridden."

The admiration was mutual. "Paul has been more than a boss," Frost said later in the season. "I turn to him for everything and he has looked after me perfectly. He's found me the right horses at the right time and had the backbone to put me up on horses and fought my corner, telling owners 'she'll show you what she can do'. It's all about repaying that faith and I know I can."

The 23-year-old rider ended the season in 25th place in the British jump jockeys' list with 38 winners from 204 rides and almost £650,000 in prize-money. Most of the riders who finished above Frost had at least 50 per cent more rides and her 19 per cent strike-rate was bettered by only four of them, all of whom finished in the top eight overall.

Unfortunately the 2018-19 season took a bad turn when Frost suffered the first serious injury of her career at Newton Abbot in July. She was unseated from Billy My Boy and trodden on by another horse, causing internal injuries including a fractured sternum, a liver tear and a bruised pancreas, and was sidelined for three months. She was soon back in the winning groove, however, scoring on her fifth ride after her return in October.

Frost's standing in the British table was surpassed in Ireland by Rachael Blackmore, who finished 11th in her first full season after making history as Ireland's first female champion conditional jockey in 2016-17.

Blackmore, 29, had her best season in 2017-18 with 34 winners, including a first Graded success on the Gordon Elliott-trained novice hurdler

Blow By Blow, and kicked on to great effect in the 2018-19 season, reaching a new career high before the end of September.

Only three and a half years after turning professional, Blackmore was trading blows with Paul Townend at the top of the table in an unlikely challenge to the established order. "The season so far has been incredible. I've got so much support from so many different trainers," she said.

"I remember what it was like when I had one ride a week. You might ride a horse on a Sunday and be disgusted with yourself for doing something wrong and you'd have to wait until the following Sunday or even longer for your next ride to try to put things right. I never thought it would get to the stage where I'd have a couple of rides at each meeting. I will never take that for granted."

****

BLACKMORE is clear about the debt she owes to Nina Carberry and Katie Walsh in blazing a trail for women jockeys. "Nina and Katie were amazing to me when they were riding. They were so

▲ Rising star: Rachael Blackmore is climbing ever higher in Ireland

▼ Katie Walsh, Bryony Frost and Blackmore at Aintree, where all three rode in the Grand National

talented and so professional and you have no idea how much I looked up to them. Their achievements were phenomenal. They both won Irish Grand Nationals and had winners at Cheltenham, so I have an awful long way to go before I get near their level. It's nice to hear people compare me to them, though."

In April, as Blackmore, Frost and Walsh prepared to ride in the Grand National – the first time three women had done so since 1988 – Tom Kerr wrote in the Racing Post: "It is often said, especially by exasperated women jockeys, that it would be better if their participation in a race like this was entirely unremarkable – just jockeys doing a job, their sex as irrelevant as their hair colour or shoe size.

"That day will come, make no mistake, and welcome it will be too, but before the involvement of women riders becomes so commonplace it is not worth mentioning, there must first come the pioneers who go where no-one has gone before, who achieve what no-one has achieved."

Where Walsh and Carberry led, Blackmore and Frost have followed. All of them have proved that, with the right support, the barriers can be broken.

Image courtesy of Hong Kong Jockey Club

BORN IN SOUTH AFRICA - BRED FOR THE WORLD

South African bred Singapore Sling, winner of the HK$10 Million
Hong Kong Classic Cup. Purchased as a yearling for HK$150 000.
Just another example of the exceptional value that
South African Thoroughbreds represent on the world stage.

BLOODSTOCK SOUTH AFRICA SALES DATES 2019

CAPE YEARLING SALE

17th March
Mistico Estate • Western Cape

KZN YEARLING SALE

4th & 5th July
Sibaya Casino • KZN

NATIONAL 2YO SALE

15th & 16th August
TBA Sales Complex • Johannesburg

NATIONAL YEARLING SALE

24th, 25th & 26th April
TBA Sales Complex • Johannesburg

READY TO RUN BREEZE-UP SALE

3rd November
TBA Sales Complex • Johannesburg

Contact Catherine Hartley
+27 83 640 1155 • catherine@tba.co.za

www.tba.co.za

**THE THOROUGHBRED BREEDERS'
ASSOCIATION OF SOUTH AFRICA**

XPRESSIONS ADV & DESIGN

'We know Richard was right there with us'

Lalor's Grade 1 success at Aintree sparked emotional scenes in the winner's enclosure

By Lee Mottershead

THERE was not a sadder story all year than the death in January of Richard Woollacott. The hearts of all who follow the sport went out to his loved ones then and again in April when Lalor's Grade 1 victory at Aintree provided an emotional reminder of his former trainer's immense talent as a horseman.

This was the second consecutive year Lalor had been successful at the Grand National meeting. It was also the second consecutive year that the celebrations were of a bittersweet nature.

In 2017 Woollacott was still coming to terms with the death six days earlier of good friend James McNeile, who lost his life following a point-to-point accident aboard a horse trained by Richard's wife Kayley. To make matters even harder for the winning trainer, Kayley was absent from the racecourse as the couple's daughter Bella was poorly in hospital.

On Lalor's return to Aintree, Kayley was forced to do the talking herself, separated from the man who so tragically was found dead at the age of 40 on January 23.

With commendable bravery, she had spoken in the days after Richard's death about his long battle with mental illness. She noted that suicide is the single biggest cause of death of men aged between 18 and 45, and stressed: "We must do more."

Richard Woollacott achieved much in his short life, including being crowned Britain's champion point-to-point jockey in 2010, a title that complemented nine Devon and Cornwall titles. As a trainer he had made a tremendously bright start, highlighted when Beer Goggles captured the prestigious Long Distance Hurdle at Newbury in December 2017.

That was a Grade 2, as had been Lalor's first Aintree triumph. When David Staddon's exciting prospect struck at Aintree for the second time, once again under Richard Johnson, it was a debut mission in Grade 1 company. By that point it was Kayley's name on the licence.

Richard had known how good Lalor might be one day and had said so after the first Aintree win. "As soon as I saw him I fell in love with him," he told the press corps, adding: "We'll take him home, give him a cuddle and then turn him out."

▶ Top performance: Lalor jumps the final flight under Richard Johnson to win the Top Novices' Hurdle at Aintree

◀ Kayley Woollacott alongside Johnson in the winner's enclosure

That patient, caring approach reaped handsome dividends when the horse cheered on by so many powered to an authoritative two-and-a-half-length defeat of Vision Des Flos on his return to Aintree in the Betway Top Novices' Hurdle.

"It's unbelievable," said Kayley. "I don't know how that just happened. It's a really emotional day. I obviously had a little bit of help from up there. This is a really special course for me and Richard. We had some of our best days here. It's unreal. I don't know what to say. We love the horse. He's amazing."

Also amazing was Steph Jones, who left her home in Australia to be at her sister's side in her darkest hour. She had been with her at Cheltenham when Beer Goggles ran at the end of the week in which Richard died. On that occasion Kayley looked understandably fragile. Come April she was slightly stronger but still in need of support. She made clear that support had been given not simply by those closest to her but also from the sport in general.

"The horses have kept everything going and kept me on the straight and narrow," she said. "Racing is one of the toughest games at times

but over recent months it has shown how amazingly supportive it can be. People get behind you and look after you. They have really helped me find my feet."

Help also came from loyal owners like Staddon. He described Richard as like a family member and observed: "It's an utter tragedy. He was such a good boy." Staddon, and many others, have continued to give their backing to the Devon yard, whose website proclaims the motto: "Passionate. Patient. Persistent." That website also contains a section named "Richard's Legacy".

In it, Kayley writes: "Lalor is a

true credit to him. He will always be the Grade 1 winner he couldn't hang on for, but we know Richard was right there with us at Aintree.

"We've all struggled in recent months to come to terms with why, and it's devastating we were unable to make him believe in himself in the same way we all did, but we're not giving up now – that would be hypocritical."

Over the years ahead there will hopefully be many more notable wins for the Woollacott horses, Lalor included. There may always be tears, as there were at Aintree. Increasingly, though, may they primarily be tears of joy.

'A throwback to a half-forgotten age of steeplechasing when giants strode the earth'

Two of the best and most-loved chasers of recent times were remembered fondly in 2018 as Denman died at the age of 18 and Cue Card was retired at the age of 12. This tribute to Denman appeared in the Racing Post the day after his death was announced

By Steve Dennis

DEATH shall have no dominion. How could it, when Denman had gained racing immortality long ago? Death takes a moment and is gone, but a life so well lived is everlasting.

The final kindness of the needle, gently and mournfully wielded, ushered Denman from his quiet field into the Elysian Field where all the horses go, the great and the good and the only ordinary.

Now, just out of our earshot, a strong, steady voice is announcing his arrival, and from the depths of the long, sweet grass Kauto Star has pricked up his ears and is walking quickly towards his old neighbour, old rival, old friend.

Denman's gone. No more will he lift his head as pheasants rise from the hedgerows with a clatter of wings, no more will he carefully present his backside to those seeking an audience, his silent, eloquent method of deterring conversation.

But what a treasury he leaves us. Death takes life but it cannot subtract from it, can't diminish that which came before. Denman's legacy is inviolable.

We know about the Cheltenham Gold Cup, the two Hennessys, the RSA Chase, the Lexus, the Racing Post Rating of 184, all the enduring excelsior of a career that never failed to excite.

What the bare statistics cannot convey, though, and what will form the main strand of a million reminiscences, is the way Denman went about his work. Some horses glide across the turf, others plod sturdily over it, but Denman hammered it into

▸ *Continues page 158*

◂ Rare breed: Denman (left) and Cue Card, two of the best in a golden era of steeplechasing

DENMAN FACTFILE

Foaled April 17, 2000

Pedigree Presenting - Polly Puttens (Pollerton)

Breeder Colman O'Flynn in Ireland

Owners Paul Barber and Margaret Findlay

Trainer Paul Nicholls, Ditcheat, Somerset (Adrian Maguire for Irish point-to-point)

Grade 1 wins 2006 Challow Novices' Hurdle, 2007 Royal & SunAlliance Chase, Lexus Chase (Leopardstown), 2008 Cheltenham Gold Cup

Best performances (RPR) 184 in 2008 Cheltenham Gold Cup; 183 in 2007 and 2009 Hennessy Gold Cup (both under 11st 12lb)

Four meetings with Kauto Star, all in Cheltenham Gold Cup 2008 (1 Denman, 2 Kauto Star), 2009 (1 Kauto Star, 2 Denman), 2010 (2 Denman, fell Kauto Star), 2011 (2 Denman, 3 Kauto Star)

Most wins in succession 9 (2006-08)

Richest prize £268,279 (2008 Cheltenham Gold Cup)

Total prize-money £1,141,347

Total races under rules 24; won 14 (5 at Newbury, 4 at Cheltenham), 2nd 5, 3rd 1

Compiled by John Randall

submission. At his great and glorious peak, he was an elemental force like no other.

He was a big horse, a throwback to a half-forgotten age of steeplechasing when giants strode the earth. We called him The Tank, in tribute to his size, but also to his relentlessness. He was the irresistible force, and woe betide any immovable object that lay in his way. Sometimes it was a rival, sometimes a long-established record, sometimes it was simply the bulwarks of belief that were turned to matchwood by his might.

His victory in the Gold Cup was a good example. Not only did he steal the crown from Kauto Star, he wrenched it away with barely credible brute force, alloyed with a rough-edged elegance and economy of effort. To watch him come barrelling down the Cheltenham hill, turning for home full of

▸▸ *Continues page 160*

WHERE DENMAN RANKS

3m+ chasers on RPR since 2008

Kauto Star 191, Denman 184, Bristol De Mai 182, Don Cossack 182, Imperial Commander 182

WHERE CUE CARD RANKS

2m4f-3m chasers on RPR since 2008

Kauto Star 191, Sprinter Sacre 190, Don Cossack 181, Cue Card 180, Long Run 180, Vautour 180

▲ Friends and rivals: Denman (left) and Kauto Star frolic in their paddock at Paul Nicholls' yard in 2009

◀ Denman in action in the Hennessy Gold Cup at Newbury, which he won twice under 11st 12lb

HORSERAIL
SAFE • STRONG • ELECTRIFIABLE

W: horserail.co.uk
E: horserail@mmg.ie
P: 0808 2344766

HOTCOTE WIRE

Safe: Wont cut, wrap or burn.
Durable: 20 Year Guarantee.
Fully Electrifiable: Very low resistance.
Economical: Significantly cheaper.
Easy Installation: Easy to set up.

HORSERAIL

Safe: Smooth and Flexible.
Durable: 30 Year Guarantee.
Strong: Wont break or splinter.
No Maintenance: No painting or
cleaning required.
Fully Electrifiable: Eliminates chewing
and rubbing.
Economical: Costs less and lasts longer.

DO IT ONCE...... DO IT RIGHT......

running, was to witness the perfect exposition of equine power. He would have run through a brick wall that day and not turned a hair.

Together with his stablemate he helped change the aspect of his sport. Denman and Kauto Star were like United and City, like Federer and Nadal, like Coe and Ovett, opposing styles, opposite poles of brilliance.

Between them they transcended the mere technicalities of their sport, seemingly spurred each other to greater heights, victory for one more sweet and more meaningful when gained at the expense of the other.

Ostensibly, you were implacably either for Denman or for Kauto Star, but that did not preclude a warm and genuine appreciation of the other's talents, nor the unavailing arguments about who was the better.

****

PERHAPS it was in his two Hennessy wins that we truly saw the greatest of Denman, though. They were similar in execution – he mercilessly crushed the opposition – but different in context.

His first victory, in 2007, was peak Denman, the mighty athlete in his pomp. He was still unbeaten over fences, his limits unknown, and he carried his 11st 12lb burden as a weightlifter might carry a small child on his shoulders. We thrilled to him, struck by all sorts of awe.

Two years later it was a different Denman. He had been made to seem mortal, a shell of his former self, laid low by his heart problems, his proud record in tatters, his crown lost for good.

On his previous start he had fallen for the first time. Now his 11st 12lb looked like a millstone around the neck of a war-wearied veteran.

Yet his spirit remained intact. He summoned up 'old Denman' for the final time, put his shoulder to the wheel, wore his battered old heart on his sleeve, and he didn't shrink from the task until it was done.

It would be his last victory, his last hurrah, and as he returned to his adoring public there were not a few of them with tears rolling down their cheeks.

Now those tears are falling again,

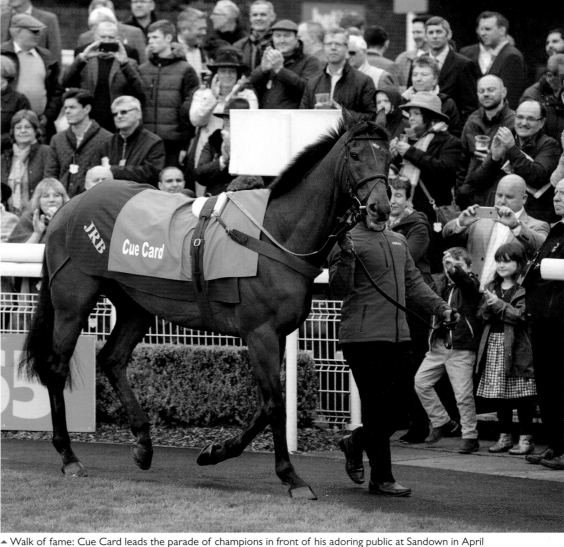

▲ Walk of fame: Cue Card leads the parade of champions in front of his adoring public at Sandown in April

now that great heart is stilled. Denman is no more. One more long, luxurious summer at grass would have been a blessing, but it was time to go.

But as long as horses race, whenever the dust is blown in clouds from ancient record books, wherever men and women come together to talk about their champions, Denman will be brought bewitchingly to life. Years hence, when younger faces light up at the exploits of the next great star (for there is always a next great star), old heads will nod and then these words will follow: "Ah, but you never saw Denman, did you?"

And the stories will be told again. Denman will never die, you see; in this way he will live forever.

CUE CARD FACTFILE

Foaled April 30, 2006

Pedigree King's Theatre - Wicked Crack (King's Ride)

Breeder Rowland Crellin

Owners Jean and Bob Bishop

Trainer Colin Tizzard, Venn Farm, Milborne Port, Sherborne, Dorset

Nine Grade 1 wins
2010 Champion Bumper, 2013 Ascot Chase, Ryanair Chase, Betfair Chase, 2015 Betfair Chase, King George VI Chase, 2016 Betfred Bowl, Betfair Chase, 2017 Ascot Chase

Champion staying chaser (Racing Post Ratings) 2016-17 (rated 176)

Best performances (RPR) 180 in 2015 King George VI Chase (won) and 2016 Cheltenham Gold Cup (fell 3 out)

Richest prize £156,612 (2013 Ryanair Chase)

Total prize-money £1,447,454

Total races 41; won 16 (3 at Cheltenham, 3 at Haydock, 2 at Aintree, 2 at Ascot), 2nd 11, 3rd 2

Compiled by John Randall

FOND FAREWELL AS 'THE PEOPLE'S HORSE' IS RETIRED

By Jonathan Harding

ONE month after Native River arrived at the pinnacle of steeplechasing for Colin Tizzard, the horse who led the way and made it all possible departed the scene.

Cue Card, Tizzard's first Cheltenham Festival winner and hero of so many big days, was retired at the age of 12 and no-one was left in any doubt about the important role he had played for the stable in nine captivating seasons.

"He set up my career, he's been the flagbearer. He's paid for a lot of these new buildings that are going up – he's done everything for all of us," Tizzard said.

The sense of gratitude was echoed by Racing Post readers, who flocked to pay tribute to 'the people's horse'. "Every time he stepped out, the emotions would be all over the place. Cue Card, you've been the horse of a lifetime," said Ann Aspery, while Matthew Smith said: "One of the best chasers in the past ten years and would have won two Gold Cups if not for coming down. There probably won't be as popular a horse as Cue Card in a long time."

In the last of his 41 races, Cue Card was pulled up in the Ryanair Chase at the Cheltenham Festival in March and the following month the decision was taken to retire him before his planned send-off in the Oaksey Chase at Sandown on the final day of the jumps season.

"He wasn't showing the sparkle he'd shown," Tizzard said. "It's a weight off my mind – it would have been a big call to race him again. I kept looking at him and saying 'this isn't the Cue Card we know'."

Owned by Jean Bishop and her late husband Bob, Cue Card won 16 races, nine at Grade 1 level, and established Tizzard as a major training force.

After impressing on his debut at Fontwell, Cue Card came to prominence as the shock 40-1 winner of the Champion Bumper at the 2010 Cheltenham Festival. "The best memory and the longest-lasting one was the Champion Bumper," Tizzard said. "I'll never forget that for the rest of my life. He sluiced away from them. It was fantastic."

He ran at six more festivals, winning the Ryanair Chase in 2013 but agonisingly falling in two Gold Cups. He also won three Betfair Chases and a King George VI Chase.

With £1,447,454 in earnings and a best Racing Post Rating of 180, Cue Card was among the leading jumps horses of recent years but what really set him apart was his longevity. The son of King's Theatre earned an RPR of 170 or better on 14 occasions, which compares favourably with the likes of Istabraq (12), Hurricane Fly (12) and Denman (ten).

His career-defining season came in 2015-16, when he won the Charlie Hall Chase, his second Betfair Chase, the King George and the Betfred Bowl.

But this was the same season Cue Card suffered the first of his two heartbreaking Gold Cup falls, when he had looked full of running and was on the brink of winning the Jockey Club's £1 million triple crown bonus.

His big-race rider Paddy Brennan, one of five jockeys fortunate enough to partner Cue Card, reflected on that fall and his relationship with the chaser. "It was my lowest moment as a jockey," he said. "He was the best horse I've ridden not to win a Gold Cup and I was just as gutted for the owners and connections as myself – I just wanted to disappear.

"But the thing that separated him from the rest, aside from his longevity, was his ability to bounce back, and to do so in a very short space of time."

Less than three weeks after the fall, Cue Card destroyed Don Poli in the Betfred Bowl, once again proving the doubters wrong.

While he was unable to go out with a victory at Sandown, the red carpet was rolled out nonetheless as Cue Card was paraded in front of his adoring public, who clutched scarves in the owner's colours as they witnessed the end of an era.

They could be happy in the knowledge that Cue Card has a loving retirement home with the Tizzards. "He won't leave the farm, he's going to stay here," the trainer said. "I'm going to ride him round a bit to keep him active. He can stay here as long as he lives."

▼ First chapter: Cue Card spreadeagles the field with a 40-1 triumph in the Champion Bumper at Cheltenham in 2010

SUPER**SUB**

Paul Townend had a string of big wins in place of the injured Ruby Walsh

By David Jennings

PAUL TOWNEND won more Grade 1s in the 2017-18 season than the top eight riders in Britain put together. Richard Johnson, Harry Skelton, Brian Hughes, Noel Fehily, Sam Twiston-Davies, Aidan Coleman, Sean Bowen and Tom Scudamore accumulated nine Grade 1s between them. Townend won ten on his own.

Townend always needs to be on his toes and, when Willie Mullins looked to his bench after Ruby Walsh was stretchered off at Punchestown 24 hours before Faugheen was due to return in the Morgiana Hurdle last November, Townend had his tracksuit top off and socks pulled up. He was ready to be thrown into the thick of the action.

"I got some kick out of Faugheen winning the Morgiana," Townend recalls. "Ruby was just after getting injured and to ride a horse like Faugheen at that time was pretty special. He was electric that day." Electric indeed. Townend sent Faugheen straight to the front and he thrashed his three rivals. Jezki got closest but only within 16 lengths. It was just like old times.

It set the tone for a season that was just like old times for Townend too. The champion jockey at the end of the 2010-2011 season proved to be the most able of deputies for Walsh, whose season was ruined when he broke his leg on Let's Dance.

There was the last-gasp lunge on Total Recall in the Ladbrokes Trophy at Newbury, the flawless

▶ *Continues page 164*

performance of Footpad in the Racing Post Novice Chase at Leopardstown over Christmas, followed by a fruitful January during which Next Destination won the Lawlor's of Naas Novice Hurdle and Un De Sceaux scooped the Clarence House Chase at Ascot.

February wasn't bad either with Footpad once again foot-perfect in the Frank Ward Solicitors Arkle Novice Chase at Leopardstown and Mr Adjudicator landing the Spring Juvenile Hurdle the following day.

****

WHEN Walsh returned for Cheltenham, it looked as if Townend would have to take a back seat for the festival. Not for long, though. Al Boum Photo's second-last-fence spill in the RSA Chase meant Walsh's Cheltenham Festival was finished.

Once again Townend was ready to step up on the big occasion. He is used to the bright lights and was reacquainted with an old friend in the Sun Bets Stayers' Hurdle.

Twelve months previously Penhill and Townend had sneaked up behind Monalee and pounced after the last to land the Albert Bartlett. Under a carbon-copy ride, the speedy stayer saw off Supasundae in the Stayers', a first success for Townend in one of the festival's big four races. It was exquisite stuff. Laurina's Mares' Novices' Hurdle success later that afternoon was less tricky. She was 18 lengths too good.

"I love riding Penhill, I just love it," the 28-year-old says. "It's a bit of a challenge in that you have to get it right. You have to do things to suit him. That's why we ride him the way we do. He's been good to me twice at Cheltenham now and he doesn't owe me anything, that's for sure."

Nor does Laurina. She took the step up to Grade 1 company in her stride to score at Fairyhouse over Easter. That made it eight Grade 1s in less than six months. Townend could do no wrong. Everything he touched was turning into a Grade 1 winner.

That was until April 24 – the day that will torment Townend for the rest of his life. The Growise Champion Novice Chase was going perfectly to script for Townend on Al Boum Photo, who had won the Ryanair

Gold Cup at Fairyhouse earlier in the month. His mount had jumped beautifully and when Invitation Only and Monalee came down at the second-last, Townend found himself in front. What happened from there was something never before seen on an Irish racecourse.

Townend made the decision to try to go around the final fence rather than jump it. Nobody knew why. The fence was not dolled off and there was no indication the fence was not to be jumped. In making a beeline to go

▲ Magic moments: clockwise from top left, Faugheen, Footpad, Next Destination (right), Penhill (right), Laurina, Un De Sceaux, Benie Des Dieux and Mr Adjudicator (nearside) were all Grade 1 winners for Paul Townend in 2017-18

inside the wing of the fence, he took Robbie Power and Finian's Oscar with him. It caused utter carnage on the track and on the exchanges.

It was sensational. It was surreal. But it was split-second stuff, a genuine misjudgement by a jockey whose previous errors you could count on one hand. It was completely out of character. Townend does not want to dwell on that day. It is in the past. He would rather leave it there than dig it up again.

▸ *Continues page 166*

LOVE BEING AN OWNER?

****

IT IS the following day that defines Townend, not Al Boum Photo. The eyes of the racing world were fixed on him for his first ride of the day on Pravalaguna in the Louis Fitzgerald Hotel Hurdle. Now that's what you call pressure.

Townend left that pressure in his tyres out in the car park and was coolness personified in producing Pravalaguna to lead approaching the last on the way to an eight-length win. He wasn't finished there either. Next Destination dug deep to deny Delta Work in the Grade 1 Irish Daily Mirror Novice Hurdle and Patricks Park won the Guinness Handicap Chase. Seldom has a hat-trick been scored under such intense scrutiny.

"I had a job to do the next day. It was as simple as that," he says. "I had a couple of good people looking out for me. Those people had my back and were there when I needed them. That was important, very important. I was relieved more than anything. That was the overriding emotion."

The Al Boum Photo episode may have made front-page headlines but Townend's reaction to the turmoil was a measure of the man. It was a season to remember, not to forget. He won ten Grade 1s, so the one that got away should not define him.

"I was very lucky really. I was in the hotseat because of Ruby's misfortune for a lot of the season and got a good few Grade 1 winners while I was there and even managed to bag myself two Cheltenham winners. When Ruby gets hurt, all the owners are very supportive of me. In fairness to Willie, he always allows me to step in there."

Why wouldn't he when you ride ten Grade 1 winners for him? Townend is a vital cog in the Mullins machine and the champion trainer knows his value better than anyone.

RUBY PUTS ON A SHOW – FOR ONE DAY ONLY

WHAT has come to be known as the core jumps season – the period from October to April – was virtually non-existent for Ruby Walsh in 2017-18. After two lengthy periods on the sidelines with a broken leg, what was left of his hollowed-out core amounted to little more than a day of the Cheltenham Festival.

▶ Foot perfect: Ruby Walsh celebrates victory on Footpad

In that day Walsh was as dominant as ever, scoring two Grade 1 victories, but over the months he lost a lot. All those other Grade 1 winners, his Irish title, his status as the king of Cheltenham and Punchestown.

The first blow came in November when he broke his right tibia in a fall on Let's Dance at Punchestown. He was out for four months, returning on the Thursday before Cheltenham with a winning ride at Thurles. "I needed a target," he said. "I needed something to keep me going, something to get me through the tough days. I suppose some people might book a holiday to get them through tough times. For me it was thinking about the Tuesday of Cheltenham."

It looked like Walsh's season would be saved, especially when he got straight into his Cheltenham groove on the opening day of the festival. His judgement was perfect on Footpad in the Grade 1 Racing Post Arkle Chase as he let the 5-6 favourite sit off the fast pace set by Saint Calvados and Petit Mouchoir before picking them off to score by 14 lengths. "Experience and racecraft – he's a legend," said winning trainer Willie Mullins.

Two races later Mullins had more praise after Walsh pulled the Grade 1 OLBG Mares' Hurdle out of the fire, coming from fourth approaching the final flight on Benie Des Dieux to get up by half a length. "It's early days but I thought that was ride of the week. Ruby was so good on her, to get her up the hill like that," Mullins said.

The euphoria did not last long. In the RSA Chase, the second race on the Wednesday, Walsh took a heavy fall on Al Boum Photo at the second last. The injury was later confirmed by the rider as "a very similar fracture on the inside of the original one" and this time he would be out for even longer, four and a half months. Even then his injury woes were not over, as he had another six weeks on the sidelines with badly bruised ribs and vertebrae after a fall at Killarney in August.

All this led to retirement talk, though not by Walsh himself. "I'm 39. I still think I've a good few years left in me yet, although I'm not stupid enough to think there's more ahead of me than behind me," he said in the summer.

"I'm still as hungry as ever and would love to find another great horse. I suppose my main goal now would be to try to get on the next Hurricane Fly or Kauto Star – that would be magic."

FIGHTBACK

Faugheen looked down and out but picked himself up off the canvas to deliver a knockout blow at Punchestown

By Richard Forristal

IF someone were to tell you that Faugheen returned from nearly two years off with one of his signature wide-margin annihilations in a Grade 1 and departed at the end of the season in similarly emphatic fashion, you would be naturally inclined to think everything had gone to script.

When the 2015 Champion Hurdle hero reappeared as a nine-year-old in the Unibet Morgiana Hurdle at Punchestown in November 2017, having been sidelined since thrashing a high-class Irish Champion Hurdle field by upwards of 15 lengths in January 2016, it was like he had never been away. In his debut link-up with Paul Townend, Willie Mullins' remorseless force of nature was sent off a 4-11 shot and proceeded to justify those odds with a trademark front-running demolition of Jezki.

Jessica Harrington's 2014 Champion Hurdle winner was left spluttering on Faugheen's fumes to the tune of 16 lengths, as one of the most gifted hurdlers in recent times recorded the widest-margin success of his career over jumps.

"The Machine is back in full working order," boomed commentator Dessie Scahill. Roll the clock forward to Punchestown in April. This time David Mullins was in the hotseat, but the outcome was similar. They never saw another rival en route to a 13-length destruction of opponents who had accumulated 23 Grade 1s.

Despite the injuries that conspired to keep him out of competitive action for so long, the chapters that bookended the 2017-18 campaign suggest everything was rosy in the garden. If only. It's a summary that doesn't reveal the trials and tribulations, more like the opening and closing scenes of a romantic fairytale that had some X-rated plot twists along the way.

That Morgiana curtain-raiser lured us all into a false sense of security. "He just jumped out and took the race from them," Mullins exuded of his returning star. "He had tons in the tank. That was great to see."

Faugheen's trouncing of Jezki took his tally to 13 wins in 14 racecourse starts and he was promptly promoted to 7-2 ante-post favouritism for the Champion Hurdle, usurping the reigning title-holder Buveur D'Air. All of a sudden it looked as though Nicky Henderson's youngster might have merely been keeping the throne warm in his absence. Not quite.

Closer inspection of that April swansong back at Punchestown points to what went on in between. First of all, Faugheen returned an SP of 11-2, bigger than he had ever done before, and Townend eschewed the chance to ride him in favour of the Mullins-trained favourite Penhill. Then there was the race itself, a stayers' championship event. No longer king of the two-mile hurdling realm, Faugheen had been relegated to the three-mile ranks in a desperate last-ditch attempt to salvage something from the debris of the previous months. It might have been an ignominious departure – if it hadn't turned out to be such a glorious redemption.

"He didn't work well last Saturday and this was sort of a last-chance saloon," Mullins admitted in the aftermath. "Myself and Ruby Walsh were on the gallop that morning and we looked at each other, thinking, 'That's him gone'."

▸▸ *Continues page 170*

****

GOOD job they opted for a final throw of the dice. After thriving on the slower fractions over three miles, Faugheen was even being discussed as a future Gold Cup prospect after Mullins threw in a curveball about the old boy going chasing now that he had got his groove back.

That constituted some turnaround, as he looked a spent force for much of the campaign. When he turned up in the Ryanair Hurdle at Leopardstown over Christmas, Faugheen was sent off at his usual short odds-on to dispense with four decidedly inferior rivals.

However, while he began in his customary forceful fashion, he could never get the opposition on the ropes. He was swinging away but he wasn't landing any punches and when they began the turn out of the back straight for the final time, it became clear Townend knew he was in trouble.

The jockey sent out the distress signals but there was no response. Within a matter of strides he had thrown in the towel, pulled up Faugheen and dismounted before the third-last flight.

Mick Jazz, whose official rating of 150 was 22lb lower than Faugheen's, went on to beat Cilaos Emery. The world had been turned on its head, yet no plausible reason ever emerged.

"He was fine after the race. We got him home and he's normal, which is good news," owner Rich Ricci said subsequently. "Paul did the right thing in pulling him up. It's one of those

things where he didn't feel right and Paul didn't want to take any chances with that."

It was just a listless display that connections ultimately put down to the bounce factor and they resolved to plough on.

Come the BHP Insurance Irish Champion Hurdle on February 3, Faugheen at least went out on his shield, finishing nearly five lengths ahead of Mick Jazz but unable to cope with the youth in Supasundae's legs from the back of the final flight.

That was a far cry from the indomitable beast who owned the Morgiana, but it hinted there was still some life in the old dog. Subsequent events would upgrade the performance further, with the smart winner going on to claim a second two-mile Grade 1 at Punchestown in the spring.

Mick Jazz also enhanced his status as an unlikely improver by finishing third to Buveur D'Air at Cheltenham, where Faugheen simply couldn't raise his game enough to figure. With Walsh back up, the old partnership eventually boxed on to be sixth. It was a respectable enough effort, but a 22-length beating still rankled as an ignominious fate for a star with such a glittering legacy. He had gone from extra-terrestrial to also-ran. The magic was gone – or so we thought.

****

ENCOURAGED that Faugheen was at least running respectably again,

> 'That victory was something else. It just shows the horse has the heart and I don't know where he got that from'

Mullins decided his now ten-year-old deserved one more shot at redemption and pinned his hopes on the more leisurely nature of the three-mile Grade 1 at Punchestown.

The same tactic had failed to fire up Hurricane Fly in similar circumstances three years earlier, but this time it proved an inspired move. David Mullins pinched an inch on the field at the start, and from there his mount was able to dictate.

Penhill, fresh from his Stayers' Hurdle triumph at Cheltenham, threatened to challenge under Townend as they swung for home. It was a fleeting threat. Mullins had filled his mount's lungs and Faugheen surged clear, the vanquished old bruiser back with a stirring vengeance. Cue the Rocky music.

It was certainly a dramatic arc befitting the emotional rollercoaster of a rousing Hollywood sports biopic, and the man behind the lens deserved all the plaudits that came his way. Willie Mullins didn't write the script, but he directed the picture and got the best out of an ageing A-lister who had looked past it.

"That victory was something else," he said at Punchestown. "It just shows the horse has the heart and I don't know where he got that from. If he had finished down the field we probably would have said it was time to retire him, but it didn't happen."

It didn't, and it all made for a suitably epic climax to another blockbuster jumps campaign.

▼ Back in business: Faugheen puts his troubles behind him with a storming victory in the Ladbrokes Champion Stayers Hurdle at Punchestown

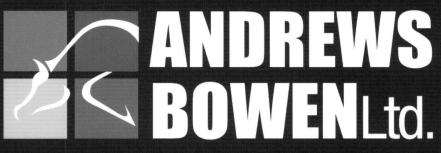

FULL BLOOM

Penhill's Stayers' Hurdle victory and Brighton's Premier League heroics gave owner Tony Bloom a spring double to savour

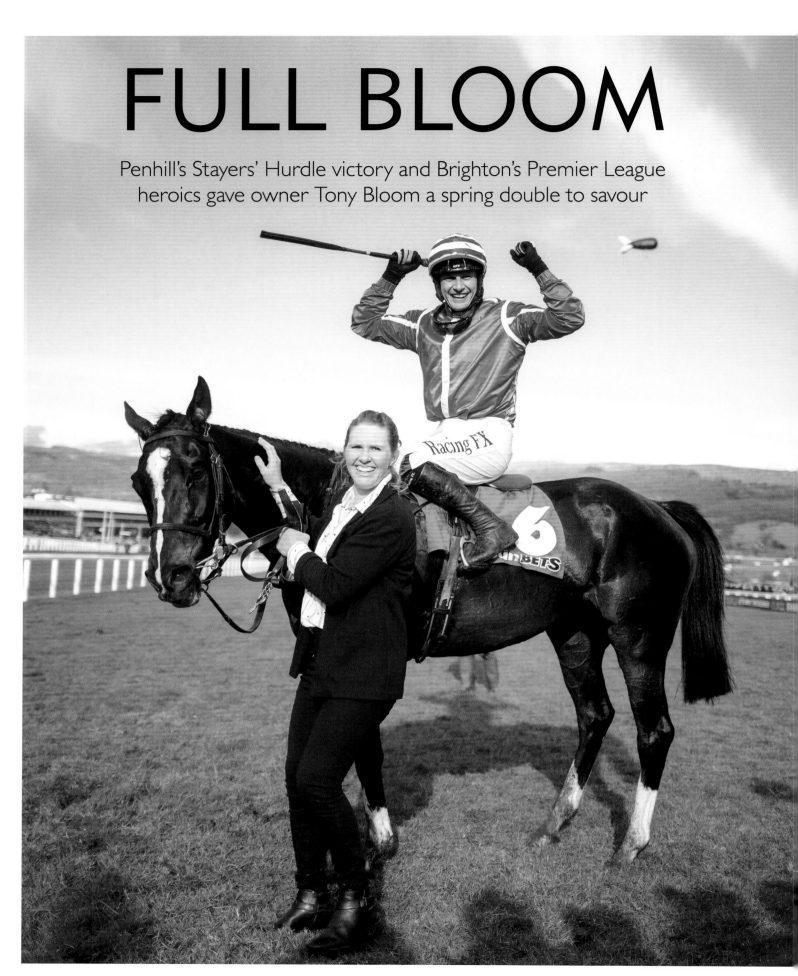

By Peter Thomas

TONY BLOOM has been called many things in his gambling career, but 'sentimental' is an epithet that rarely gets an outing. The man they call 'The Lizard' is famed for his gimlet-eyed expertise at the poker table and his data-driven success as a 'betting consultant' and high-staking punter, but every now and then the mask slips and he makes an investment that defies monetary logic and strays into the realms of the fanciful.

Who, for example, in the midst of a financial crisis and flying in the face of impartial banking advice, would buy a lowly League One football club like Brighton and Hove Albion and attempt to turn it into a going concern where before it was on the brink of extinction?

Set against such a speculative backdrop, the purchase of the 88-rated three-year-old Flat handicapper Penhill for 230,000gns at the Tattersalls Autumn Horses-in-Training sale in 2014 must have seemed a relatively risk-free venture, with no danger of incurring either financial ruin or the wrath of an army of Seagulls fans.

In the event, both ventures came good, with 2017-2018 being the season when Brighton, having moved to a new ground funded by Bloom, joined the Premier League and Penhill, having switched codes for a jumps career, landed the Sun Bets Stayers' Hurdle to complement his Albert Bartlett Novices' Hurdle success of the previous season.

From a relatively small holding – around a dozen horses and just one football club – Bloom has mustered considerable success at a high level, from the 2017 Cesarewitch win of the heavily backed Withhold to the same year's British Champions Sprint glory for Librisa Breeze. Penhill and 'the Albion' simply confirmed that the sports-loving owner has the Midas touch, even when he allows sentiment to cloud his judgement.

"Buying Brighton and Hove

‹ Bloomin' marvellous: owner Tony Bloom leads in Penhill after his Stayers' Hurdle success

Albion was certainly not a business decision," he confessed, recalling the days of his youth when he would make the short journey to the old Goldstone Ground to see the club of which his grandfather Harry was chairman. "I was faced with a very stark choice. Either I put my head above the parapet, financed the building of the new stadium and took over the football club; or we wouldn't be able to afford to build the stadium and the club would probably cease to exist.

"When I looked at it in those terms, it was a very easy decision for me to make. Some people ask if my heart ruled my head and was it an emotional rather than a business decision; the truth is I knew exactly what I was getting myself into, but if it wasn't for the emotion of Brighton being my lifelong football club, I wouldn't have considered it.

"In comparison to football, buying racehorses is a lot simpler. It's a pastime for me, and the primary objective is certainly not to make money. My best days on the racecourse are when I'm celebrating a winner, particularly a big-race winner, with family and

friends. It's like scoring a winning goal in football. You feel on top of the world."

Bloom's success in racing seems to revolve around a policy of surrounding himself with the best people and letting them do their job. Penhill, for example, having improved steadily during his Flat days as a four-year-old with Luca Cumani, was sent to Willie Mullins, for whom he won six times before injury struck and forced the trainer into arriving at Cheltenham in March after a 323-day absence.

For the master of Closutton and his staff it was a routine piece of genius to have the fragile seven-year-old ready to win a championship race off such a preparation. The son of Mount Nelson crept closer and closer from the back of the field under a stealthy Paul Townend – deputising for the injured Ruby Walsh – before hitting the front heading for the last hurdle and making light of his troubles to see off the potent challenge of Supasundae.

Bloom hailed the trainer's "magnificent effort" with a 12-1

shot whose career had looked in jeopardy; Mullins characteristically praised the painstaking work of Penhill's groom Holly Conte, who he said had "virtually trained him herself"; and whoever was responsible, it was a victory that took Mullins level with Nicky Henderson as the festival's all-time leading trainer.

"I never dreamed he'd win and I was surprised how fit he was," admitted Mullins. "I think Paul was blowing more than the horse, so that just shows what an engine he has. If I can keep him right, hopefully we can bring him back for a few more years."

Bloom – who eight weeks after the festival was celebrating Brighton's 15th-place finish that kept them in the Premier League – would no doubt be delighted to be at jumping's top table again in 2019, but he has other priorities, truth be told.

"Winning the FA Cup final would be amazing and, of course, I'd love to win the Derby," he said, "but if it came down to a straight choice, it's not even close. It would be Brighton and Hove Albion winning the Cup final every time."

IN THE LEAD

Penhill's victory put Willie Mullins level with Nicky Henderson at the top of the all-time Cheltenham Festival trainer standings and two races later the Irish champion moved into a clear lead when Laurina won the Grade 2 Trull House Stud Mares' Novices' Hurdle.

Mullins ended the 2018 festival on 61 winners with Henderson, who had led by four going into the meeting, on 60. Next in the list is Paul Nicholls with 43.

On reaching that milestone, Mullins said: "It's unbelievable. When you start training you hope for one winner here – that's the greatest aspiration most Irish trainers have. This isn't something we ever dreamed of because we thought we couldn't do that with a base in Ireland."

COMING OF AGE

James Bowen landed the Welsh National on his way to the British conditionals' title – and remarkably he was only three years older than his winning mount

By Lewis Porteous

ONE of them can look forward to a long and fulfilling career, whereas the other is nearing the end, yet on a bleak afternoon in January, when thermal underwear and woolly hats were the order of the day, the two combined for a heartwarming success in Wales's biggest horserace.

They may be at different ends of their working lives, yet just three years separated fresh-faced rider James Bowen, 16, and his experienced partner Raz De Maree, 13, as the duo lined up for a belated running of the Coral Welsh Grand National.

Traditionally the perfect cure for a Christmas hangover on December 27, the race was initially lost without trace at a waterlogged Chepstow but a break in the storm meant the annual staying slogfest came under starter's orders on the first Saturday of the new year with all the traditional fanfare and under-foot squelch to boot.

"The delay was annoying," says Bowen, who had been rerouted to Kempton for day two of its Christmas fare when Chepstow was initially called off. "I was declared on Raz De Maree first time around but there's always a bit of a worry you might lose the ride once it gets postponed. It was probably the best thing that could have happened, though, because there were certain horses who didn't get declared the second time and it worked out well in the end."

With top agent Dave Roberts in his corner, Bowen was safely booked for the new date, although at that stage the young rider had not spoken a word to trainer Gavin Cromwell and the first time they talked tactics was in a windswept paddock at Chepstow.

"I'm not really sure if connections were confident or not as I only saw them 20 minutes before the race," the rider recalls. "Gavin told me to let him warm into it as he doesn't travel the best in his races."

True to Cromwell's words, Raz De Maree had gone from front rank as the tapes went up to stone cold last by the time they approached the fourth obstacle and even at that early stage of the 3m5½f marathon, success looked unlikely as the 16-1 shot struggled to find any rhythm in the Monmouthshire mud.

"We ended up last and I had to sit and suffer," Bowen says. "He's not the quickest and we got left behind a little bit. But with a circuit to run he started to pick one or two off and started to enjoy himself."

At that stage Bowen's focus was on nothing more than completing the course but, after much pushing, shoving and navigation of the in-running mishaps up ahead, his expectations were on the rise turning for home.

"The race started to fall apart and coming to four out he started to run on again and was coming good. As he started to get to the leading group and pass a few of them his confidence was building and, when there was only one left to pass, he was always going to get there."

The last of 19 rivals Raz De Maree overcame was fellow 13-year-old Alfie Spinner, partnered by another rising star of the weighing room in Richard Patrick, with the veteran chasers showing the whippersnappers how to conquer Chepstow's war of attrition.

"You probably need a horse like him who is behind the bridle," Bowen says. "That way they're never doing too much and can last it out. He's a relaxed horse and a strong stayer."

Bowen, for whom this was a home win having been raised on racing at his family's yard in rural southwest Wales, became the youngest winning rider of the race in modern times, while Raz De Maree equalled the record of Snipe's Bridge, the only previous 13-year-old winner of the race in

1927, when it was still run at Cardiff.

"I wasn't expecting to win but it's a race I grew up watching and it was exceptional to do it – it was the best day of my career so far," says the now 17-year-old, whose memories of the immediate aftermath remain a blur, although he does recall that parents Peter and Karen were on hand to celebrate a groundbreaking success for the youngest of their three sons.

****

THERE are many reasons why Bowen's success in the Welsh National was extraordinary, yet remarkable achievements have been a common theme throughout the early days of his career, which had not even begun when Raz De Maree chased home Native River in the Welsh National the previous year. At that stage the teenage tyro still had no experience of riding under rules.

Looking back further still, Bowen was barely out of novice

status on horseback when Raz De Maree started his career in 2010 for Dessie Hughes, yet just eight years later he was leaving experienced riders like Barry Geraghty, Paddy Brennan and Tom Scudamore in his wake in one of the biggest jumps races.

"I'd obviously sat on a horse earlier but I was never hugely interested and didn't start riding properly until I was eight," he says. "But once I started I couldn't stop and it was great to be brought up in an environment where we could ride whenever we wanted. I was almost ten when I started pony racing, which was a good experience, and after that it was all about becoming a jockey."

Riding comes naturally to Bowen, although the same cannot be said for his patience, which was pushed to its limit as he counted down the days for his point-to-point licence to drop through the
▸▸ *Continues page 176*

▸ James Bowen and Raz De Maree head to victory in the Welsh Grand National

letterbox on his 16th birthday, not helped by the fact older brother Sean had already landed the conditional jockeys' title he craved.

"I was getting itchy feet watching Sean win the conditional championship and I wanted to be there straight away but it's nice now to have my brother in the weighing room and I look up to him," he says.

In his first three months of being eligible to ride in points, James notched an unprecedented 30 winners, including a double on his 16th birthday.

His first winner under rules came on May 27, 2017 aboard Curious Carlos at Cartmel, while July 5 at Worcester was the day Get Home Now gave him a first winner as a conditional rider. By the end of the 2017-18 season he had racked up a phenomenal 58 winners to follow in Sean's footsteps, not to mention those of Sir Anthony McCoy, Richard Johnson, Mick Fitzgerald and Aidan Coleman among others, as he lifted the conditionals' title by a wide margin.

"The season was incredible and I couldn't have done it without the support of my parents, Mr Henderson and all the trainers who have supported me," says Bowen, who dreams big without letting his feet off the ground.

Along with his National win, the Welsh wizard scooped Listed prizes on William Henry and Thomas Campbell in his first season, as well as a Grade 3 hurdle at Ascot in January aboard Jenkins. All three of those wins

were for his boss, champion trainer Nicky Henderson, who has not been scared to throw the youngster in at the deep end.

His big-race victors also include Exitas, Limited Reserve and Rons Dream, while he came close to opening his Cheltenham Festival account at the first attempt in March when a neck second on Shantou Flyer in the Ultima Handicap Chase.

New riding sensations come and go but Bowen has been relentless from the off, shedding his claim before the middle of June and, considering his drive, ambition and undoubted talent, little imagination is required to picture him as a future champion jockey.

"He's very focused and really believes in himself," says dad Peter, no stranger to big-race success himself and perhaps best qualified to explain what sets his son apart.

"I remember the first pony race he rode in when he was little – he finished third and was devastated. He's always been very competitive and

▲ Band of brothers: the Bowen sons (from left, Mickey, Sean and James) steaming up the gallops at dad Peter's stables in November 2011

▼ Six and a half years later the youngest of the trio would be crowned champion conditional rider in a season that saw him win the Welsh National on Raz De Maree (9, below, trailing the field on the first circuit)

won't give in to anything. He trains hard as well and he knows the form, not just of his horse but every other horse in the race as well, so he deserves it. He looks top class, doesn't he?"

Despite shedding the safety blanket of his conditional rider's allowance so soon in his career, there has been no let-up since Bowen joined the professional ranks and, like Jack Kennedy and Harry Cobden, there is no apparent ceiling to what the latest addition to an exceptional crop of young riders on both sides of the Irish Sea might achieve.

"This is what I dreamed about, I really enjoy it and really appreciate the position I'm in," says the teenager, before casting an eye to the future. "Being champion jockey is definitely my ambition but it's the number one target for a lot of people and I'm a long way off it, but hopefully one day I'll be there."

That day might not be as far off as he thinks. After all, he did win the Welsh National at his first attempt.

IN THE PICTURE

Gold Cup winner Thornton calls time after 28 years

ANDREW THORNTON, the senior jump jockey in the British weighing room, was given a rousing sendoff at Uttoxeter on June 6 having ridden a winner on his final day in the saddle after a 28-year career.

Thornton, 45, announced only two days earlier that Uttoxeter would be his last meeting and, while he could not win the rapidly renamed Andrew Thornton Congratulations On Your Retirement Handicap Hurdle, he was successful on evens favourite Amirr – trained by his great friend Seamus Mullins – in a two-mile maiden hurdle. It was the 1,007th winner of a career that began in 1990 and, as he hung up his saddle, he ranked eighth on the winners list among current jump jockeys and 22nd among jump jockeys to have ridden 1,000 winners in Britain and Ireland.

"If you'd sat down for a year, you couldn't have planned it any better," said an emotional Thornton, who was given the traditional drenching after his final ride. "The main thing for me is that all the lads are here. My wife Yvonne and son Harry are here and my parents are here." In all, 50 of his nearest and dearest gathered to witness his last day in the saddle.

With almost 10,000 career rides, the County Durham-born jockey inevitably compiled a long list of injuries but he was always determined to choose his own moment to stop, having long prepared for a second career as a racing pundit.

"In those long periods when I was injured I always said nobody was going to tell me when I was going to do it, and that it was important to me to do it on my own terms," he said. "I'm lucky that I've been able to edge my way out of the riding side towards media work, because I know how difficult it is for those who have gone from riding flat out to stopping completely."

The highpoint of Thornton's career was Cool Dawn's 25-1 success in the 1998 Cheltenham Gold Cup for Robert Alner, who also gave him a Welsh Grand National winner with Miko De Beauchene in 2007. Other big-race victories included the 1997 King George VI Chase on See More Business and the 2001 Scottish Grand National and 2002 Hennessy Cognac Gold Cup on Gingembre.

Another treasured moment was his 1,000th jumps victory on Kentford Myth at Wincanton on Boxing Day 2016. He admitted reaching that milestone had been an important incentive in prolonging his career well into his 40s but added: "I didn't retire after my 1,000th winner because I didn't want to turn the best day of my life into the worst. But I've eked it out for as long as I dared."

Picture: **EDWARD WHITAKER** (RACINGPOST.COM/PHOTOS)

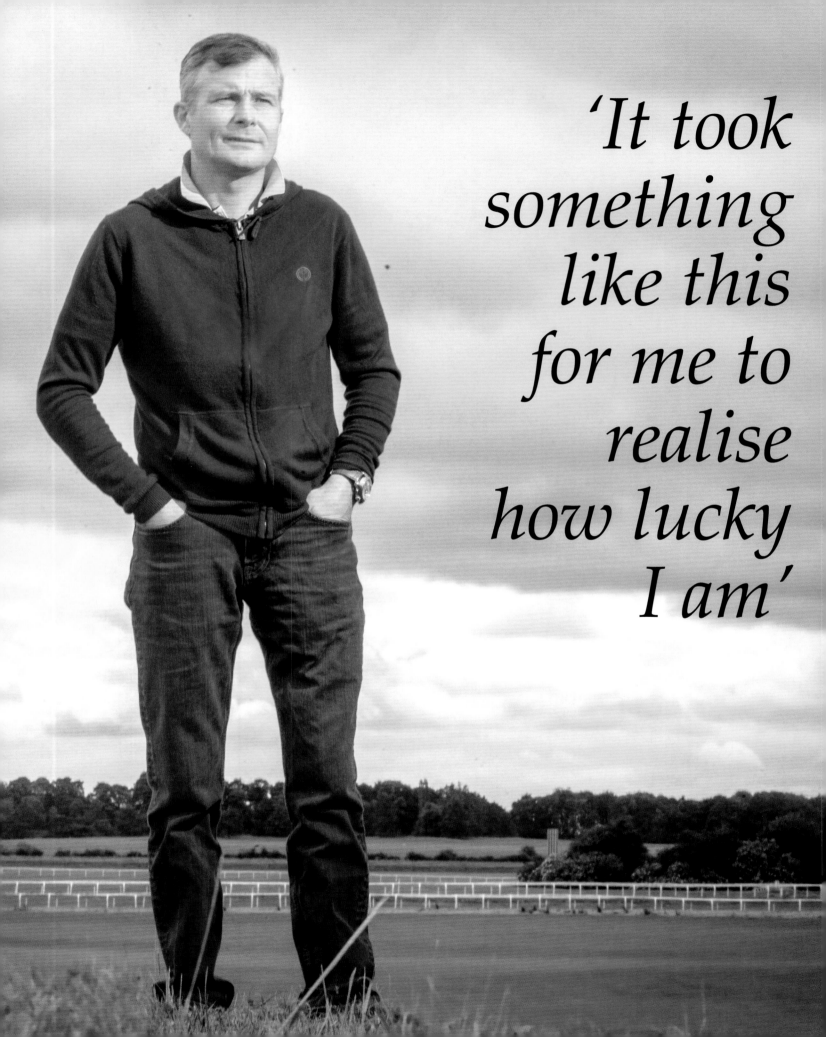

'It took something like this for me to realise how lucky I am'

Pat Smullen's fight with cancer cast a shadow over the Irish Flat season. In this Racing Post interview in July, the nine-time champion jockey spoke openly about his illness

By Richard Forristal

ON THE Sunday of Irish Guineas weekend, Pat Smullen decamped to the Curragh. You could say it was the first time he'd been there. The nine-time champion jockey Pat Smullen had graced the grand old plains countless times over the previous 25 years en route to plundering nine Irish Classics, but the guy who stepped through the makeshift entrance at headquarters on May 27 wasn't the same man.

He was liberated. There was a lightness of being and a relaxed air to Smullen as he mingled at his leisure, sporting an easy smile as people gravitated towards him to wish him well. Every approach was gratefully received, including two television interviews in which his new-found lack of inhibition resonated stirringly. Smullen lit up the place.

In the preceding two months, life had come to mean something very different to the 41-year-old son of a County Offaly farm labourer whose ferocious ambition took him to the summit of his sport aboard Dermot Weld's Harzand at Epsom in 2016.

On March 23, he was diagnosed with pancreatic cancer when a malignant tumour was finally identified as the source of the back and chest pain that had escalated over a period of months. Smullen's view of the world would never be the same again. In that moment, his mind was concentrated on what he had. Not what he wanted.

"I'm surprising myself and everyone belonging to me," he says of his response to such shuddering adversity, something that even his wife, the Classic-winning trainer Frances Crowley, didn't foresee. "Frances only recently said to me she was very concerned about me not being able to ride, and how I'd take it all, because I was very driven to succeed. But I think that's how you need to be to get on.

"People say you can be relaxed or laid back, but personally I don't think so. Deep down all the very top riders are driven and have that bit of madness, or whatever you want to call it. You have to have that. I did it for years, probably to the extent that I was taking my own family for granted, and everything in life for that matter."

When his diagnosis was confirmed that inauspicious Friday afternoon, two days before the start of the Flat season, he made a determination to stay strong. "From the previous few days, when I just wanted to get whatever it was done and dealt with so I could ride on the Sunday, my mindset literally changed there and then," Smullen reflects of that initial spell in the Beacon Hospital.

"I know it's hard to believe, but on the Saturday morning when I woke up on my own, lying in bed, it just dawned on me. From that day until now, my mindset changed, and thankfully it did, because it's the only way I could deal with this.

"If I was watching racing every day pining after it, it wouldn't help my recovery or be good for me mentally. Of course I miss it, but I had to make a conscious decision to put racing on hold for now and, to be honest, I'm enjoying watching it all from the other side.

It would be wasted energy if I was looking through my fingers watching a race, thinking I would love to be riding that horse. This is something I need to put all my energy in to fight.

"As I say, it's a shock to everyone, including myself, that I'm coping as well as I am, and Frances thought it might even be adrenaline or a high of some sort that I would come down off. I have had days where I felt a bit sorry for myself, but that was only ever for a few hours. I've given myself a kick up the arse and shaken it off."

****

HITHERTO, Smullen lived his life by the quasi-scientific method of hard work reaping rewards, values that still underpin everything he does. It doesn't sound like he has become especially spiritual all of a sudden, but he is a walking, talking epitome of the power of a positive attitude.

"I would have been sceptical of that kind of thing before," he concedes as he sips on a glass of water at the TRI Equestrian café on the Curragh. "I thought you got on and did what you had to do to make things happen, but now I realise the mind is a very strong – and fragile – thing. You have to be positive. I have a wonderful medical team looking after me, but you have to bring a strong mental approach as well and that's what I'm trying to do."

If that was Smullen's private pledge, his public response has been similarly emphatic. A few days after the cancer was identified, he contacted Tony O'Hehir to get the message out there and convey that he would not be riding for the foreseeable future.

"I wanted to get it out there from the word go, that's why I contacted the Racing Post," he says. "I was hearing stories, that it was dreadful news, and I wanted to put a stop to that. I wanted to get it out there for my family that there was nothing to be hidden.

"This is something that unfortunately has darkened many people's doors, and it's nothing to be embarrassed about. Getting it out there was the best thing I ever did, because the goodwill and good wishes and support flowed in that minute from around the world.

"The support has been brilliant, and it just proves the great industry we work in. We all started with horses because we love them, and then it becomes a business, and you lose sight of what you got into the business for. That affinity, it unites the whole industry and I can see that now.

"Frances and I come from very level-headed families. I'm from a working-class family and we know what hard work is. I had the conversation with two of my brothers the day after the diagnosis and I said, 'You either lie down and give up, or get up and give it everything'.

"It doesn't matter who you are, and that is something that is very clear in my mind. Being a nine-time champion jockey means nothing now. Humbling isn't the right word probably, but it makes you realise that everyone is equal."

Is he aware of how much his buoyancy has reverberated with

▸▸ *Continues page 182*

people? "I suppose, but people who have gotten through this have got in touch with me and they have given me inspiration, so it works both ways. That has been unbelievable. Please God, when I do get through this, and am back healthy and well, I will be able to help people in a similar position, or even if someone wanted to ring me now they could. I have no issues speaking about it."

****

ON the day of the Irish 2,000 Guineas, Smullen attended his youngest daughter Sarah's first holy communion ceremony. He and Frances have two older kids, Hannah and Paddy, both of whose equivalent celebrations he missed.

From his current perspective, he savours the way in which his eyes have been opened to the joys of such family occasions, although he recognises that we all find a level at which we are comfortable doing what we do.

Smullen operated in an elite echelon where the demands were considerable and few ever get off the wheel when it's in motion. He is philosophical now as opposed to revisionist.

"It wouldn't have even been because it was Guineas weekend," he muses of his absences from his first two children's landmark ceremonies. "You have a job and Dermot has runners, so you just go and ride them. Nothing stopped me. I missed my brothers' weddings, communions, confirmations – all because I wanted to ride horses. When you're riding for an operation like Dermot's, you have to be 100 per cent committed and that's what I was. Yes, I was doing it for my family, but I was doing it for myself as well.

"The kids were growing up and thankfully I have a wife who was born into the business who understood how you had to be, but I don't think you have to be as bad as I was. Maybe that's the price you pay to survive and succeed, but there's a silver lining to everything and it's only now I realise how lucky I am to have it all.

"I loved every day of race-riding but it took something like this for me to stand back and see what life is all about. I have no regrets and I don't mean to sound like I'm contradicting

myself, but I'm a different person now to the one I was in March. I've done a complete 180-degree turn.

"Up to then, I wanted to ride in every race, every day. It's an embarrassing thing to say now but riding winners was all that mattered. There is more to life than I thought. When you're faced with something like this, it gives you complete clarity in your mind. I'm 41 years of age with three young kids, a great wife and plenty to look forward to. Lying down isn't an option."

Smullen has completed the first phase of his treatment, comprising six rounds of chemotherapy at fortnightly intervals. "Tough going," he says of that gruelling process. The ultimate objective is to have the tumour reduced to the point that he can undergo surgery, and to look at him you wouldn't think he is a man with a health problem.

He says his hair is getting thin, but to the naked eye it looks a fine thatch, and his weight and complexion are probably better than when he was starving himself for a living. There is the inevitable sickness and nausea that comes with chemo, but he is living as

▲ Changed man: Pat Smullen says his illness has given him a different perspective on life

cleanly as possible, not a drop of caffeine or alcohol passing his lips since his diagnosis.

Their stud farm in Rhodes is proving suitably therapeutic, and some mornings are spent on the Curragh watching the Weld string at work. He even rode out for the first time since March last Friday week, Leigh Roche's snap of a beaming Smullen sending Twitter into a din of glee.

"I have possibly never felt as well in my life," Smullen ponders. "It's extremely tough going, but my fitness and my age are a help, and Frances has been a rock. I know that's a cliche, but she's a tough woman – I couldn't do this without her.

"We try to keep things as normal as we can and just get on with it. That's another reason why it's important to stay positive. Even on my bad days, I still push myself to get up and get out. I don't want my kids seeing me lying on the couch or in bed, thinking, 'Oh, Dad is sick', so I push myself to get up. That's what you have to do and that's the type of person I am and the type of person Frances is too. Just get up and get on with it."

He can't do any more than that, and he wouldn't know how to do any less. A champion in the purest sense of the word.

This is an edited version of an article that appeared in the Racing Post on July 1

'Even on my bad days, I still push myself to get up and get on with it. That's the type of person I am'

Proud to promote the responsible use of horses in sport

Advisor on horse welfare to the British Horseracing Authority and International Equestrian Federation (FEI).

WorldHorseWelfare

Could you rehome from World Horse Welfare?

SPC Holdings

9

www.worldhorsewelfare.org/rehoming
Registered charity no: 206658 and SC038384

WorldHorseWelfare

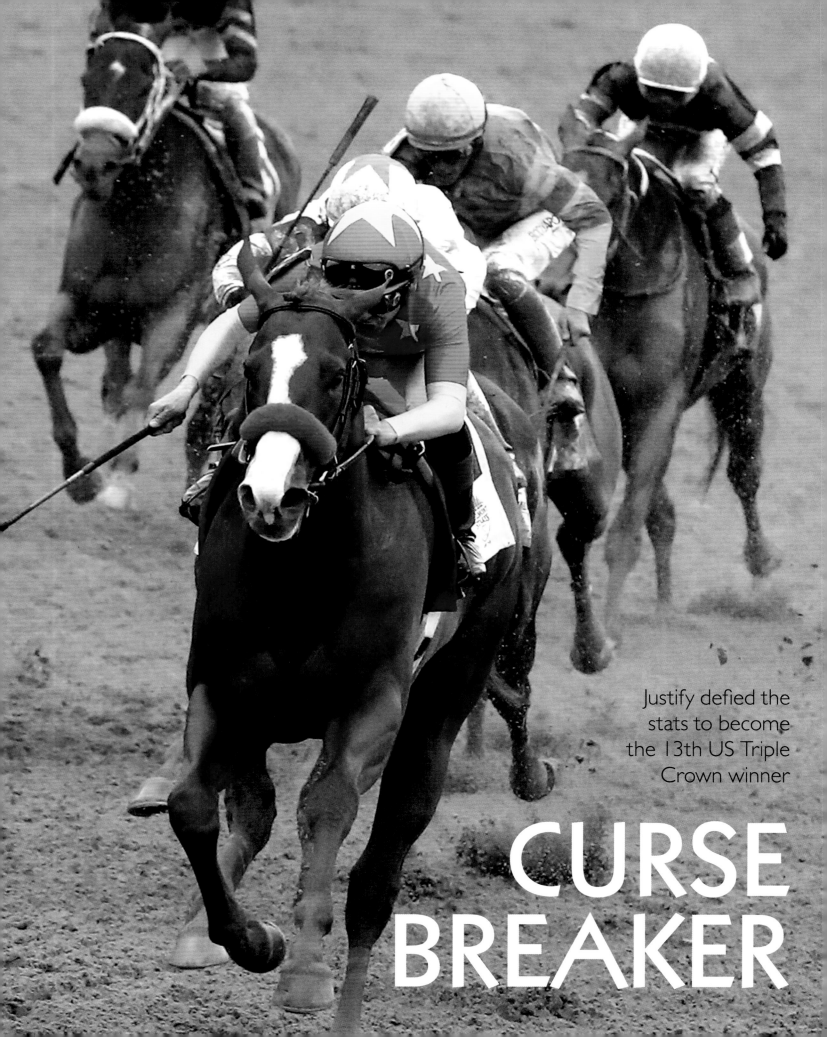

Justify defied the stats to become the 13th US Triple Crown winner

CURSE BREAKER

By Tom Kerr

WHEN Justify ran pillar-to-post to win the 150th Belmont Stakes and become the 13th US Triple Crown winner, it was not just the setting sun that cast long shadows over the venerable New York racecourse. It was impossible to reflect on the chestnut colt's achievement without invoking American Pharoah, whose triumph on the same dirt just three years previously had lifted a Triple Crown curse that stood for almost four decades.

The 37-year wait for a 12th Triple Crown champion that followed Affirmed's win in 1978 had come to obsess American racing, which viewed the annual five-week circus spanning the Kentucky Derby, the Preakness Stakes and the Belmont with a mixture of hope, longing and desperation. Some began to believe there would never be a 12th, while the inability to produce a hero on the one occasion the American public paid serious attention to racing seemed almost a form of impotency, a reflection of a sport whose glorious heyday belonged, like the Triple Crown winners, to a sepia-tinged past.

So American Pharoah was not just a champion, he was a release. Four decades of hurt and hope came pouring out when he flashed past the line a winner at Belmont, the delirious crowd crying and screaming, a nation watching transfixed. Justify, whose own Triple Crown triumph followed so soon after, could never recapture the aftermath of 2015. Through no fault of his own, his victory was overshadowed by proximity to an exquisite moment of unique sporting history.

Yet every Triple Crown winner gains their chapter in history and Justify more than earned his. He may not have ended a desperate

▲ Fully justified: Mike Smith celebrates his Belmont Stakes win on Justify

wait for greatness like American Pharoah or redefined greatness like Secretariat, but he became just the 13th colt to make the mad, gruelling march from Kentucky to New York undefeated. That alone would earn him immortality, but unusually what made Justify a fascinating addition to the Triple Crown pantheon was not necessarily what he did, but what he didn't.

****

TO UNDERSTAND that we must go back to

his debut on the track, the moment the world got its first glimpse of a champion in the making. For every Triple Crown winner in history that came several months before they lined up beneath the famous twin spires of Churchill Downs for the Kentucky Derby; from Sir Barton in 1919 through to American Pharoah in 2015, all of the Triple Crown winners made their debut at two.

Justify, by contrast, did not make his competitive debut until February 18, 2018, when the big, muscular chestnut colt appeared at Santa Anita for trainer Bob Baffert, the same man who handled American Pharoah. Under 23-year-old jockey Drayden Van Dyke, the 1-2 favourite produced an explosive performance, blitzing
▸▸ *Continues page 186*

more than nine lengths clear down the straight despite getting embroiled in an early duel for the lead.

It was enough to make track-watchers take notice and for Van Dyke to be replaced with the safer hands of 52-year-old Mike Smith, the near-ageless riding marvel who had teamed up with the silver-haired Baffert during Arrogate's stunning five-month romp through several of the world's richest races in 2016-17.

With less than three months until the Kentucky Derby, Baffert knew he had to turbocharge Justify's season. A few weeks after his debut he found him an easy allowance race, then a month before the Classic pitched the swaggering colt into the Grade 1 Santa Anita Derby: Justify tore up, thundering home a three-length winner from his main challenger, Bolt D'Oro.

It was a perfect Kentucky Derby preparation but doubts persisted about his suitability for Churchill Downs, not least since no horse that went unraced as a juvenile had won the Derby in 136 years. The so-called 'Curse of Apollo' – named after the 1882 winner, the last greenhorn to land the Classic – was one of the longest-running streaks in sport, accounting for dozens of contenders over the years, but all that history didn't stop Justify going off 29-10 favourite.

At Churchill Downs, on a drenched track officially described as sloppy, Justify powered through the mud, his long, powerful stride making short work of the conditions and his rivals. It was a fifth Derby for Baffert, placing him second in the all-time trainers' list, and in his eyes his finest yet. "I was just in awe of the performance," he said. "That's the best Kentucky Derby-winning performance that I've brought up here. He just put himself up there with the greats."

****

JUST two weeks later the Triple Crown circus rolled into Pimlico, a battered racecourse in a tired corner of north Baltimore, for the Preakness Stakes. Again, the weather was little short of diabolical. For four days before the race the rain had hammered the old track, turning the

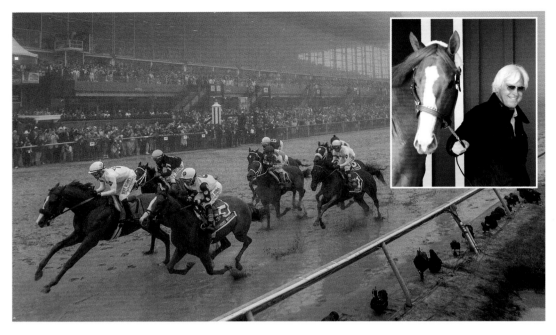

surface into a sucking slop, and as the big race approached a thick grey mist fell over the racecourse, obscuring much of the oval from the grandstand.

In the Preakness, Justify again used his opening burst to power to the front but as the field swung round the bend and into the rear straight they disappeared from the grandstand's view, swallowed by the fog, and the watching thousands could only hold their breath and hope. When the field reappeared like ghosts they did so with Justify narrowly at their head and he held off the closer Bravazo down the sopping stretch for a hard-fought half-length victory.

There was little of his previous wins' irresistible dominance about it, but after the disorientating, uncertain blindness of the fog, and the stamina-sapping misery of the rain and mud, there was just relief that he had won at all. It was not a commanding performance this time but a courageous one, and perhaps that mattered more.

Then on to Belmont, hope tempered by the knowledge that so many had fallen at the final hurdle, expectation lifted by the fact Baffert seemed to be developing a unique ability to defy racing's many curses. Between him and glory: the mile and a half of the Belmont Stakes, the longest of the three races, and nine rivals, more than any other Triple Crown winner had faced in the final

TRIPLE CROWN WINNERS

1919 **Sir Barton**
1930 **Gallant Fox**
1935 **Omaha**
1937 **War Admiral**
1941 **Whirlaway**
1943 **Count Fleet**
1946 **Assault**
1948 **Citation**
1973 **Secretariat**
1977 **Seattle Slew**
1978 **Affirmed**
2015 **American Pharoah**
2018 **Justify**

▲ Muddy marvel: Justify lands the Preakness Stakes and (inset) with trainer Bob Baffert after arriving at Pimlico; below, winning the Kentucky Derby at Churchill Downs

reckoning. Justify was the best horse in the race, no doubt, but would he be undone by fatigue following his demanding schedule?

Breaking from the inside draw (from which the last winner was Secretariat, 45 years before) Justify roared to the lead. Down the back and into the far turn he led, those muscular limbs powering him almost effortlessly over the dirt. Then in the stretch Smith squeezed, quickly opening up a near two-length lead he would not relinquish. Chased in vain by dirt-covered rivals, Justify breezed home, his white blaze and copper coat as spotless as if he had just come out of his barn.

It was to be the 13th Triple Crown winner's last race. A month later, connections announced a minor injury had ended Justify's career. In total, his undefeated six-race career spanned just 112 days, a furious, frenetic and fabulous campaign the like of which had never been seen in US racing. "He just came on there and broke every curse there was," Baffert said. "It was meant to be."

IN THE
PICTURE

Thunder Snow storms to scintillating victory in Dubai World Cup

WHEN Thunder Snow is good, he's very good. But when he's bad, he's no Mae West – he's terrible.

The talented but temperamental Godolphin four-year-old has shown both aspects of his character on some of the world's biggest racedays and it was his very good side that came out on Dubai World Cup night at Meydan as he scorched to victory in the $10m showpiece race in track-record time.

Thunder Snow had seemed compromised by an outside draw but jockey Christophe Soumillon manoeuvred him into a front-running position and there was no stopping the 8-1 shot as he came home five and three-quarter lengths clear of red-hot favourite West Coast.

This victory was the best of Thunder Snow's career, with a Racing Post Rating of 123, and was in stark contrast to his performance in the 2017 Kentucky Derby, when he put in a mini-bucking bronco routine and had to be pulled up soon after leaving the stalls, and his last of 15 in the Queen Elizabeth II Stakes at Ascot on his final start that season.

Soumillon was ecstatic after his first victory in the Dubai World Cup. "I can't quite believe I've just won this amazing race. I was screaming and crying watching horses like Cigar and jockeys such as Jerry Bailey and Frankie Dettori winning this race, so for me to do it is incredible," he said.

No jockey knows Thunder Snow as well as Soumillon, who was riding him for the 12th time in 18 starts on World Cup night. "He's a funny horse – he's very talented but when he doesn't want to do something there's nothing you can do about it," he admitted.

But on this occasion the jockey was able to get the best out of his mount. "I never thought I'd be able to make the running from that draw but it couldn't have gone any better," Soumillon said. "The track really suits front-runners but, even still, he's a true champion. He proved it as a two-year-old, a three-year-old and now today he was amazing."

Thunder Snow's scintillating success was a seventh victory in the race for Godolphin with six of those winners trained by Bin Suroor, who has enjoyed eight in all including Dubai Millennium and Street Cry. "This horse is brilliant," the trainer said. "Christophe rode a great race. We spoke beforehand about what to do from the outside draw and he rode him to perfection."

As for West Coast's jockey, Javier Castellano, he looked down at trainer Bob Baffert after the race, shook his head and said: "The other one [Thunder Snow] – the other one was too good."

Picture: **EDWARD WHITAKER (RACINGPOST.COM/PHOTOS)**

Joanna Mason, part of the Easterby clan, is making her mark in Arabian racing

FAMILY VALUES

By Kitty Trice

THE Easterby family has a rich heritage at all levels of racing, from famous festival triumphs at Cheltenham to big-race glory on the Flat, and right down to the grassroots of the sport. They are a strong force in point-to-pointing and amateur riding, and now even in Arabian racing through the exploits of Joanna Mason.

The 28-year-old granddaughter of legendary trainer Mick Easterby has established herself as one of Britain's leading amateur jockeys. She shared the lady riders' championship with Serena Brotherton in 2015 and more recently has won the prestigious

Ladies' Derby at Epsom twice and the Queen Mother's Cup at York on Tapis Libre, trained by her cousin Jacqueline Coward.

Mason has added another string to her bow with her developing prowess in Arabian racing. She was the leading female jockey for the third year in a row in 2018 and relishes the challenge of riding Arabians.

"They're renowned for being quite quirky but I like that as it makes them more of a tactical ride. You have to coax them along and use patience rather than strength and force," says Mason, who has formed a strong association with the Newmarket yard of James Owen, one of the top trainers in the sport.

Owen trains for Sheikh Hamdan Al Maktoum, a leading patron of Arabian racing, and two runners in the famous blue and white colours have particularly caught Mason's eye. "Al Kaaser and Farhaa are two very nice Arabians I've had the chance to ride and they're destined for better races," she says.

"I've been lucky enough to enjoy another good season. To finish fourth in the [overall] championship against the boys has been fantastic. This is the third year [winning the ladies' title], so it's an amazing achievement and I'm very grateful to James Owen's team."

Mason also pays tribute to the Arabian Racing Organisation, the sport's governing body. "The ARO are so good at giving amateur jockeys more opportunities and a chance to race ride. There are a lot of full cards for us to ride in, so we can have up to seven rides in a day. They are also very good at getting the younger people into racing as a step up from pony racing to riding under rules."

There is another important element that makes Arabian racing attractive to Mason. "Under the ARO we can ride against the professionals," she says. "I've been given the opportunity to ride in a couple of Group 1s at Goodwood and Sandown, and it's a good feeling to compete against the top jockeys."

Arabian races have become an established part of major

◀ Clockwise from left: Joanna Mason and Mazyoonah; Vindetta and James Harding win at Chelmsford; Joudh and Olivier Peslier take the Group 1 Shadwell Arabian Stallions Hatta International Stakes; Peslier in the winner's enclosure again at Newbury's big meeting after riding Nafees to victory in the Group 1 Shadwell Dubai International Stakes

thoroughbred racedays, with many top jockeys taking part. The Group 1 Arabian race at Goodwood on Sussex Stakes day was won by Jim Crowley, Sheikh Hamdan's retained rider, and the Group 1 on St Leger day at Doncaster went to Christophe Soumillon.

On the all-Arabian raceday held at Newbury in late July, one of the sport's biggest events, Olivier Peslier was the star with a four-timer, including all three Group 1 contests.

Mason took her own chance to shine on another all-Arabian card at Chelmsford in August, winning the Group 1 UK Arabian Derby Handicap on the Owen-trained My Boy Sam. This was another of the most important days in the calendar, featuring the Wathba Stallions Handicap won by James

Harding on Vindetta for trainer Adam Newey.

The Wathba Stallions race was part of the HH Sheikh Mansoor Bin Zayed Al Nahyan Global Arabian Horse Flat Racing Festival, which travels the globe throughout the year before concluding with a hugely valuable finals night at Abu Dhabi in November.

As well as being a showcase for the best Arabian horses, the festival also offers valuable opportunities to riders with the HH Sheikha Fatima Bint Mubarak Ladies World Championship and HH Sheikha Fatima Bint Apprentice World Championships.

The ladies' races were a gateway into the sport for Mason. "I got the opportunity to ride in the Sheikha Fatima series, which puts on races all over the world. I rode

in Texas and just got beaten a short head," she says. Her link with the Owen stable then came about as a result of a conversation with Sarah Oliver, chief executive of the Amateur Jockeys Association, about her desire to get more involved in Arabian racing.

Mason is always looking for more opportunities and a winter break is the last thing on her mind as she focuses her attention on riding out for Godolphin in Dubai. "This will be my second winter working for Charlie Appleby – there's no time for rest."

She will be back on the Arabian circuit next year too and shooting for the top. In true Easterby spirit, she says: "I don't think a girl has won the overall championship before and I'll be aiming to beat the men next year."

Our selection of the horses and people
– some established, some up-and-coming –
who are likely to be making headlines in 2019

ANNUAL
20

TOO DARN HOT

THE Group 1 Dewhurst Stakes was billed as one of the best editions in years and, while only time will tell us the strength of the form, Too Darn Hot could hardly have been more eyecatching in winning by two and three-quarter lengths.

The even-money Dewhurst favourite was getting close to the same odds for the 2,000 Guineas next May after his remarkable victory under Frankie Dettori. Keen early in the seven-furlong contest, he looked in trouble when he hit a flat spot in the Dip but roared clear up the rising ground.

He was simply too darn fast for Group 1 winner Advertise and Anthony Van Dyck, runner-up to Quorto in the Group 1 National Stakes, and earned a Racing Post Rating of 126, equalling Frankel's mark when he won the Dewhurst in 2010.

"He was getting knocked about a bit and was running in snatches and then, like he does, the turbo kicks in and away he goes," Dettori said. "He's an amazing horse and in the end I was able to ease him down. He's among the best two-year-olds I've ridden."

That was the fourth straight win for the unbeaten colt, trained by John Gosden for owner-breeders Lord and Lady Lloyd-Webber. He worked his way up from maiden to Group 3, Group 2 and finally Group 1 level, with his smallest margin of victory being one and three-quarter lengths in the Champagne Stakes at Doncaster.

The Guineas looks the obvious next step for the son of Dubawi even though he is bred to stay – his dam is Yorkshire Oaks and Dubai Sheema Classic winner Dar Re Mi and his year-older sister, Lah Ti Dar, landed the 1m4f Galtres Stakes impressively before finishing second in the St Leger.

"He's blessed with an awful lot of speed and it would be lovely to come back for the Guineas," Gosden said. "His mother got a mile and a half and his father was a phenomenal miler and, at this stage, he seems to be taking more after his father."

If he takes after either of his parents, he will be pretty good. If he takes after both, he might be exceptional.

JASON WATSON

WITH just two winners on the board in 2017, few would have anticipated Jason Watson's rapid ascent up the riding ranks in the last 12 months. He reached a century in 2018 by British Champions Day, when he took the apprentice title by an emphatic margin from Rossa Ryan.

Watson, 18, became the latest champion apprentice to emerge from the Andrew Balding stable but even he was pinching himself at his spectacular progress. "It's just been insane," he said. "I can't believe how well everything has gone and, although I've enjoyed a bit of luck along the way, I've put in a lot of hard work, which has been rewarded."

The highlight was his last-gasp Stewards' Cup victory at Glorious Goodwood on Gifted Master for Hugo Palmer, which saw his claim reduced to 3lb. His claim was completely gone by the end of the season but Watson is not worried about competing with the big boys on level terms.

"Losing the claim is of little concern to me," he said. "I have the right people around me and a very good agent in Tony Hind. I want to be champion jockey next year."

With continued support from Balding, and with Saeed Bin Suroor and Charlie Hills among the other top trainers supplying rides, Watson could well follow in the footsteps of William Buick and Oisin Murphy, former champion apprentices out of the Balding stable who took their careers to new heights in 2018.

KHAADEM

CHARLIE HILLS was quick to catch on to the Commonwealth Cup, winning the inaugural running in 2015 with Muhaarar, and he might have another strong candidate in Khaadem.

Muhaarar's Royal Ascot success was the first of four Group 1 wins that propelled him to the champion sprinter title and, while it would be a huge stretch to suggest Khaadem can reach the same level in his three-year-old campaign, Hills's latest sprint prospect in the Sheikh Hamdan Al Maktoum colours has shown plenty of promise.

After a distant third to subsequent Coventry winner Calyx on his debut at Newmarket in June, Khaadem returned to the July course ten weeks later for a clear-cut novice victory and improved again to win a six-furlong conditions race at the Doncaster St Leger meeting.

Reportedly he had worked impressively in preparation for an intended tilt at the Group 1 Middle Park Stakes before being ruled out by a minor setback and put away for the winter.

"He got cast in his box and it looks like he's pulled a muscle, but it's nothing major and has just come at the wrong time," Hills said. "He's a nice horse and we just need to make sure he's okay. There's definitely a lot to look forward to next year."

Hills has shown his skill with top sprinters, having also trained Battaash for Sheikh Hamdan, and Khaadem could not be in better hands.

KALASHNIKOV

AMY MURPHY featured in this list two years ago after becoming Britain's youngest trainer and she has justified her inclusion by making significant strides. The biggest came in the 2017-18 jumps season when Kalashnikov ran away with the Betfair Hurdle by four and a half lengths and then was agonisingly denied by Summerville Boy in the Supreme Novices' Hurdle.

Those were huge performances by a five-year-old whose frame suggests he will be much better over fences and he looks set to keep Murphy, 26, in the spotlight as he tackles his novice chasing season.

Although Kalashnikov is bred to be suited by further than two miles, he had an impressive cruising speed over hurdles and the Newmarket trainer sees no reason to move him up in trip, with the ultimate target being the Racing Post Arkle back at the Cheltenham Festival in March. If the ground is quicker there than last season, all the better.

"He's a lovely-actioned horse and all his family were better on good ground," Murphy said. "He hasn't really had it yet, but he's shown his toughness by slogging through heavy ground. Hopefully he'll show a turn of foot you haven't seen yet when he gets good ground.

"He's bred to be a chaser, he's a huge horse and I think it'll play to his strengths. The Racing Post Arkle is the dream."

With Kalashnikov, Murphy has every right to dream big.

HARRY COBDEN

STILL only 19, Harry Cobden has had a meteoric rise from champion conditional in 2016-17 to a successful first season in the senior ranks that included a Cheltenham Festival winner and now he tackles the 2018-19 season as the new number-one jockey for Paul Nicholls.

Cobden won the Grade 1 Tingle Creek Chase on Politologue for Nicholls last December but now he will have his temperament and talent tested in the glare of the TV spotlight every Saturday and at the big festivals, having stepped into the role vacated by Sam Twiston-Davies in May.

"I definitely feel I can thrive on the pressure that comes with the number-one spot and it'll be important to keep the winners flowing," Cobden said. "It'll be nice to have a choice of the many good horses in the yard."

There was a bump in the road in June when Cobden had a heavy fall at Market Rasen that resulted in a fractured vertebra in his neck and sidelined him for four months.

Cobden was back in early October and looking to build on last season, when he had 76 winners and finished ninth in the championship table. His wins included the Albert Bartlett Novices' Hurdle on Kilbricken Storm for Colin Tizzard, who will continue to be a strong supporter.

It will be a big season too for Twiston-Davies, 26, now a freelance but still in line for plenty of rides from the Nicholls yard. A little friendly rivalry with Cobden might spur on both of them.

SANTINI

"I CAN'T wait to ride him over fences. He's going to be some horse next season." Nico de Boinville has surfed a wave of chasing talent in recent years, including Cheltenham stars Coneygree, Sprinter Sacre, Altior and Might Bite, and he is clearly excited by Santini, the latest to roll along the Seven Barrows conveyor belt.

With good reason. Nicky Henderson has plotted a careful route with chasing in mind for Santini and instead of bumpers the champion trainer sent him for a year of hunting in the West Country, where he won his sole point-to-point. He won on his hurdles debut last December, stepped up to land a Grade 2 the following month, finished third in the Grade 1 Albert Bartlett at the Cheltenham Festival and then kept going to win the Grade 1 Sefton Novices' Hurdle at Aintree.

That was a bonus, with Henderson saying: "He ran such a good race at Cheltenham we thought we ought to put him away, but the horse has said all along, 'I'm up for this again'."

The going was heavy for his Cheltenham win – "ground I can't believe he wants," Henderson said – and soft for his other runs, with the feeling that De Boinville did not push him too hard in the Albert Bartlett.

The six-year-old's hurdles RPR of 153 – achieved twice in his four runs – is likely to be left well behind over fences.

Nobody plays the long game better than Henderson and Santini's novice chasing season should be exciting.

As early as January, the trainer said: "You'd think of him as an RSA horse next year and if he improves as much as he did from last year to this year he'll be an absolute machine – he's a proper horse."

NORWAY

COUNTRIES could be a big thing for Ballydoyle in 2019 – Japan is another to watch –- and the Norway option looks a good one for Aidan O'Brien following his Zetland Stakes success at Newmarket.

O'Brien won the 1m2f race for the first time the previous year with Kew Gardens, who went on to land the St Leger, and the trainer predicted Norway will be "a lovely middle-distance horse next year" after his one-length victory.

Norway is a full-brother to 2013 Derby winner Ruler Of The World and after the Newmarket win rider Seamie Heffernan said: "He's a little bit more forward than Ruler

Of The World was and hopefully could end up winning a Derby. There's plenty to like about him."

After a few years in the doldrums, the Zetland is on the up again as a significant juvenile contest. The 2016 edition featured

O'Brien's Wings Of Eagles (fourth), who went on to Derby glory, as well as classy Coronet, Permian and Defoe, while the 2017 runner-up to Kew Gardens was Dee Ex Bee, who was second to Masar in the Derby.

CAREFULLY SELECTED

KATIE WALSH'S last big win as a jockey came on Relegate in the Champion Bumper at the Cheltenham Festival, but the neck runner-up was significant for her too. Carefully Selected, the middle part of a one-two-three for Willie Mullins in the race, was snapped up at the sales as a yearling by Walsh and guided to point-to-point success before being sold on in June 2017.

The first steps with Mullins came in bumpers and, in going close at Cheltenham and then finishing third in the Grade 1 event at Punchestown, the giant six-year-old took bigger strides than expected. When a debut win over 2m4f at Leopardstown was followed by a drop back to 2m and another victory, he had earned his ticket to the big days with Mullins admitting "he's better than I thought he was at Christmas".

Carefully Selected may be built like an oil tanker but he has been fitted with a sports car engine and the trainer has already talked about the Albert Bartlett Novices' Hurdle as a target in 2019. As a stayer with a bit of toe, the son of Well Chosen should excel over fences eventually but he has the attributes for a productive season in Graded hurdles on the way.

BEN COEN

IN A racing version of a fantasy football league, Ben Coen would be a young jockey to have on your side. He scored heavily in 2018, mounting a concerted challenge for the Irish apprentice title in his first full season, and his statistics look set to sky-rocket as he gains more experience.

The 17-year-old from County Tipperary is a good judge of pace, he's tactically astute and, most importantly, he has the head for the game and a coolness beyond his years.

None of this came out of the blue. Coen hails from the well-known Slattery family – he is apprenticed to his uncle Andy, the Killenaule-based trainer – and gained an invaluable grounding preparing horses for breeze-ups and racing ponies.

He was more than ready when he became eligible for an apprentice licence and can only get better. Make no mistake, he's the real deal.

ARCHIE WATSON

HAVING started with only three horses in August 2016, Archie Watson, 29, has quickly emerged as one of the best young Flat trainers. He enjoyed a fabulous first full season with 56 winners and made even more impressive progress in 2018.

His Lambourn string started the year in good form with a strong challenge for the winter all-weather title but it was on turf where Watson really made his mark, particularly with his juveniles.

The young brigade was led by Soldier's Call, who gave him a first Royal Ascot success in the Windsor Castle and ended up a close third in the Group 1 Prix de l'Abbaye behind Mabs Cross. Along the way he won the Group 3 Prix d'Arenberg and Group 2 Flying Childers Stakes, both firsts at that level for the trainer.

Watson ranked in the top four for two-year-old winners along with Mark Johnston, Richard Hannon and Richard Fahey, with his results in that category alone virtually matching his 2017 overall tally. That suggests he will have plenty of firepower in 2019, with Soldier's Call set to lead the way again in his bid for top sprint honours.

TOM LACEY

DUBBED 'the strike-rate king', Lacey finished 36th on the British jumps trainers' list in the 2017-18 season with a career-best 39 winners and looks set to carry on climbing given his skill at developing young jumpers. From his base at Cottage Field Stables in Woolhope, Herefordshire, Lacey had a strike-rate of 25 per cent that was bettered only by champion trainer Nicky Henderson among the top 50 and finished the season strongly with two winners at the Aintree Grand National meeting and some noteworthy bumper performances.

Lacey, 48, was a late starter as a full trainer, having previously concentrated on pre-training, point-to-pointing and buying and selling horses, but has virtually doubled his tally of winners in each of the past four seasons, going from five in 2014-15 to nine, 21 and 39.

"I pride myself on individual runners to winners because it's about finding the races that the horses can win," said Lacey, who had around 35 horses for the start of the core jumps season and seems sure to keep churning out winners.

QUORTO

QUORTO'S career as a two-year-old mirrored that of his sire Dubawi – debut victory followed by a successful step up to Group company in the Superlative Stakes at Newmarket and then a Group 1 win on his third start in the National Stakes at the Curragh.

Godolphin, owner of both colts, will be hoping Quorto *(below)* makes a smoother transition to the Classics than Dubawi, who was fifth behind Footstepsinthesand when favourite for the 2,000 Guineas in 2005 before bouncing back to take the Irish 2,000 and later the Prix Jacques le Marois.

As with Dubawi, the National turned out to be Quorto's last run as a two-year-old. "The 2,000 Guineas has always been the long-term plan and, following discussions with His Highness Sheikh Mohammed, we have decided to put him away for the year," said trainer Charlie Appleby.

After the National, in which Quorto showed some signs of inexperience but quickened impressively to beat Ballydoyle's highly touted Anthony Van Dyck by a length and a quarter, Appleby said his colt was a more obvious contender for the Guineas than the Derby.

"There's a lot of stamina on the dam's side – Volume was placed in the Oaks – but he travels very well through his races. If you were to pin me down now I'd say a mile was his trip," he said. "A mile and a quarter might be his maximum. He's very much a Dubawi – the stamp of him, the way he travels through his races, his mentality."

Appleby and Godolphin, though, will be hoping Quorto turns out different when it comes to 2,000 Guineas day.

JAMIE GORMLEY

HAMILTON'S champion jockey award may not seem much of an accolade but beating leading northern lights such as Joe Fanning and David Allan was a notable feather in the cap of apprentice Jamie Gormley, confirming him as a rider to watch on the Flat.

A lack of ammunition – relative to his southern-based rivals – meant his challenge for the British apprentice title fell away in 2018 but Gormley nevertheless attracted attention from shrewd trainers other than Iain Jardine, with whom he is based in Dumfries.

The 26-year-old from Langholm partnered the Tim Easterby-trained Eeh Bah Gum to win a valuable sprint handicap at York's Ebor meeting and was trusted by Jim Goldie to ride Theglasgowwarrior in the Cesarewitch, finishing a fine fifth.

Described by Goldie as "a late developer and a great talent", Gormley is likely to ride out his claim in the first half of 2019 but, with the burgeoning Jardine stable as a principal backer, he should continue to enjoy plenty of success even without a weight allowance.

STEP BACK

THE small Oxfordshire operation of Mark and Sara Bradstock has won the Cheltenham Gold Cup with Coneygree and the Hennessy with Carruthers in the current decade, and now they have the Grand National in their sights with bet365 Gold Cup winner Step Back.

If their 20-horse yard pulls it off, it would be another incredible triumph to rank with the big-race victories of Coneygree and Carruthers, both bred by Sara's late father Lord Oaksey. The family has National history too: in his riding days, the noble lord was noted amateur Mr John Lawrence and in 1963 he went heartbreakingly close to Aintree glory on Carrickbeg, who was overtaken by 66-1 shot Ayala in the final strides.

Step Back is made of the right stuff, as he showed in his big-race victory at Sandown by leading all the way and coming home 13 lengths clear under Jamie Moore. He went there off a novice-chase win at Fakenham and, having suffered numerous problems that had limited him to six starts under rules by the end of last season, the eight-year-old is expected to improve further.

"He's the most lovely horse and he just jumps and gallops forever," said Sara Bradstock. "Again and again we prove we can do it if we get the horses."

Winning the National would be the ultimate proof.

CIEREN FALLON

HE IS one of the most inexperienced jockeys around, having ridden his first winner on September 24 at the age of 19, but few will be more closely watched in 2019 than Cieren Fallon.

The son of six-time British champion jockey Kieren Fallon carries a weight of expectation with his family name and his first winner attracted plenty of attention even though it came on a Monday at Leicester in a lowly hands and heels apprentice handicap. Fallon snr was on hand to see his son bring the John Ryan-trained 25-1 shot Plucky Dip with a well-timed run inside the final furlong to win by half a length.

Fallon jnr said: "That's my third ride and it feels really good to get the first winner out of the way, as you tend to start wondering if it's going to happen. It's a fair weight off my shoulders."

The apprentice, based with William Haggas in Newmarket, added: "I've been working as hard as I can. I love what I'm doing. It would be brilliant to be as good as Dad was when he was riding at his peak, but that's a really tall order."

Fallon snr said: "It's brilliant to see my son ride a winner. He decided he wanted to be a jockey and this is the first step for him. There's an awful long way to go and, as we all know about the racing game, one minute you're up and the next you're down."

COMMANDER OF FLEET

GORDON ELLIOTT may not have known a lot about Commander Of Fleet prior to the Punchestown festival but the Gigginstown-owned four-year-old may well have been moved up a barn or two nearer the stable stars at Cullentra House after his runaway victory in the Land Rover Bumper.

Commander Of Fleet led home a one-two-three for Elliott, which points to the depth of young talent in his yard, but the trainer wouldn't take any credit for the performance of the winner on the day.

"He's a nice horse and a big thanks goes to Pat Doyle, who trained him to win a point-to-point," Elliott said.

"I've only had him from the week after he won his point-to-point. I haven't galloped him, just cantered him away. Pat did all the hard work with him."

Commander Of Fleet was the only finisher when winning his point-to-point for Doyle and it was almost as if he didn't have a race at Punchestown, such was the authority of his victory by eight and a half lengths.

After that Elliott knew he had a good one on his hands.

FAIRYLAND

THE pecking order of Aidan O'Brien's juveniles is always difficult to evaluate and especially so among the fillies, with the 2018 Oaks winner Forever Together being a case in point as she was beaten in both starts as a two-year-old and achieved a Racing Post Rating of just 75.

Fairyland has done much better than that, with an RPR of 113 for her battling victory in the Group 1 Cheveley Park Stakes, and if it comes down to toughness there will be few fillies who can match her in 2019.

There is the racecourse evidence of her neck success over The Mackem Bullet in the Cheveley Park, which had been preceded by an even narrower win in the Group 2 Lowther Stakes at York where she beat the same rival by a nose.

But there is also what happened off the track in the 62 days between Fairyland's third in the Albany Stakes at Royal Ascot and her return to action at York. The daughter of Kodiac was among the most severely afflicted by the bug that swept through Ballydoyle – "they were all very sick but absolutely she was [hit hard]," O'Brien said – and she did well to come back so strongly in the Lowther.

All five juvenile starts were over six furlongs, with the Albany being the only defeat, but O'Brien is hopeful she might step up as a three-year-old. "She's a lovely, big filly. We always thought she would maybe get a mile but she's not short of speed."

Nor does she lack fighting spirit.

RICHARD PATRICK

JAMES BOWEN has been the dominant force among the British conditional jump jockeys but there are other promising young riders around and one who is beginning to make a push is Richard Patrick, who knows Bowen and his brother Sean from teenage days in pony racing and riding out at their father Peter's yard.

Patrick, 23, went close to a big win in the Welsh Grand National in January when second on Alfie Spinner, beaten by none other than James Bowen aboard Raz De Maree.

Based with Alfie Spinner's trainer Kerry Lee, Patrick looks well placed for a good winter.

WILLIAM CARVER

PONY racing, for so long a route into the grown-up game in Ireland, is becoming a more fruitful source of riding talent in Britain and William Carver is the latest promising graduate.

The 18-year-old from West Sussex has gained a place at the distinguished riding academy of Andrew Balding's Kingsclere stable and has been mentored by Oisin Murphy, the former Kingsclere star apprentice who enjoyed a Group 1 winning spree in 2018.

Carver will have to battle hard in such a competitive environment but he was quick to show he had the right temperament with a winning debut ride for Balding at Southwell in November 2017. He continued to impress on a limited number of rides in the latest season and, with his 7lb claim, could be set for a breakthrough year.

ADAM SHORT

AS BUSY as he is talented, Adam Short prides himself on accommodating the growing list of trainers who want him in to ride work on a daily basis, and his mechanic must be a happy man as this is a young Irish conditional who does a lot of miles to push his career forward.

Liz Doyle was one of the first trainers to take notice of Short's abilities and provided him with the biggest victory of his nascent career on Last Goodbye in a valuable handicap chase at the Dublin Racing Festival at Leopardstown in February. That 20th career winner brought his claim down to 5lb, which remains a considerable asset for a rider of his ability.

Short is picking up rides on a regular basis and his contacts list should bring plenty of opportunities this season. Even if the 21-year-old from County Wicklow lacks the ammunition to thwart some of the more heavily armed riders in the Irish conditional jockeys' championship, he is one to watch.

THE
BIGGER
PICTURE

Sunrise at Meydan racecourse in Dubai
World Cup week. The big night proved
to be a triumph for Godolphin with four
Group 1 winners – Thunder Snow in the
big race, Jungle Cat, Benbatl and Hawkbill
EDWARD WHITAKER (RACINGPOST.COM/PHOTOS)

Final Furlong

Stories of the year – from the serious to the quirky

Festival winner Hatch retires

CHELTENHAM Festival-winning jockey Ryan Hatch (*pictured*) was forced to announce his retirement in February at the age of 24 after doctors advised him he was at risk of paralysis in the event of another serious fall.

Hatch had not ridden since fracturing the C6 and C7 vertebrae at the base of his neck, the T6 vertebra below his shoulder blade and his sternum when Cogry fell at Cheltenham in December 2016.

"It's not been a decision I've taken on my own terms – I've had to do it on medical advice, which is frustrating," he said. "The bones have healed well but there's been what's called a signal change in my spinal cord, which puts me at massive risk of paralysis if I was to get a bad fall."

Hatch rode 78 winners over jumps, first as an amateur and then as a conditional. Sixty-six of them came for Nigel Twiston-Davies, who provided him with his two Cheltenham Festival wins, on Same Difference in the 2013 Kim Muir and Blaklion in the 2016 RSA Chase.

"The whole of the sport has been brilliant to me and it's a shame things have had to end this way," Hatch said. "However, those winning days will always mean I have happy memories."

From prison to a 'whole different life' in racing

THE Godolphin Stud and Stable Staff Awards showcase some wonderful stories but few have been as emotional as that of Adrian Stewart, who won the David Nicholson Newcomer Award in February.

Stewart, 29, from Beeston in Leeds, had a difficult start in life but has been given a second chance by racing, having been encouraged to consider a career in the sport during a spell in prison.

On his release he applied to the Northern Racing College. "It was Dawn Goodfellow [the NRC's then chief executive] who gave me the chance having never sat on a horse. I can't thank the NRC enough for what they've done for me," he said.

Stewart found his feet with trainer Kevin Frost – "he gave me a chance and got me up to scratch" – before joining Shropshire trainer Dave Loughnane when Frost switched yards. "He has taken me further. If you're working towards something and if you're working hard enough for it, he'll help you achieve what you want to achieve.

"The horses have given me a whole different life that I could only have dreamed of and wished for. They couldn't have given me a better life than I have now."

Stewart's prize was £2,000 and a five-day educational trip to Dubai to learn more about the country's racing, culture and customs.

▲ Fresh start: Adrian Stewart won the David Nicholson Newcomer Award

●On thin ice

ITV Racing betting pundit Matt Chapman has always divided opinion among viewers and it was the same story when he made his primetime debut as the announcer on Dancing On Ice in January, leading to a quicker exit for him than any of the 12 celebrities in the competition.

The ice skating show returned after a four-year break with a Sunday night slot and Chapman (below) took over the role long associated with Tony Gubba,

who died in 2013. Chapman's job was to summarise each performance as it was replayed before inviting the judges to give their scores, but his own performance was heavily criticised.

One viewer, Marion Criswell, tweeted: "Please stop that awful commentator shouting. Absolutely awful. Spoiling the show." Michael Morgan also tweeted his displeasure: "Is it just me or does Matt Chapman need to go from Dancing On Ice? So annoying."

Chapman was gone before the second show in the nine-week run, replaced by sports commentator Sam Matterface. "It's been what one could call eventful," Chapman said after his departure.

●Kian's winning favourite

RACEGOERS can get closer to the action than many other sports fans and the generosity of those at the heart of the action brightened an ice-cold afternoon at Market Rasen in February when Kian Burley cheered his favourite jockey Paddy Brennan to victory.

The Cheltenham Gold Cup-winning rider handed over his skull cap, emblazoned with the initials PB and

the date, to his biggest fan Kian, 7, who braved the arctic conditions with his mother Hannah and family.

Cerebral palsy restricts Kian to a wheelchair but does not stop the racing-mad youngster enjoying what he loves best – an afternoon at the track – and cheering on Brennan.

Hannah Burley, from Doncaster, said: "We've been at Market Rasen and all over the country, braving all weathers, and Paddy came over to us one day

and asked Kian if he was having a good day – Kian has supported him everywhere ever since. Kian eats, sleeps and breathes racing – he loves it.

"Paddy's a lovely, down-to-earth man and he and Will Kennedy have given Kian so many presents. It really is appreciated.

"We've got breeches, two whips, more goggles than you can imagine and champagne glasses at home."

Viva Las Vegas

A GENEROUS punter treated six lucky friends to a trip to Las Vegas after winning £168,751 on a £1 each-way Lucky 31 at the Cheltenham Festival.

Martin Palk, 55, struck the £62 bet at a Betfred shop in Tiverton, Devon, and roared home the final selection – Missed Approach in the Kim Muir – in the company of his pals.

"There was a great atmosphere in the shop as my choice Missed Approach led from virtually start to finish," Palk recalled. "I'm normally quite tanned but everyone says I went white as a sheet. Prior to the last race I said half-jokingly, 'If I win I'm taking all of us, all seven, to Las Vegas.'

"It was a bit of banter but I'm a man of

my word, so the Magnificent Seven are off to the Strip. It'll cost me £10,000."

Palk (pictured), who owns a cleaning company, was back at work at 5am the morning after his windfall but vowed to enjoy his winnings. "I tell you what, we

won't be saving it or anything boring like that. Money is for spending and having a good time."

Wrongs make a right

WILLIE MULLINS' Low Sun, who landed the Cesarewitch at Newmarket in October, had a bizarre win at the Galway festival in August when he was allowed to keep the race despite taking the wrong course – because all 20 runners in the €100,000 2m7f handicap hurdle had done the same.

The stewards determined the entire field went off course briefly on the first circuit, going the wrong side of a rail, before taking the correct route next time around. Having found that no horse had gained an advantage, they allowed the result to stand.

Tree felled at 1-20 in huge upset

TREE OF LIBERTY equalled the unenviable record for the shortest-priced loser in British jump racing history when beaten at odds of 1-20 at Ludlow in March.

The Kerry Lee-trained six-year-old had more than 3st in hand on official ratings in a three-runner 2m novice contest but went down to 20-1 chance Cap'N by two and a half lengths.

The only other 1-20 jumping loser was the great Jerry M over fences at Newbury in 1909, when he fell in a two-horse race and was remounted to complete the course. He won the Grand National in 1912.

Tree Of Liberty became the shortest-priced loser of any race in Britain since Triple Dip at the same odds on the all-weather at Lingfield in 2015.

A total of ten 1-20 shots have been beaten, but the record for the shortest-priced loser in British racing history is held by Royal Forest, a 1-25 chance who was second at Ascot in September 1948.

Lee said Tree Of Liberty was "beaten by a better horse" but the veterinary officer later reported the favourite had bled from the nose.

The 20-1 shock winner Cap'N, making his chase debut, was sent off the shortest price of his career, having finished no closer than 27 lengths behind the winner in five previous starts on the Flat and over hurdles.

A 'what happened next?' moment

HISTORY was made on Betfair in a lowly handicap hurdle at Wetherby in February in a dramatic finish where three horses were beaten at the minimum price of 1.01 and the winner Pookie Pekan was backed at the maximum 1,000.

The chain of events was set in motion when clear leader Northern Girl crumpled a stride after landing over the final hurdle, falling in the path of Dulce Panem and Conor O'Farrell, who were unable to avoid her and came down.

The favourite Along Came Theo sidestepped the two horses and looked all over a lucky winner. At this point £17,389 was traded on the 9-4

favourite – to go along with the £4,472 on Northern Girl and £4,431 on Dulce Panem – but he started to tread water and 11-1 outsider Pookie Pekan, who had been ten lengths behind in fifth two out, galloped past to secure the unlikeliest of victories by a length and a quarter.

Betfair's Barry Orr said: "This is a first in our

18-year history. We've had plenty of races where two horses have traded at 1.01 and got beaten but never three in one race. And then to see a 1,000 [999-1] winner is nothing short of amazing. There was plenty traded at 1.01 and a tenner at 1,000 on the winner. It's the glorious uncertainty of racing taken to an extreme."

▾ Spot the winner: Northern Girl leads from Dulce Panem and Along Came Theo but the race is about to change dramatically in favour of Pookie Pekan (circled)

RACING POST
ANNUAL
AWARDS

Our pick of the best of 2018 – plus the results of a Racing Post readers' poll in the top four categories

HORSE OF THE YEAR (FLAT) OUR CHOICE Roaring Lion
Roared back from Classic defeats to score a string of Group 1 triumphs
READERS' CHOICE Roaring Lion

HORSE OF THE YEAR (JUMPS) OUR CHOICE Tiger Roll
The little horse with the big heart conquered Aintree and Cheltenham
READERS' CHOICE Tiger Roll

RACE OF THE YEAR (FLAT)
OUR CHOICE Prix de L'Arc de Triomphe
Two fillies giving their all in a race that tugged at the heartstrings
READERS' CHOICE Prix de L'Arc de Triomphe

RACE OF THE YEAR (JUMPS)
OUR CHOICE Cheltenham Gold Cup
Native River and Might Bite head to head in a virtual match race
READERS' CHOICE Cheltenham Gold Cup

RIDE OF THE YEAR (FLAT)
OUR CHOICE James Doyle, Sea Of Class, Irish Oaks
Brilliant waiting ride that combined panache and a punchy finish

RIDE OF THE YEAR (JUMPS)
OUR CHOICE Noel Fehily, Summerville Boy, Supreme Novices' Hurdle
Never-say-die effort to overcome mistakes at the last two flights

RISING STAR OUR CHOICE Jason Watson
Stewards' Cup win showed he has the temperament as well as talent

COMEBACK OF THE YEAR OUR CHOICE Enable
Off for 11 months, one prep run, then a second Arc triumph. Amazing

UNLUCKIEST HORSE OUR CHOICE Sea Of Class
Brilliantly trained and ridden, just unfortunate to be poorly drawn in the Arc

MOST IMPROVED HORSE OUR CHOICE What A Welcome
Expertly placed by Patrick Chamings to win six out of seven while rising 28lb

FLOP OF THE YEAR OUR CHOICE Elarqam
Juvenile campaign promised fireworks but we got a Classic damp squib

BEST TV RACING PUNDIT OUR CHOICE Jason Weaver
Insightful and incisive – and our favourite for the second year running

BEST 'I WAS THERE' MOMENT OUR CHOICE Cheltenham Gold Cup
Native River v Might Bite in an epic 'one to tell the grandchildren' story

BEST RIVALRY OUR CHOICE Roaring Lion v Saxon Warrior
Six career meetings, three decided by a neck, and Roaring Lion came back to win 4-2

Photo-finish blunder – not once but twice

RACECOURSE judge Felix Wheeler called the wrong result at Kempton in March but if that seemed a misfortune, it began to look more like carelessness when he did it for a second time at Sandown four months later.

In the first case, Oregon Gift *(far side in the photo)*, sent off a heavily backed 10-11 favourite for a 1m4f handicap at Kempton, officially went down by a nose to 8-1 shot Bird For Life after hitting an in-running low of 1.1 on Betfair.

However, the result was amended five days later following further consideration of the photo-finish by Wheeler, who had been the judge on duty, and the race was awarded to Oregon Gift.

In response the BHA introduced a 'failsafe' system whereby all photo-finish decisions would be available for review by a BHA official before the 'weighed in' announcement, which is

Official Photofinish ©   **RaceTech**

the point at which a result becomes official for betting purposes.

The new system was in place by early July and almost immediately came into play when Wheeler called the wrong winner in a photo-finish to a 5f handicap at Sandown.

Initially 13-2 chance Rio Ronaldo was called the winner by a nose from

6-1 shot Vibrant Chords but the stipendiary stewards on duty at Sandown queried Wheeler's decision, which led to Vibrant Chords being given the verdict after closer examination.

This time the process was conducted before

◀ Wrong verdicts: judge Felix Wheeler

the weighed-in announcement was made, which the BHA claimed as a victory for their new system, but bookmakers were unhappy after several paid out on both results.

Paul Binfield, representing Paddy Power, said: "It's hard for us to digest yet another error by a judge, which in the 21st century shouldn't be occurring and ultimately costs us money every time."

● Horse goes into bar . . .

STAFF and customers in a Chantilly bar had a shock one Monday morning in September when a racehorse briefly ran amok after escaping on her way to the nearby gallops.

The filly, trained by Jean-Marie Beguigne, dropped her rider and, with the saddle back around the point of her hips, came bucking through Le Chantilly bar, which is opposite the train station.

Beguigne told Ouest France: "Between the training track and the stables the filly dropped her rider and escaped down the road. She crossed a roundabout before running into the bar. It was extraordinary."

The bar's owner Stephane Jasmin said: "The horse pushed in through the door and ran down the bar. She turned round at the end, breaking a table and some chairs, and ran back. Fortunately no-one was injured but we were all scared."

ALTERNATIVE AWARDS

The London Buses Award
Frankie Dettori, who had to wait 13 years for a record-equalling fourth Arc but has now had three in quick succession

The NCP Award
Sea Of Class, who almost managed to come from the car park to win the Arc

The SatNav Award
inscribed 'If possible, do a U-turn'
Paul Townend, who inexplicably went off course with Al Boum Photo at Punchestown, taking the unfortunate Finian's Oscar with him

The Who Wants To Be A Millionaire Award
Stradivarius, who was set four posers and came up with the answer every time to hit the jackpot in the Stayers' Million

The Specsavers Award *inscribed 'Should have gone to . . .'*
Racecourse judge Felix Wheeler for twice calling the wrong winner in photo-finishes, leading to the results having to be amended

The Blue Is The Colour Award
Sheikh Mohammed, who at last had a Derby winner in the Godolphin silks with Masar

The Lost Voice Award
York racecourse, whose headline act Sir Tom Jones had to cancel his concert in July owing to appalling weather

The Frankie Dettori Award for infectious enthusiasm
Bryony Frost, whose bubbly post-race personality matched her effervescent riding

The Marmite Award
Matt Chapman, who divides opinion among armchair racing fans and did not endear himself to Dancing On Ice viewers

The No Pain, No Gain Award
Harriet Tucker, who shrugged off a dislocated shoulder to win the Cheltenham Foxhunter on Pacha Du Polder

The Charlie Chaplin Award *inscribed 'Silence is golden'*
Pat Kelly, who kept out of the media spotlight and quietly went about the business of turning RSA Chase winner Presenting Percy into a star

The lastminute.com Award
Willie Mullins, who snatched the Irish jump trainers' title out of Gordon Elliott's hands in the final week for the second season running

The Generation Game Award
inscribed 'didn't he do well?'
Gordon Elliott, who didn't have such a bad season with victories in the Grand Nationals at Aintree and Fairyhouse and eight Cheltenham Festival winners

The It Takes Two Award
Might Bite, who played his part alongside Native River in a magnificent Cheltenham Gold Cup

The Some Like It Hot Award
Oisin Murphy, whose sizzling form in the summer's big races matched the weather

A-Z of 2018

The year digested into 26 bite-size chunks

A is for Alpha Centauri, the miling star of the summer in a stunning Flat campaign for jumps queen Jessica Harrington.

B is for the brothers O'Brien. Trainer Joseph and jockey Donnacha both made Classic breakthroughs and teamed up to win the Irish Derby with Latrobe.

C is for Cieren. A spelling that might become familiar as the new Fallon kid on the block (the 19-year-old son of six-time British champion Flat jockey Kieren) pursues his own riding career.

D is for dead-heat, the first in Ayr Gold Cup history between Son Of Rest and Baron Bolt.

E is for Enable, who capped a great season for John Gosden when she became the first dual Arc winner trained in Britain.

F is for fighting. Racing was rocked by outbreaks of on-course violence at Goodwood and Ascot on consecutive weekends in May.

G is for Godolphin, whose resurgence as a racing force included a first Derby triumph with the Charlie Appleby-trained Masar.

H is for Hatchfield Farm. The ten-year saga over Newmarket housing development rumbled on.

I is for infestation. Epsom and Salisbury had to abandon meetings in September owing to an invasion of chafer grubs, which feed on the root system of grass and loosen the racing surface.

J is for Justify, who became the second US Triple Crown winner in four years for trainer Bob Baffert.

K is for Kentucky Derby, a race described by Aidan O'Brien as "nearly savagery" in wet conditions after his challenger Mendelssohn finished last.

T

X

R

L is for little 'uns Stradivarius and Tiger Roll, who proved big 'uns don't always win.

M is for Micko. Cheltenham Gold Cup and Classic-winning Irish trainer Mick O'Toole – universally known by the shortening of his name - died in August aged 86. His Gold Cup winner was Davy Lad in 1977.

N is for Native River, who ended British champion jump jockey Richard Johnson's 18-year wait for a second Cheltenham Gold Cup winner.

O is for OBE, awarded to 2017 Grand National-winning trainer Lucinda Russell in the Queen's birthday honours for services to horseracing.

P is for Poet's Society, the horse who took trainer Mark Johnston to a British record 4,194 winners.

Q is for queue, as Arc-day racegoers need no reminding after the redeveloped Paris Longchamp track ran into a storm of criticism over its facilities.

R is for Redzel, who has won both runnings of The Everest sprint – the world's richest turf race – and now has prize-money of A$16 million (£8.66m/€9.83m), making him Australia's second-highest-earning racehorse behind Winx.

S is for Sydney Opera House, which became embroiled in an unlikely racing-related row when it was forced to display advertising for The Everest on its famous sails.

T is for Towcester. The much-loved Northamptonshire jumps and greyhound track was plunged into administration in August, sparking a frantic search for a buyer.

U is for Urban Sea, the 1993 Arc winner who featured as granddam or great-granddam of the first eight in the 2018 edition of the race.

V is for valedictory success as ground-breaking amateur riders Katie Walsh and Nina Carberry went out on a winning note at the Punchestown festival.

W is for wind ops. In January it became mandatory in Britain for wind surgery to be notified by trainers and included on racecards, with the Warren Greatrex-trained Boite becoming the first winner denoted in that way.

X is for X factor, the beguiling quality that will endure through the winter with Dewhurst winner Too Darn Hot.

Y is for yellow (and white). A study commissioned by the BHA found horses respond better to those colours on hurdles and fences than the traditional orange, with a possible change under consideration.

Z is for Zabriskie, who had the dubious distinction of finishing last of 12 in both the Derby and St Leger, beaten a total of 84 lengths.

FLASHBACK

1978 Shirley Heights wins the Derby for John Dunlop

Shirley Heights (right) triumphs at Epsom for John Dunlop (below)

Picture: GERRY CRANHAM

JOHN DUNLOP, who died in July at the age of 78, was one of the greatest and most respected trainers of his generation with a total of about 3,600 victories. In a 47-year career at Castle Stables, Arundel, he enjoyed consistent success at the top level, most notably with Derby winners Shirley Heights and Erhaab, champion sprinter Habibti and Irish Derby-winning filly Salsabil. He also trained Arc runners-up Balmerino and Leggera, champions Awaasif, Shadayid, Elnadim and Mujahid, Derby runner-up Sakhee and Sheikh Mohammed's very first winner, Hatta.

Shirley Heights in 1978 became the most famous horse of the trainer's career, as well as one of the toughest and classiest, by winning the Derby

and Irish Derby, both by a head. In the Derby he seemed to have an impossible task two furlongs out, but he had the good luck to find a clear run after Greville Starkey switched him to the rails, and produced a tremendous burst to catch Hawaiian Sound in the last couple of strides. In the Irish Derby he scored narrowly from Exdirectory and Hawaiian Sound.

Shirley Heights gave Dunlop the first of ten British Classic wins, with Erhaab becoming his other Derby hero in 1994. He was champion trainer in 1995, the season in which his top-class miler Bahri memorably won the Queen Elizabeth II Stakes under Willie Carson, who famously took the outside route under the trees.

Carson, whose Classic successes with Dunlop included Salsabil in the 1,000 Guineas and Oaks and Erhaab in the Derby, said on his death: "John was from the old school and was always a gentleman to ride for – I don't remember him ever raising his voice. He was a great man, a great trainer, and it's a hell of a loss to racing."

Dunlop was an active fundraiser for charities, especially those connected with stable lads' welfare, and in 1996 that work was recognised by his appointment as an OBE.

He retired in 2012 but his racing legacy lives on through sons Ed and Harry, who have been training since 1994 and 2006 respectively.